RPG WORLD

VOLUME ONE

ART AND STORY BY
IAN JONES-QUARTEY

keenspot

RPG WORLD VOLUME ONE: UNLIKELY HERO OUT FOR ADVENTURE

FOR MOM AND DAD

Most of the material in this book has previously appeared on the internet at www.rpgworldcomic.com.

RPG WORLD #74 and ADVENTURERS! #320-#324 Written and Illustrated by Mark Shallow. Used with permission.

"Clint" appears in comic #133 courtesy of Josh Mirman. www.stubblecomics.com

Published by Keenspot Entertainment
P.O. Box 1525, Temple City, California 91780
Phone: (626) 286-1007 FAX: (626) 286-1260
E-Mail: keenspot@keenspot.com
Web: www.keenspot.com

Co-CEO/Editor Chris Crosby
Co-CEO Darren "Gav" Bleuel
CFO Teri Crosby
CTO Nate Stone

ORDER KEENSPOT PRODUCTS BY PHONE
DIAL TOLL-FREE 1-888-KEENSPOT

ISBN 0-9722350-4-3 (Softcover Edition)

First Printing, January 2004
10 9 8 7 6 5 4 3 2 1
Printed in Canada

A COMPLETE COLLECTION OF STRIPS FROM THE FIRST STORYARC

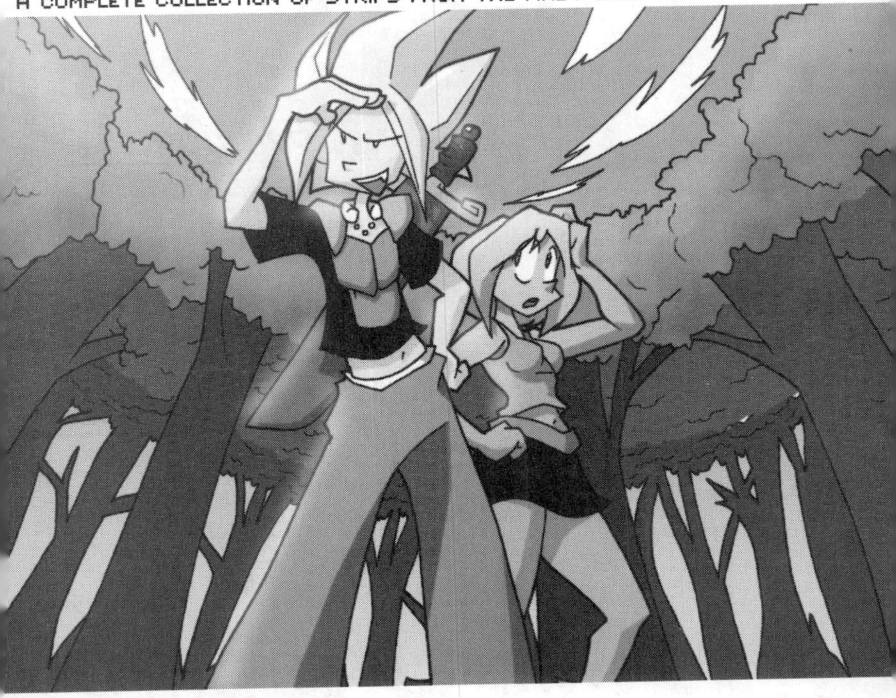

RPG WORLD

VOLUME ONE

UNLIKELY HERO OUT FOR ADVENTURE

ART AND STORY BY

IAN JONES-QUARTEY

READ THESE AND MORE FINE COMIC STRIPS AT

WWW.RPGWORLDCOMIC.COM

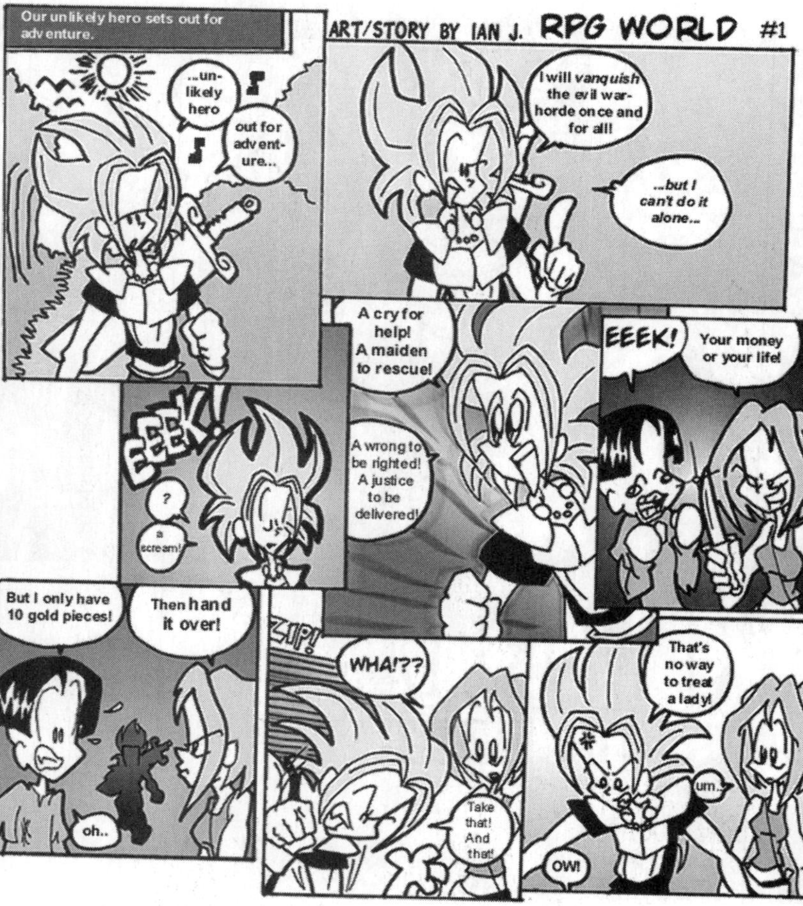
Our unlikely hero sets out for adventure.
ART/STORY BY IAN J.
RPG WORLD #1
..unlikely hero
out for adventure...
I will vanquish the evil war-horde once and for all!
...but I can't do it alone...
A cry for help! A maiden to rescue!
EEEK!
?
a scream!
A wrong to be righted! A justice to be delivered!
EEEK!
Your money or your life!
But I only have 10 gold pieces!
Then hand it over!
oh..
ZIP!
WHA!??
Take that! And that!
That's no way to treat a lady!
um..
OW!

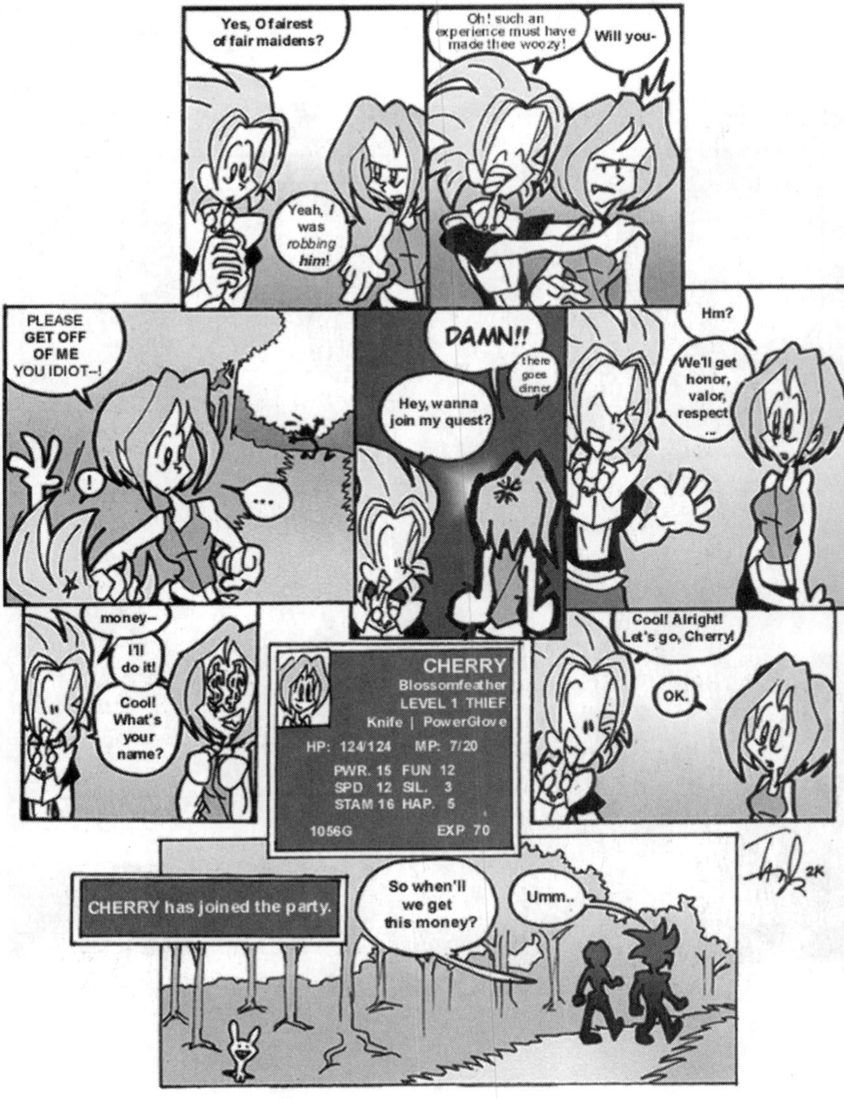
Yes, O fairest of fair maidens?
Yeah, *I* was *robbing* **him**!
Oh! such an experience must have made thee woozy!
Will you-
PLEASE GET OFF OF ME YOU IDIOT--!
!
...
DAMN!!
there goes dinner
Hey, wanna join my quest?
Hm?
We'll get honor, valor, respect ...
money--
I'll do it!
Cool! What's your name?
CHERRY
Blossomfeather
LEVEL 1 THIEF
Knife | PowerGlove
HP: 124/124 MP: 7/20
PWR. 15 FUN 12
SPD 12 SIL. 3
STAM 16 HAP. 5
1056G EXP 70
Cool! Alright! Let's go, Cherry!
OK.
CHERRY has joined the party.
So when'll we get this money?
Umm..
2K

RPG WORLD

ART/STORY BY IAN J.

"TURN-BASED STUPIDITY"

#2

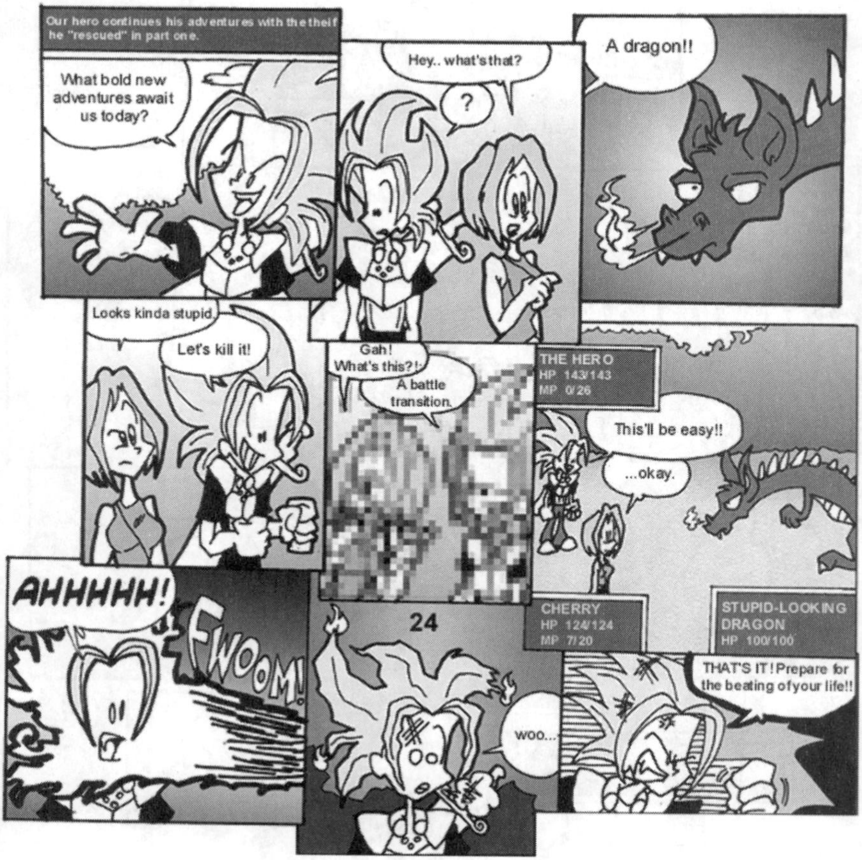
Our hero continues his adventures with the theif he "rescued" in part one.
What bold new adventures await us today?
Hey.. what's that?
?
A dragon!!
Looks kinda stupid.
Let's kill it!
Gah! What's this?!
A battle transition.
THE HERO
HP 143/143
MP 0/26
This'll be easy!!
...okay.
CHERRY
HP 124/124
MP 7/20
STUPID-LOOKING DRAGON
HP 100/100
AHHHHH!
FWOOM!
woo...
THAT'S IT! Prepare for the beating of your life!!

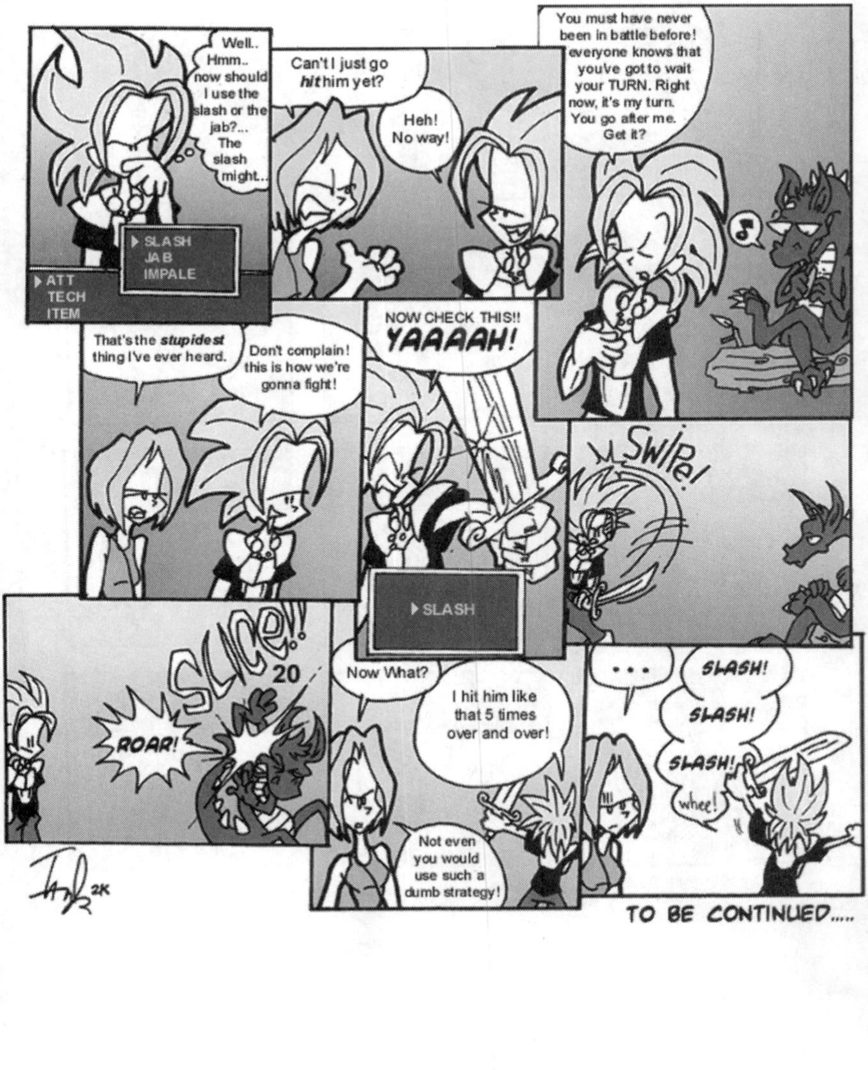

Well.. Hmm.. now should I use the slash or the jab?... The slash might...
SLASH
JAB
IMPALE
ATT
TECH
ITEM
Can't I just go *hit* him yet?
Heh! No way!
You must have never been in battle before! everyone knows that you've got to wait your TURN. Right now, it's my turn. You go after me. Get it?
That's the *stupidest* thing I've ever heard.
Don't complain! this is how we're gonna fight!
NOW CHECK THIS!!
YAAAAH!
SLASH
SWIPE!
SLICE!!
20
ROAR!
Now What?
I hit him like that 5 times over and over!
Not even you would use such a dumb strategy!
...
SLASH!
SLASH!
SLASH!
whee!
2K

TO BE CONTINUED.....

RPG WORLD
ART/STORY BY IAN J.

#3

"YOU EARNED ONE STUPID COMIC"

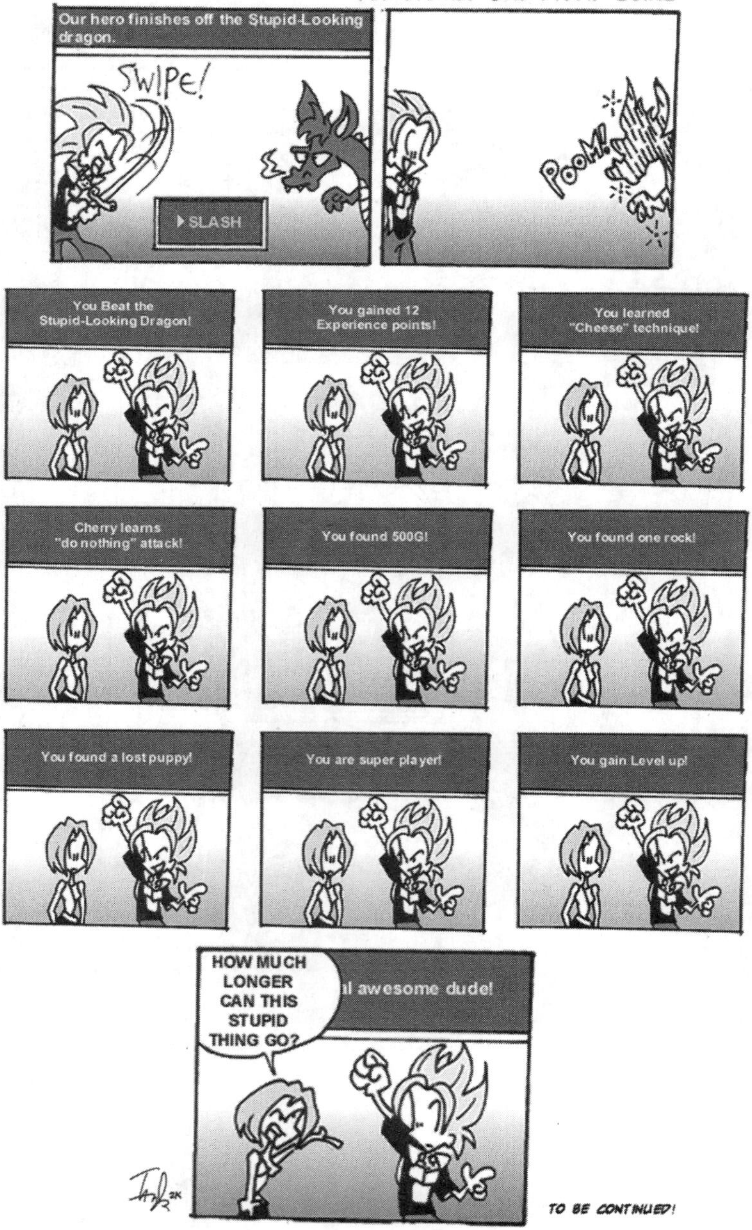

Our hero finishes off the Stupid-Looking dragon.
SWIPE!
SLASH
POOM!
You Beat the Stupid-Looking Dragon!
You gained 12 Experience points!
You learned "Cheese" technique!
Cherry learns "do nothing" attack!
You found 500G!
You found one rock!
You found a lost puppy!
You are super player!
You gain Level up!
HOW MUCH LONGER CAN THIS STUPID THING GO?
al awesome dude!

TO BE CONTINUED!

RPG WORLD

ART/STORY BY IAN J.

"ENTER THE FUZZY THING" #4

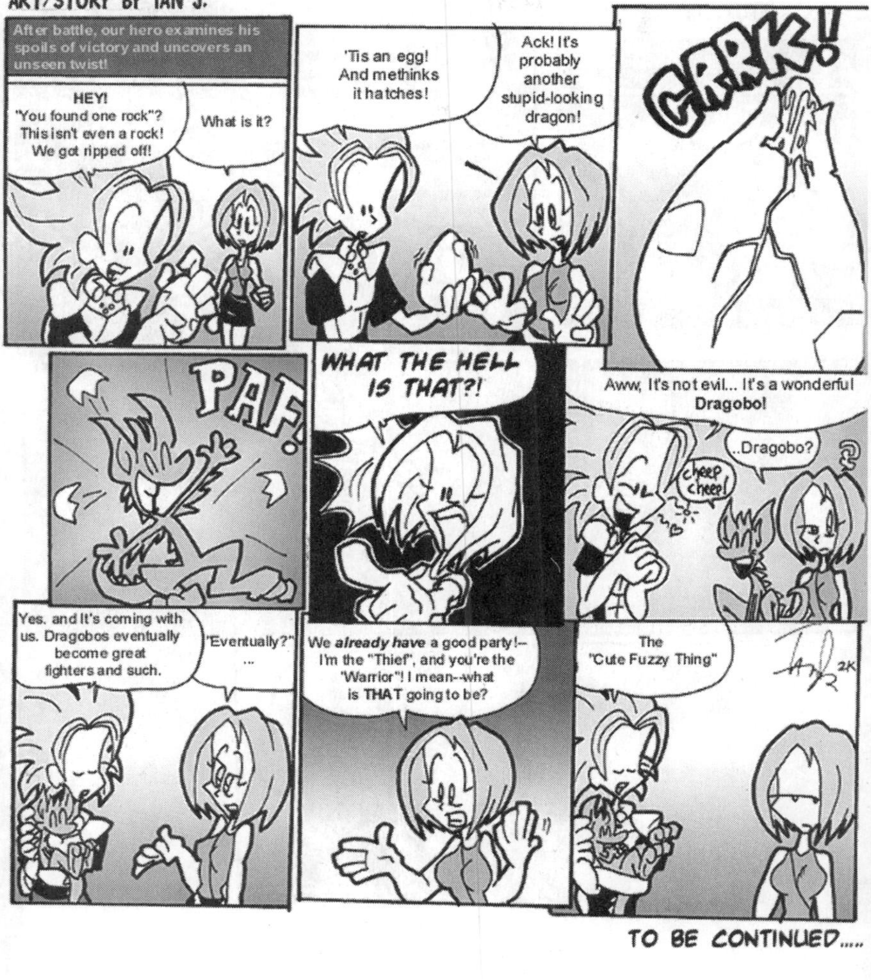
After battle, our hero examines his spoils of victory and uncovers an unseen twist!
HEY! "You found one rock"? This isn't even a rock! We got ripped off!
What is it?
'Tis an egg! And methinks it hatches!
Ack! It's probably another stupid-looking dragon!
CRRK!
PAF!
WHAT THE HELL IS THAT?!
Aww, It's not evil... It's a wonderful **Dragobo!**
..Dragobo?
cheep cheep!
Yes. and It's coming with us. Dragobos eventually become great fighters and such.
"Eventually?" ...
We *already have* a good party!-- I'm the "Thief", and you're the "Warrior"! I mean--what is **THAT** going to be?
The "Cute Fuzzy Thing"
2K

TO BE CONTINUED.....

RPG WORLD

ART/STORY BY IAN J.

#5

"TRANSITIONS ARE FUN"

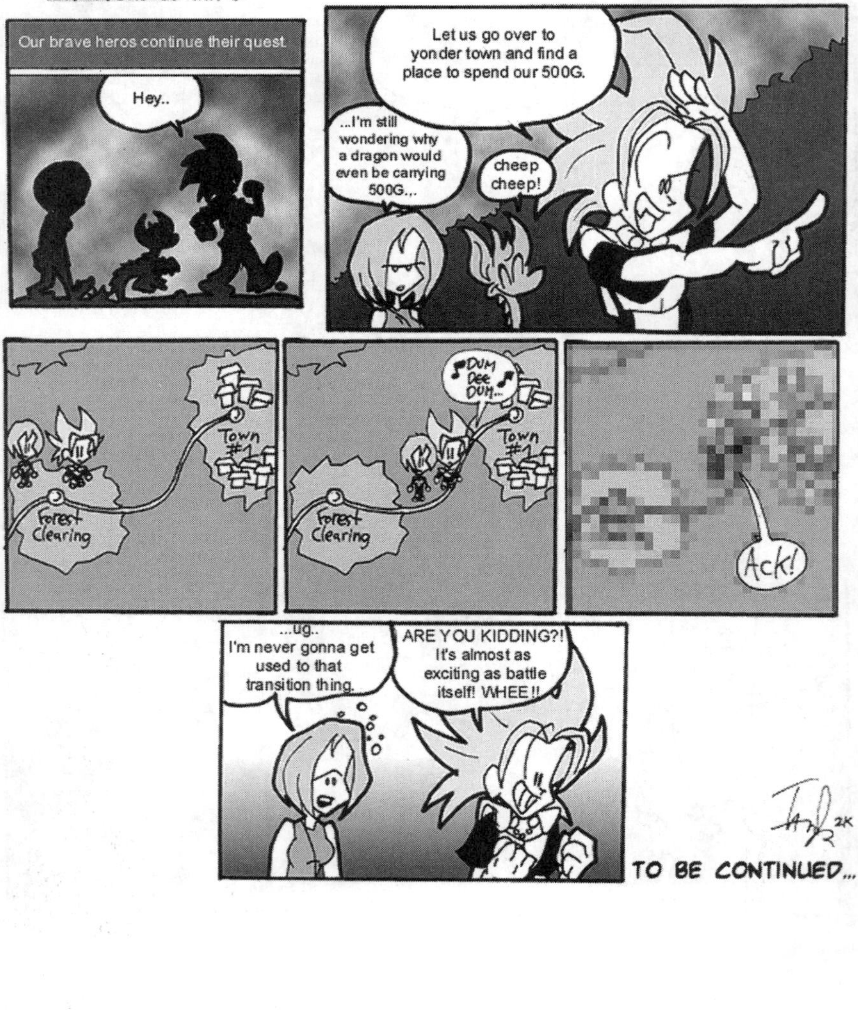

Our brave heros continue their quest.
Hey..
Let us go over to yonder town and find a place to spend our 500G.
...I'm still wondering why a dragon would even be carrying 500G...
cheep cheep!
Forest Clearing
Town #1
Forest Clearing
Town #1
DUM DEE DUM...
Ack!
...ug.. I'm never gonna get used to that transition thing.
ARE YOU KIDDING?! It's almost as exciting as battle itself! WHEE!!
2K

TO BE CONTINUED...

RPG WORLD
ART/STORY BY IAN J.

6

"THIS IS HOW I PLAY RPG'S, MYSELF.."

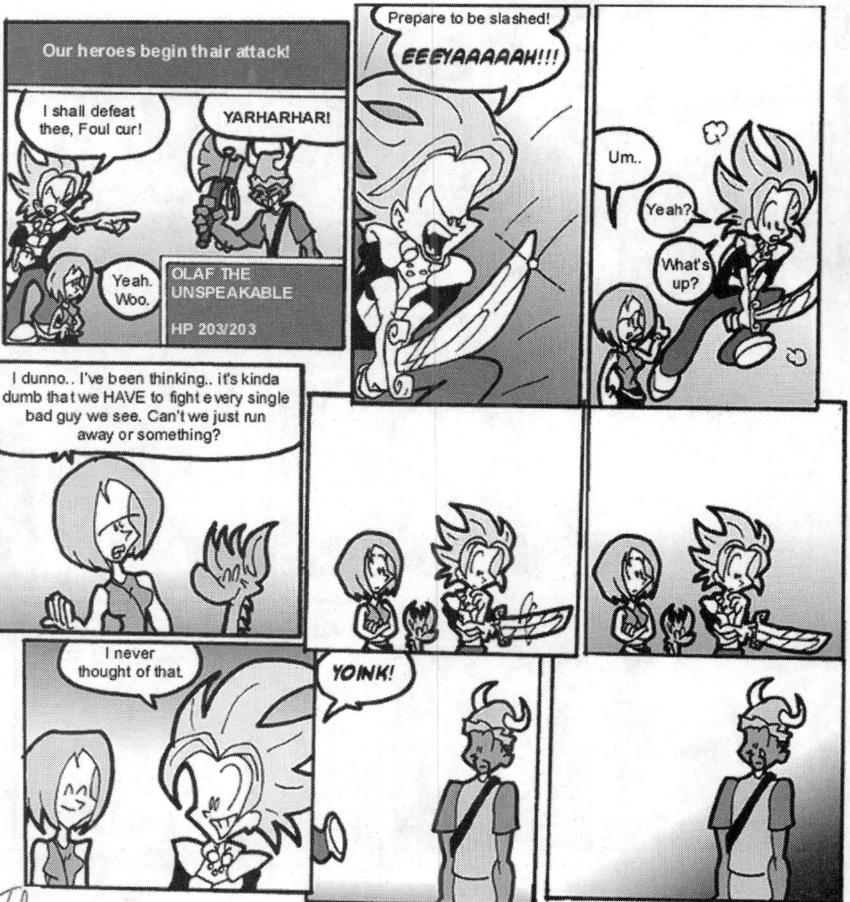

Our heroes begin thair attack!
I shall defeat thee, Foul cur!
YARHARHAR!
Yeah. Woo.
OLAF THE UNSPEAKABLE
HP 203/203
Prepare to be slashed!
EEEYAAAAAH!!!
Um..
Yeah?
What's up?
I dunno.. I've been thinking.. it's kinda dumb that we HAVE to fight every single bad guy we see. Can't we just run away or something?
I never thought of that.
YOINK!

TO BE CONTINUED!

RPG WORLD
ART/STORY BY IAN J.

"NOW LOADING......." #7

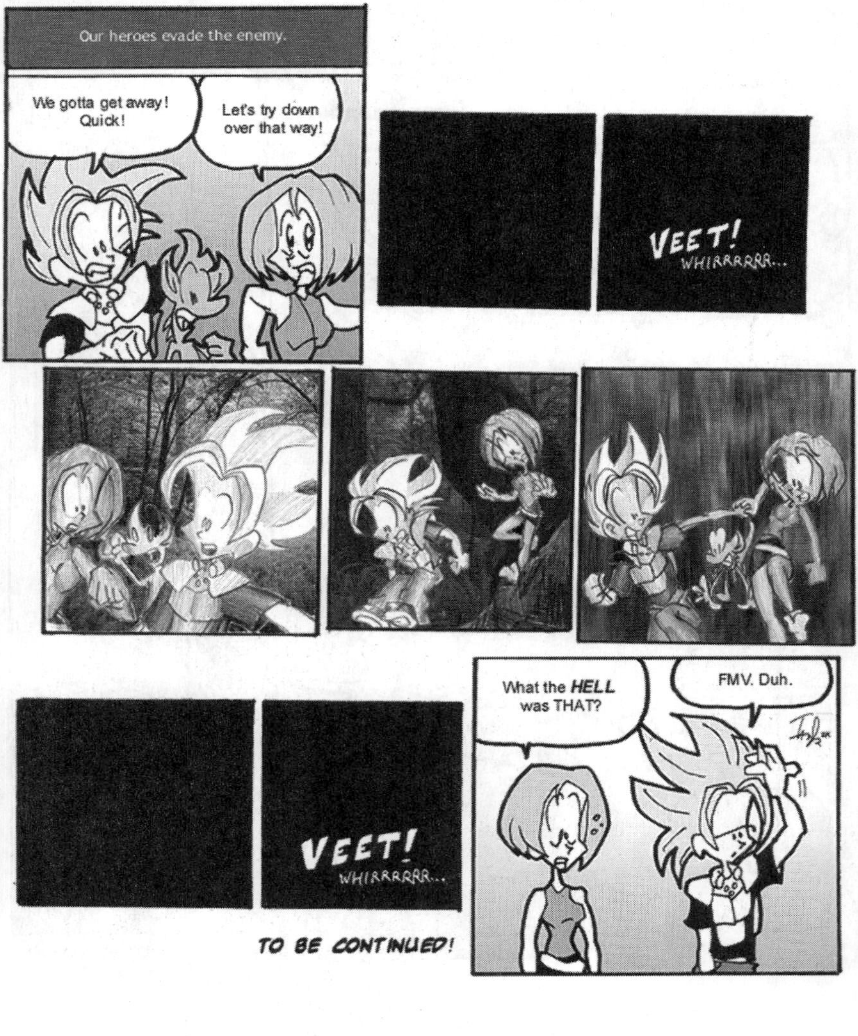

Our heroes evade the enemy.
We gotta get away! Quick!
Let's try down over that way!
VEET!
WHIRRRRRR...
VEET!
WHIRRRRRR...
What the HELL was THAT?
FMV. Duh.
TO BE CONTINUED!

RPG WORLD
ART/STORY BY IAN J.

"INVASION OF PRIVACY" **#8**

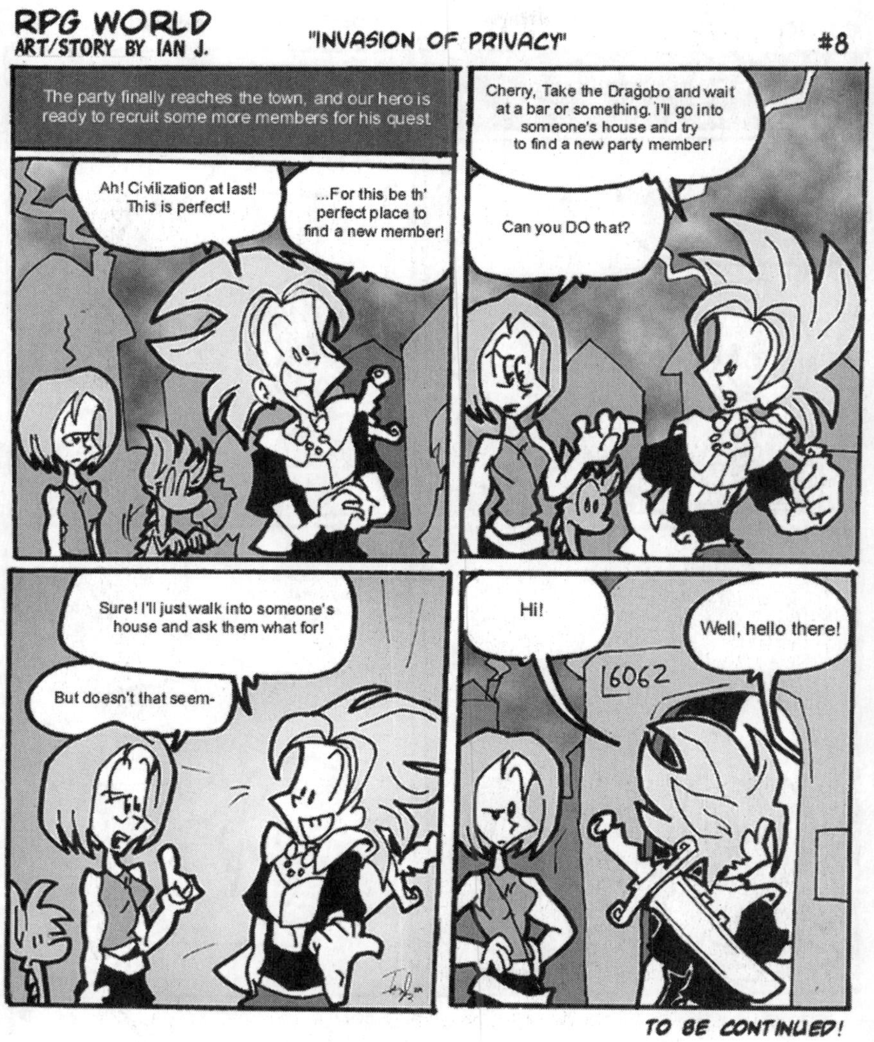

The party finally reaches the town, and our hero is ready to recruit some more members for his quest.
Ah! Civilization at last! This is perfect!
...For this be th' perfect place to find a new member!
Cherry, Take the Dragobo and wait at a bar or something. I'll go into someone's house and try to find a new party member!
Can you DO that?
Sure! I'll just walk into someone's house and ask them what for!
But doesn't that seem-
Hi!
Well, hello there!
6062

TO BE CONTINUED!

RPG WORLD
ART/STORY BY IAN J.

"THE TROUBLE WITH NON-PLAYABLE CHARACTERS"

#9

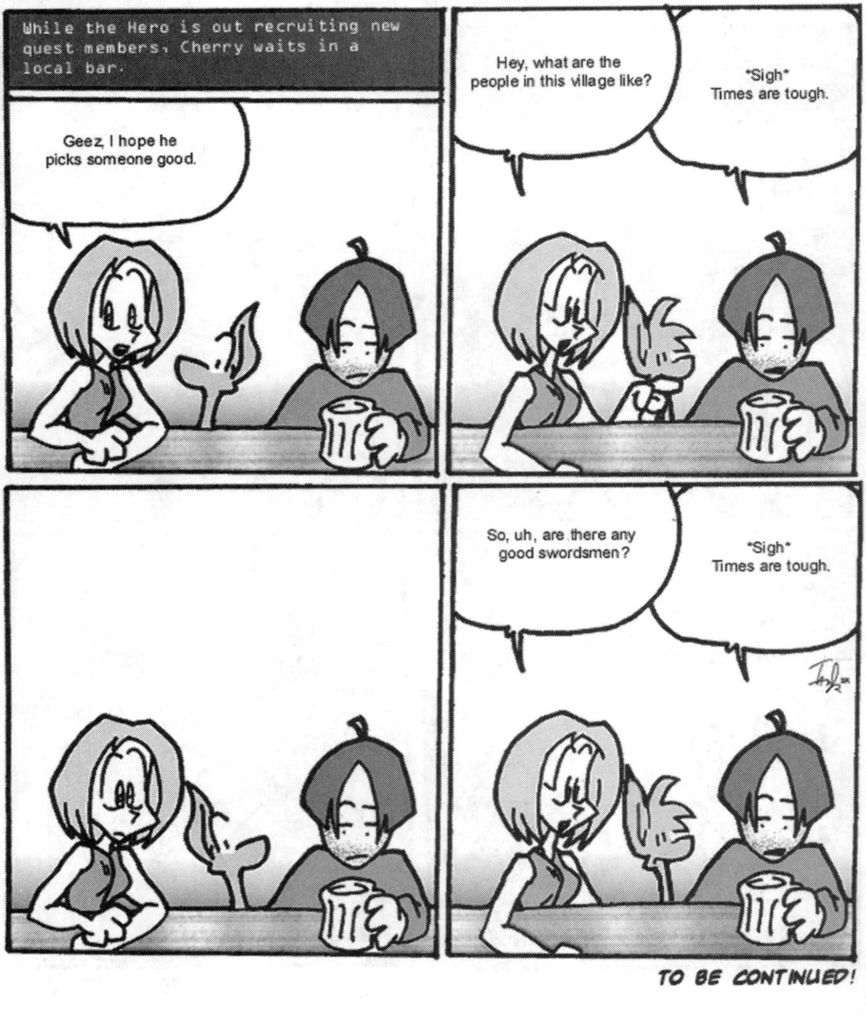

While the Hero is out recruiting new quest members, Cherry waits in a local bar.
Geez, I hope he picks someone good.
Hey, what are the people in this village like?
Sigh Times are tough.
So, uh, are there any good swordsmen?
Sigh Times are tough.

TO BE CONTINUED!

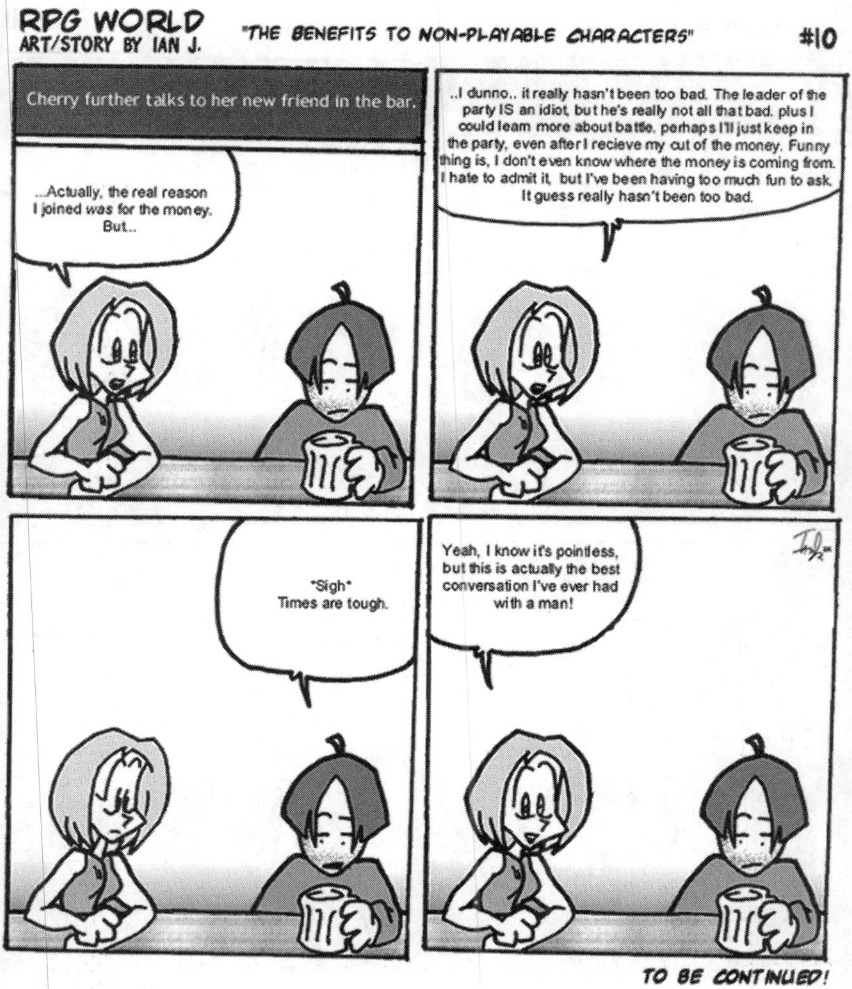
RPG WORLD
ART/STORY BY IAN J.
"THE BENEFITS TO NON-PLAYABLE CHARACTERS"
#10
Cherry further talks to her new friend in the bar.
...Actually, the real reason I joined *was* for the money. But..
..I dunno.. it really hasn't been too bad. The leader of the party IS an idiot, but he's really not all that bad. plus I could learn more about battle. perhaps I'll just keep in the party, even after I recieve my cut of the money. Funny thing is, I don't even know where the money is coming from. I hate to admit it, but I've been having too much fun to ask. It guess really hasn't been too bad.
Sigh Times are tough.
Yeah, I know it's pointless, but this is actually the best conversation I've ever had with a man!
TO BE CONTINUED!

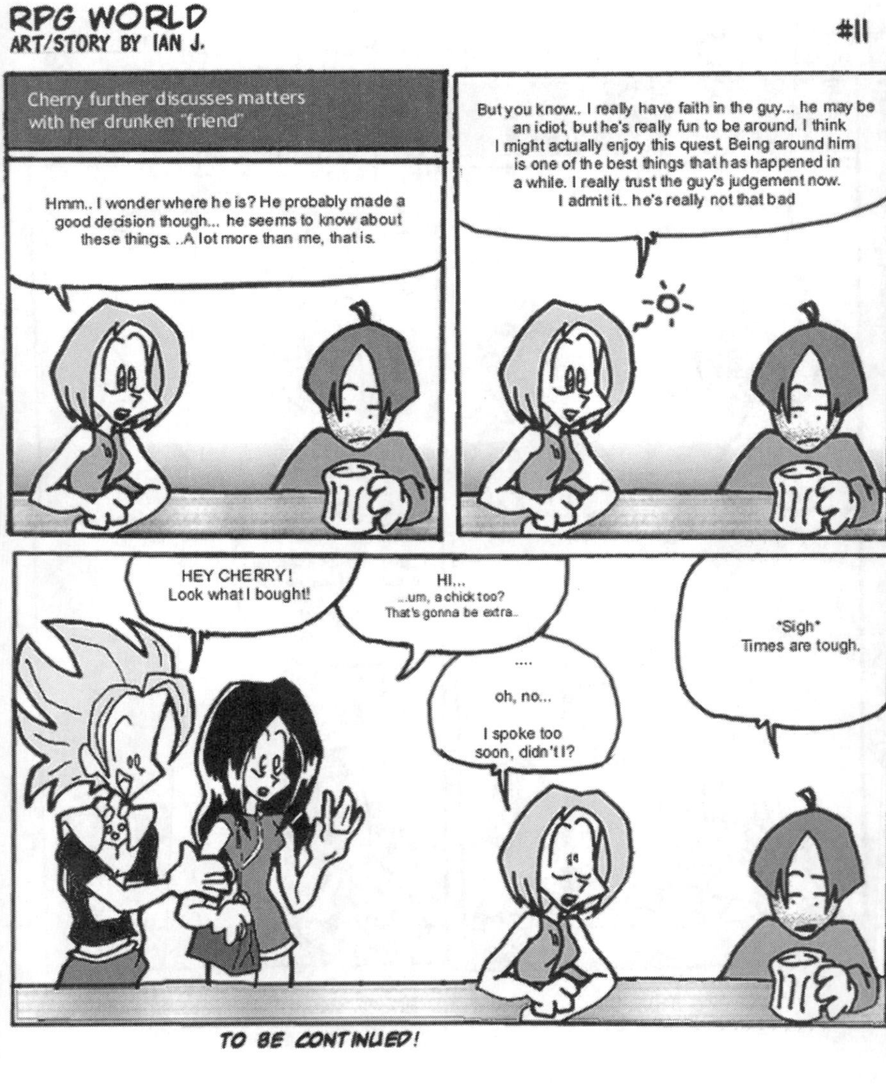
RPG WORLD
ART/STORY BY IAN J.
#11
Cherry further discusses matters with her drunken "friend"
Hmm.. I wonder where he is? He probably made a good decision though... he seems to know about these things. ..A lot more than me, that is.
But you know.. I really have faith in the guy... he may be an idiot, but he's really fun to be around. I think I might actually enjoy this quest. Being around him is one of the best things that has happened in a while. I really trust the guy's judgement now. I admit it.. he's really not that bad
HEY CHERRY! Look what I bought!
HI... ...um, a chick too? That's gonna be extra..
.... oh, no... I spoke too soon, didn't I?
Sigh Times are tough.
TO BE CONTINUED!

RPG WORLD
ART/STORY BY IAN J.

"A WHOREIBLE SITUATION"

#12

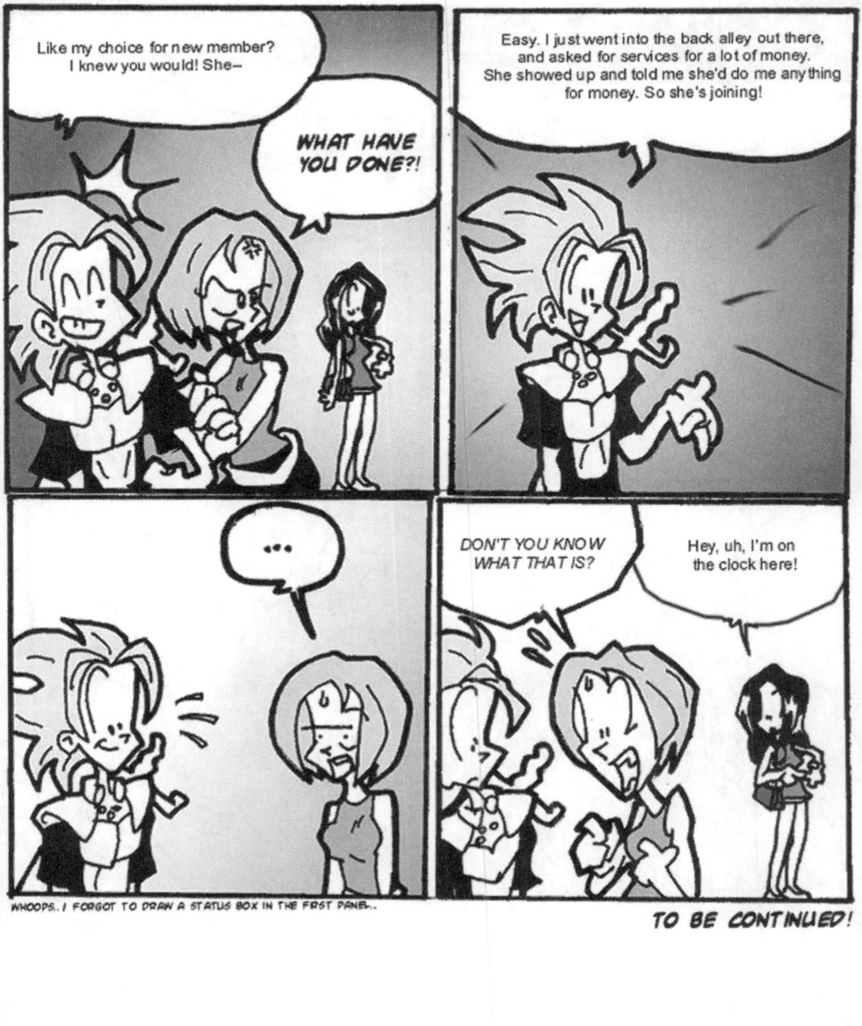
Like my choice for new member? I knew you would! She–
WHAT HAVE YOU DONE?!
Easy. I just went into the back alley out there, and asked for services for a lot of money. She showed up and told me she'd do me anything for money. So she's joining!
...
DON'T YOU KNOW WHAT THAT IS?
Hey, uh, I'm on the clock here!

WHOOPS.. I FORGOT TO DRAW A STATUS BOX IN THE FRST PANEL..

TO BE CONTINUED!

RPG WORLD

ART/STORY BY IAN J.

"HEY, WANNA GIMME SOME HP?"

#13

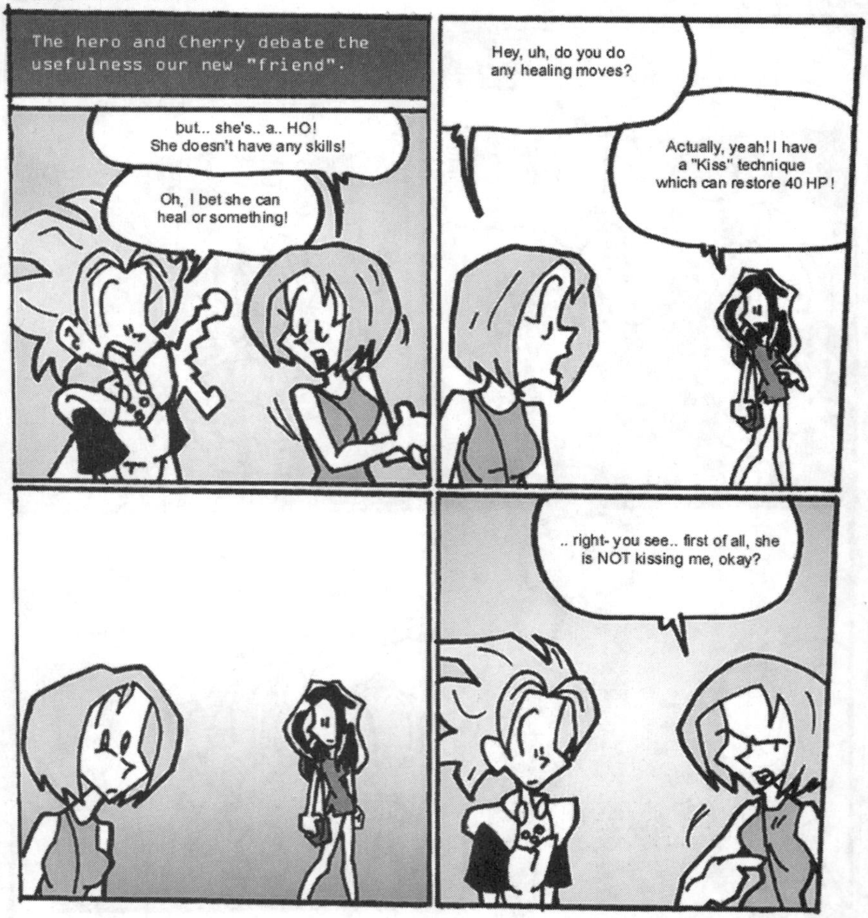

The hero and Cherry debate the usefulness our new "friend".
but.. she's.. a.. HO! She doesn't have any skills!
Oh, I bet she can heal or something!
Hey, uh, do you do any healing moves?
Actually, yeah! I have a "Kiss" technique which can restore 40 HP!
.. right- you see.. first of all, she is NOT kissing me, okay?

TO BE CONTINUED!

RPG WORLD
ART/STORY BY IAN J.

"FUN WITH NAMES"

#14

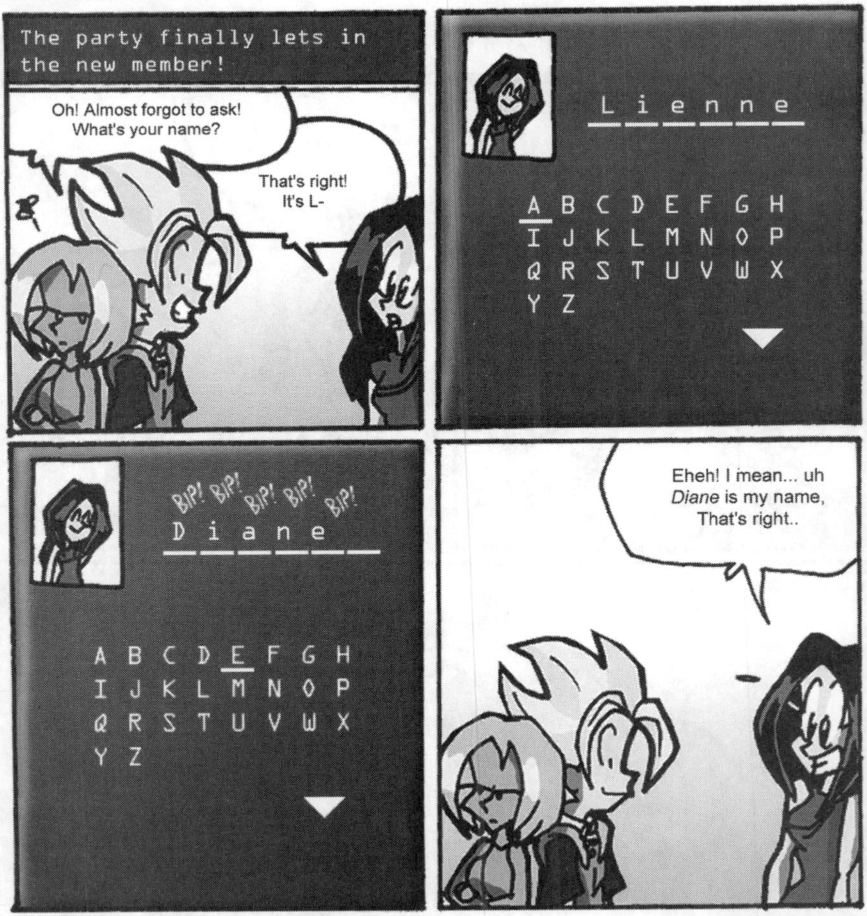

The party finally lets in the new member!
Oh! Almost forgot to ask! What's your name?
That's right! It's L-
L i e n n e
A B C D E F G H
I J K L M N O P
Q R S T U V W X
Y Z
BIP! BIP! BIP! BIP! BIP!
D i a n e
A B C D E F G H
I J K L M N O P
Q R S T U V W X
Y Z
Eheh! I mean... uh *Diane* is my name, That's right..

TRY RENAMING FFT'S CLOUD AS 'DILDO', IT'S FUN!

TO BE CONTINUED!

RPG WORLD
ART/STORY BY IAN J.

"WHAT *ARE* INNS GOOD FOR, ANYWAY?"

#15

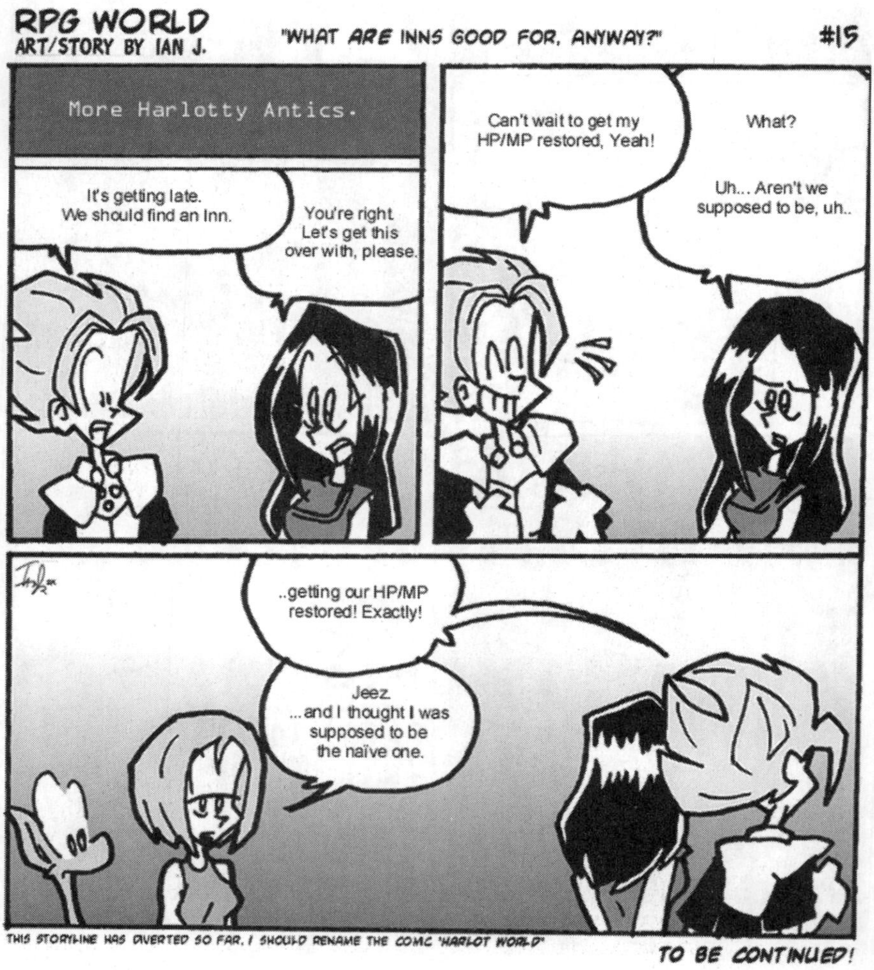

More Harlotty Antics.
It's getting late. We should find an Inn.
You're right. Let's get this over with, please.
Can't wait to get my HP/MP restored, Yeah!
What?
Uh... Aren't we supposed to be, uh..
..getting our HP/MP restored! Exactly!
Jeez. ...and I thought I was supposed to be the naïve one.

THIS STORYLINE HAS DIVERTED SO FAR, I SHOULD RENAME THE COMC 'HARLOT WORLD'

TO BE CONTINUED!

RPG WORLD
ART/STORY BY IAN J.

"SLEEPY TIME"

#16

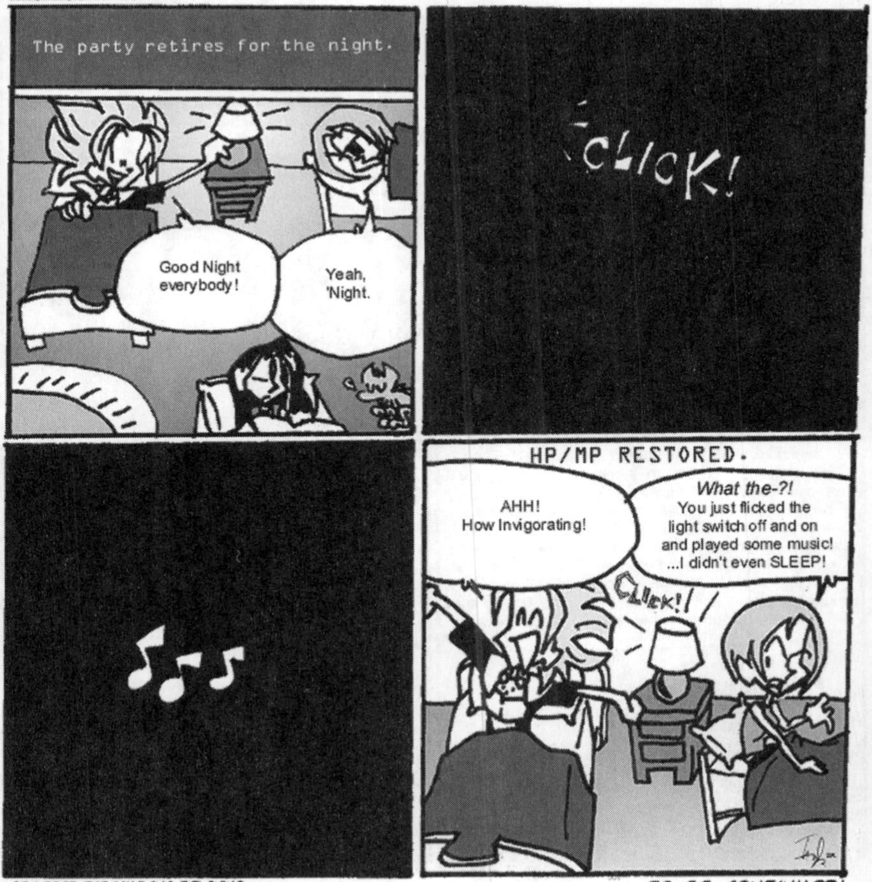

The party retires for the night.
Good Night everybody!
Yeah, 'Night.
CLICK!
HP/MP RESTORED.
AHH! How Invigorating!
What the-?! You just flicked the light switch off and on and played some music! ...I didn't even SLEEP!
CLICK!

AT LEAST THE MUSIC IS RELAXING.

TO BE CONTINUED!

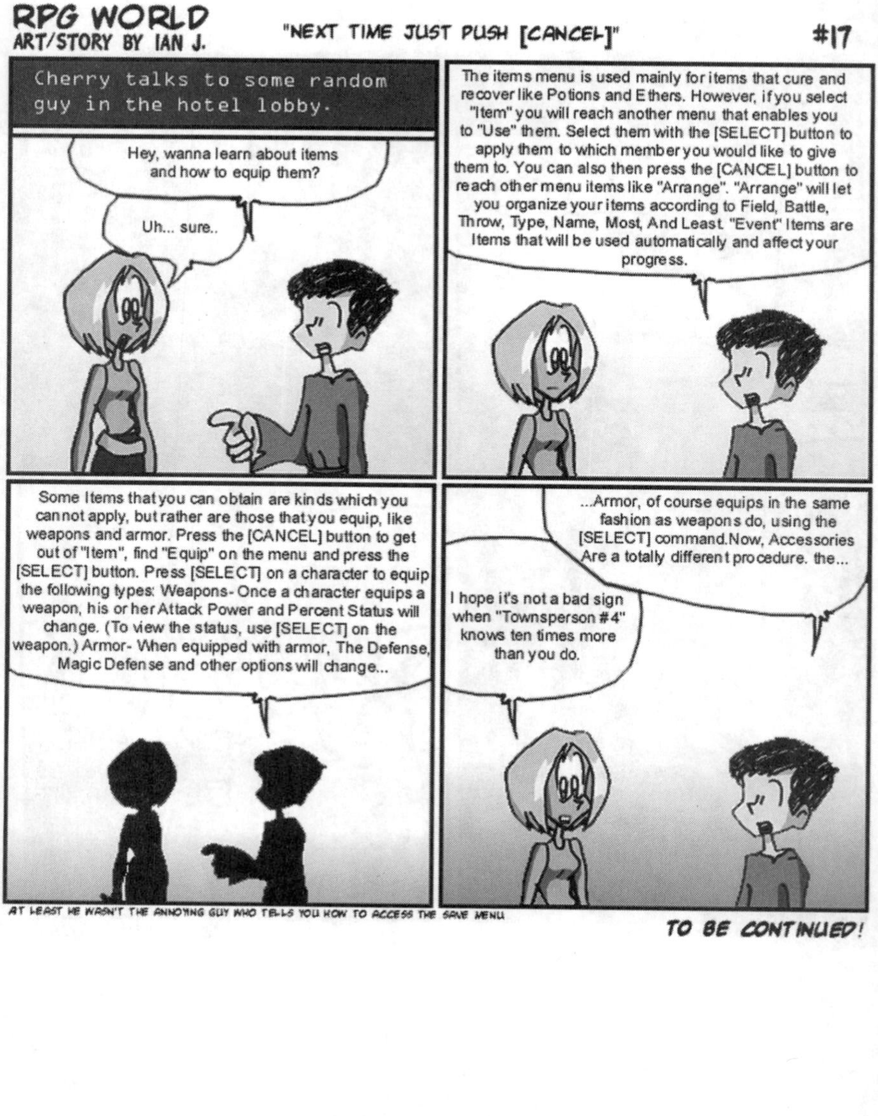
RPG WORLD
ART/STORY BY IAN J.
"NEXT TIME JUST PUSH [CANCEL]"
#17
Cherry talks to some random guy in the hotel lobby.
Hey, wanna learn about items and how to equip them?
Uh... sure..
The items menu is used mainly for items that cure and recover like Potions and Ethers. However, if you select "Item" you will reach another menu that enables you to "Use" them. Select them with the [SELECT] button to apply them to which member you would like to give them to. You can also then press the [CANCEL] button to reach other menu items like "Arrange". "Arrange" will let you organize your items according to Field, Battle, Throw, Type, Name, Most, And Least. "Event" Items are Items that will be used automatically and affect your progress.
Some Items that you can obtain are kinds which you cannot apply, but rather are those that you equip, like weapons and armor. Press the [CANCEL] button to get out of "Item", find "Equip" on the menu and press the [SELECT] button. Press [SELECT] on a character to equip the following types: Weapons- Once a character equips a weapon, his or her Attack Power and Percent Status will change. (To view the status, use [SELECT] on the weapon.) Armor- When equipped with armor, The Defense, Magic Defense and other options will change...
...Armor, of course equips in the same fashion as weapons do, using the [SELECT] command.Now, Accessories Are a totally different procedure. the...
I hope it's not a bad sign when "Townsperson #4" knows ten times more than you do.
AT LEAST HE WASN'T THE ANNOYING GUY WHO TELLS YOU HOW TO ACCESS THE SAVE MENU
TO BE CONTINUED!

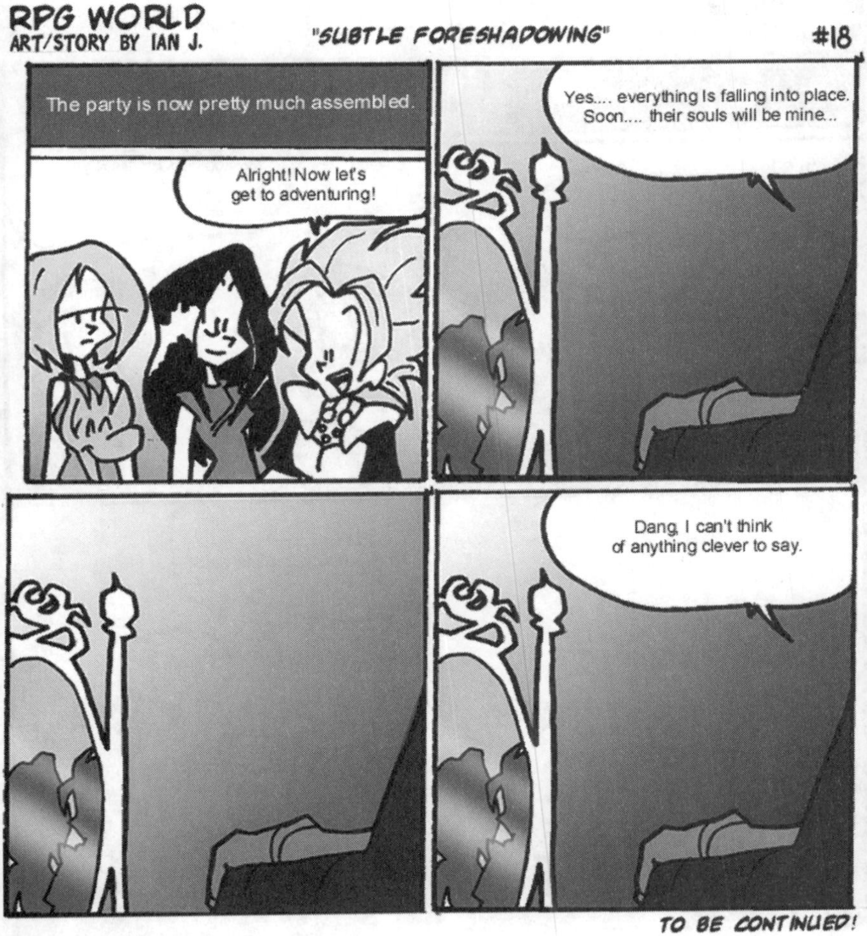
RPG WORLD
ART/STORY BY IAN J.
"SUBTLE FORESHADOWING"
#18
The party is now pretty much assembled.
Alright! Now let's get to adventuring!
Yes.... everything Is falling into place. Soon.... their souls will be mine...
Dang, I can't think of anything clever to say.
TO BE CONTINUED!

RPG WORLD
ART/STORY BY IAN J.

"JUST THOUGHT YOU'D LIKE TO KNOW..."

#19

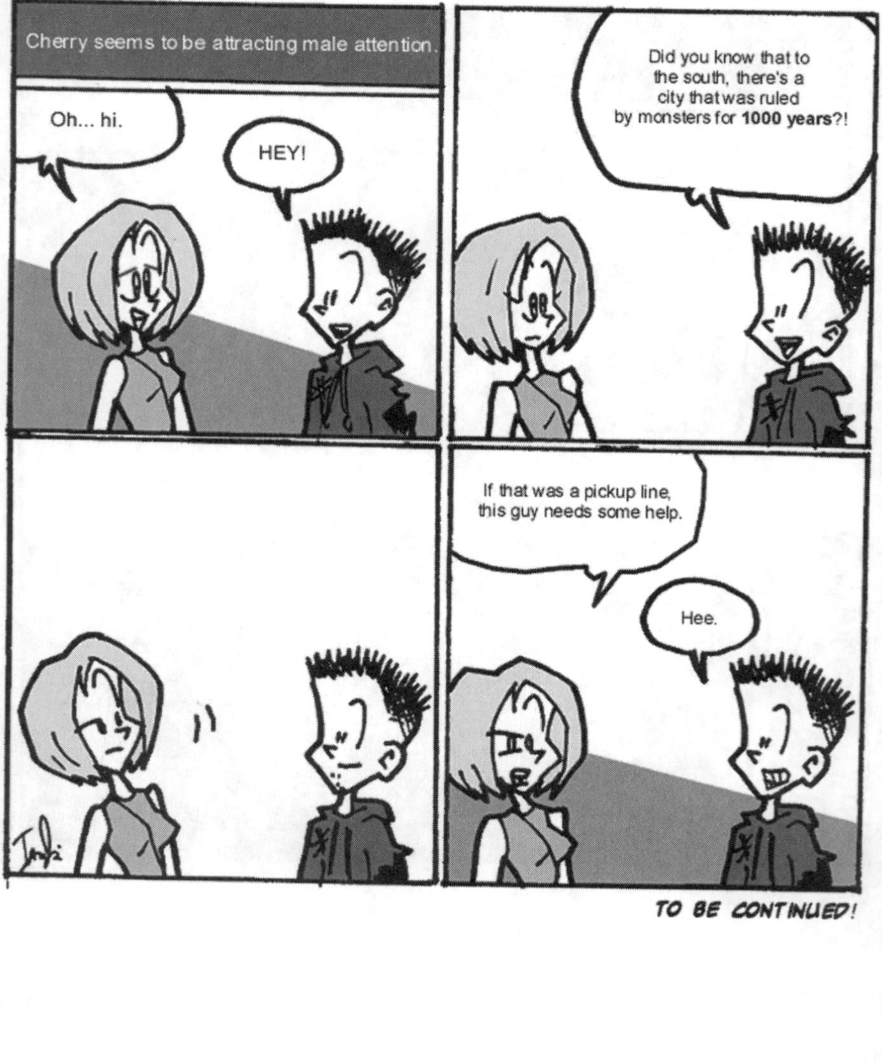
Cherry seems to be attracting male attention.
Oh... hi.
HEY!
Did you know that to the south, there's a city that was ruled by monsters for **1000 years**?!
If that was a pickup line, this guy needs some help.
Hee.

TO BE CONTINUED!

RPG WORLD

ART/STORY BY IAN J.

"RECCOMENDED DESTINATION"

#20

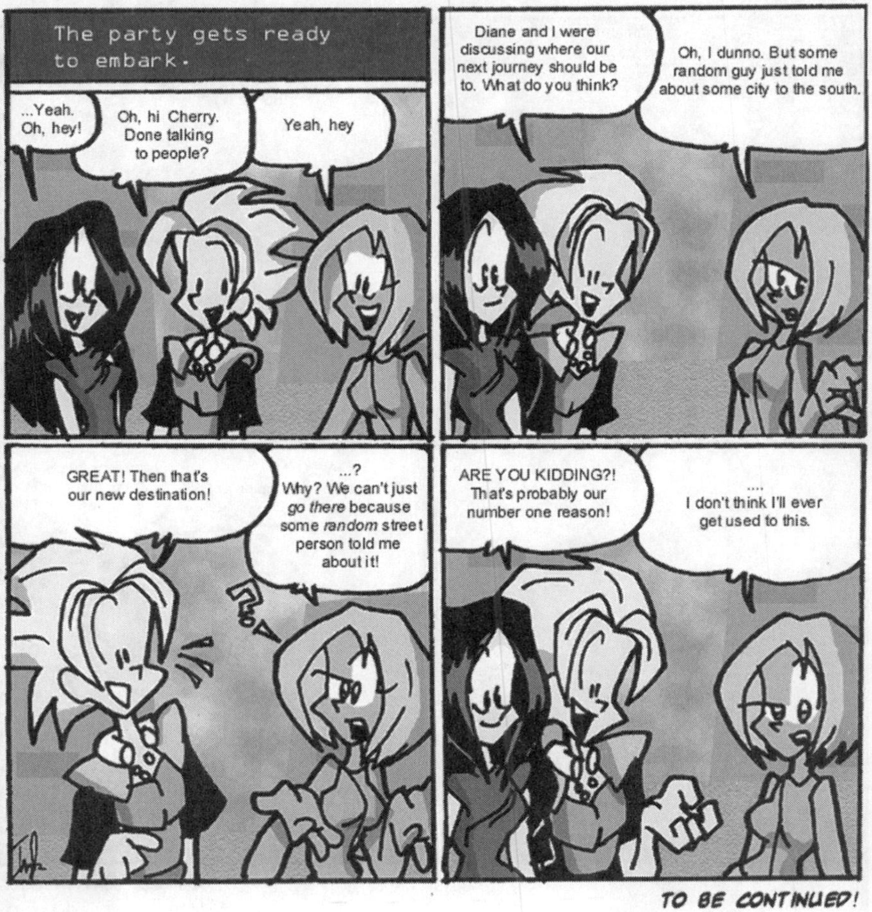

The party gets ready to embark.
...Yeah. Oh, hey!
Oh, hi Cherry. Done talking to people?
Yeah, hey
Diane and I were discussing where our next journey should be to. What do you think?
Oh, I dunno. But some random guy just told me about some city to the south.
GREAT! Then that's our new destination!
...? Why? We can't just *go there* because some *random* street person told me about it!
ARE YOU KIDDING?! That's probably our number one reason!
.... I don't think I'll ever get used to this.

TO BE CONTINUED!

RPG WORLD

ART/STORY BY IAN J.

"SNEAKY ENEMIES"

#21

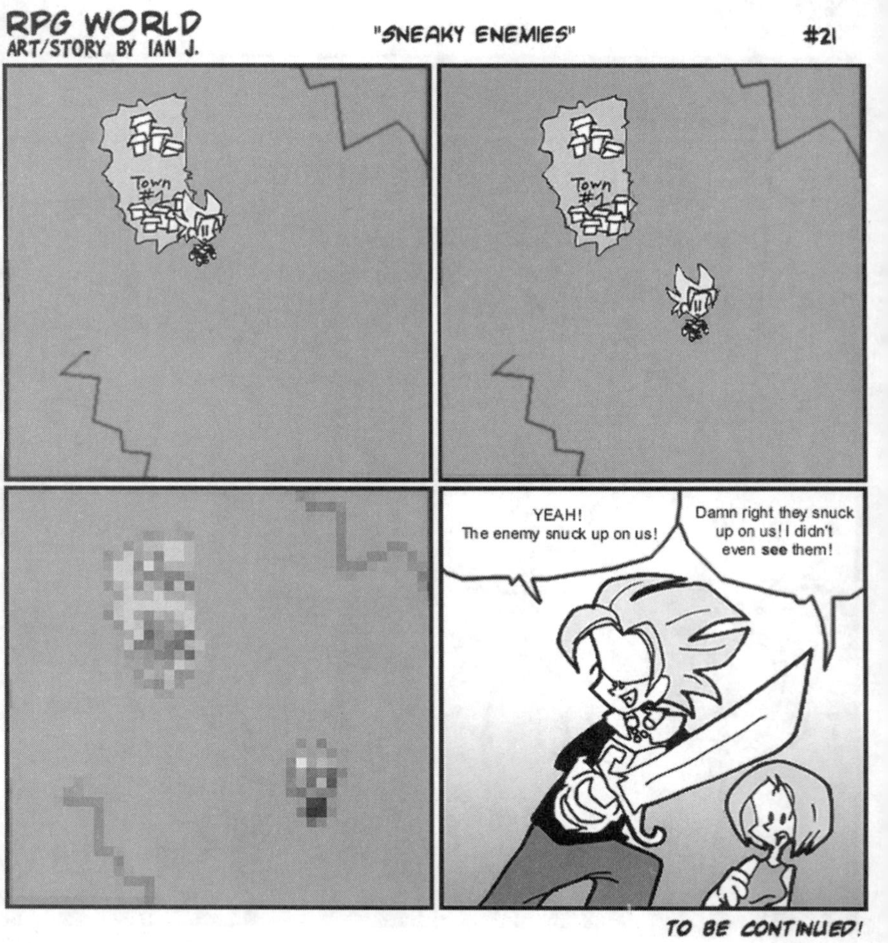
Town #1
Town #1
YEAH! The enemy snuck up on us!
Damn right they snuck up on us! I didn't even **see** them!

TO BE CONTINUED!

RPG WORLD
ART/STORY BY IAN J.

"THAT'S GOTTA HURT"

#22

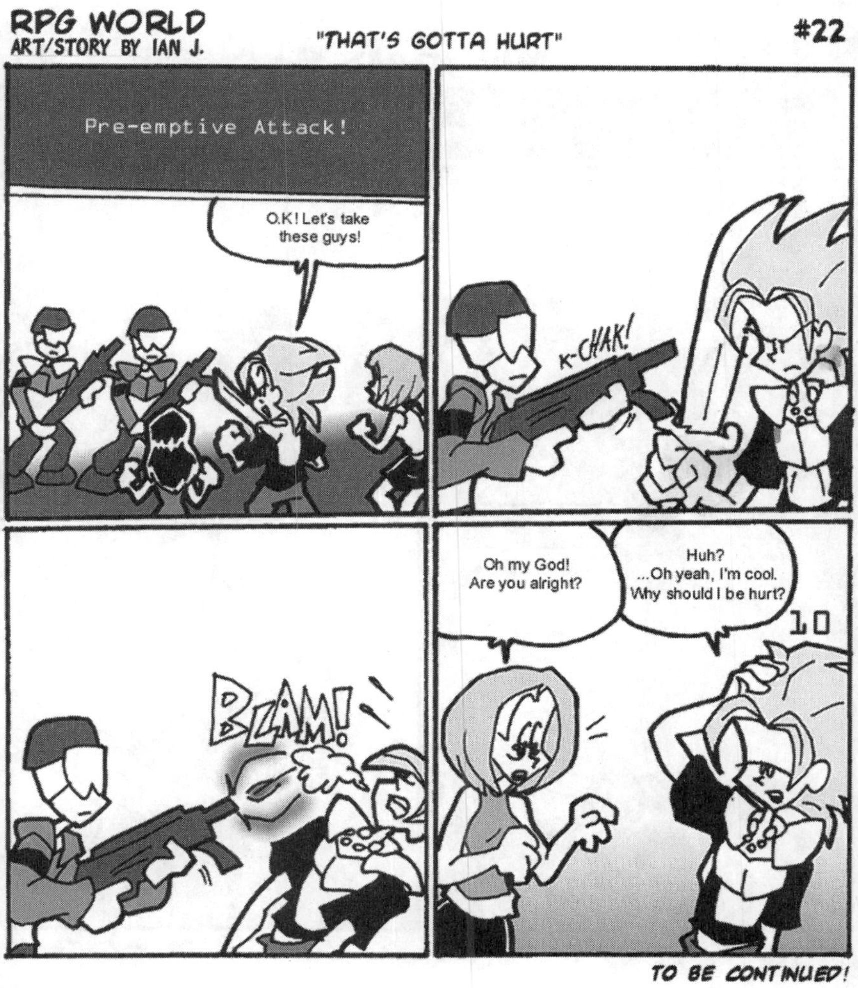
Pre-emptive Attack!
O.K! Let's take these guys!
K-CHAK!
BLAM!
Oh my God! Are you alright?
Huh? ...Oh yeah, I'm cool. Why should I be hurt?
10

TO BE CONTINUED!

RPG WORLD
ART/STORY BY IAN J.

"HOLD ON..."

#23

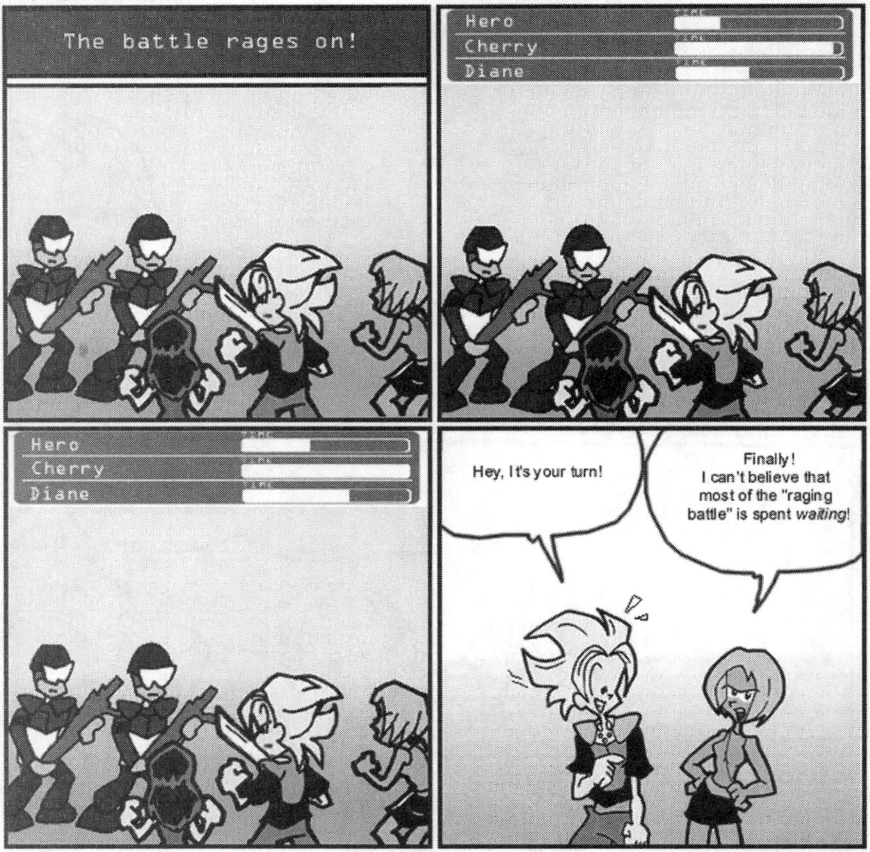
The battle rages on!
Hero
Cherry
Diane
Hero
Cherry
Diane
Hey, It's your turn!
Finally! I can't believe that most of the "raging battle" is spent *waiting*!

TO BE CONTINUED!

RPG WORLD
ART/STORY BY IAN J.

"SEXIST ATTACK" #24

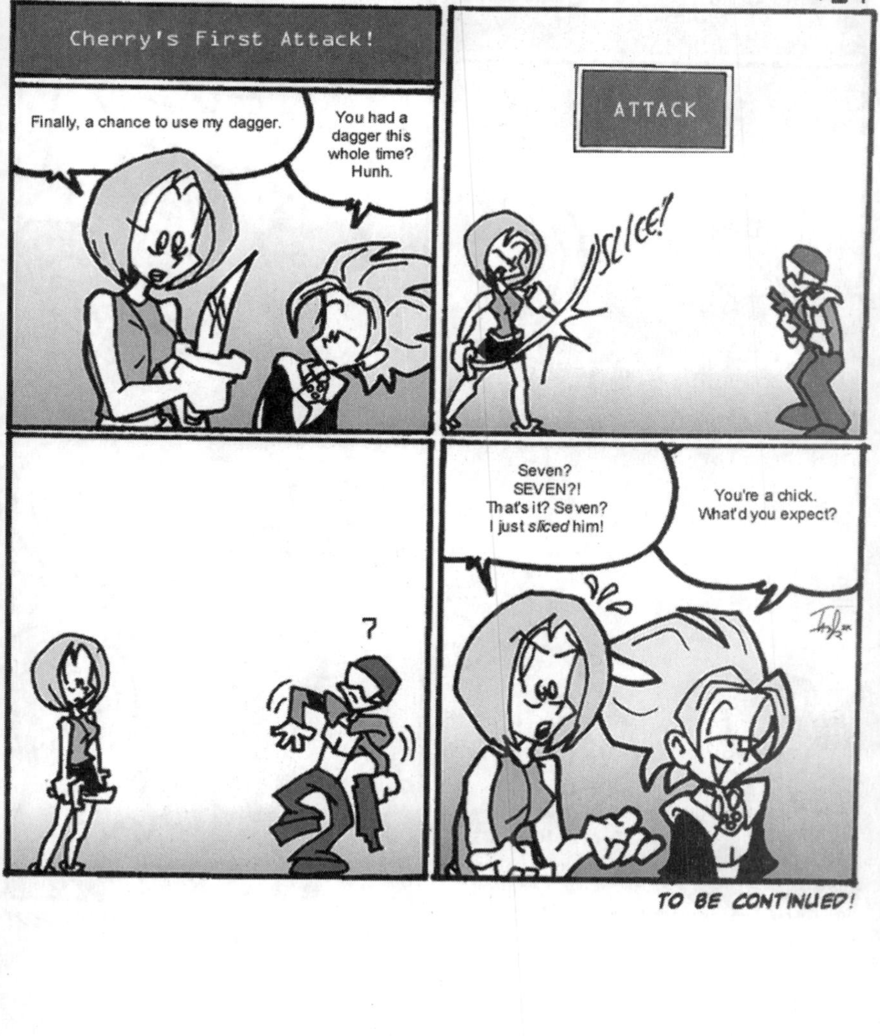
Cherry's First Attack!
Finally, a chance to use my dagger.
You had a dagger this whole time? Hunh.
ATTACK
SLICE!
7
Seven? SEVEN?! That's it? Seven? I just *sliced* him!
You're a chick. What'd you expect?

TO BE CONTINUED!

RPG WORLD
ART/STORY BY IAN J.

"BANG!"

#25

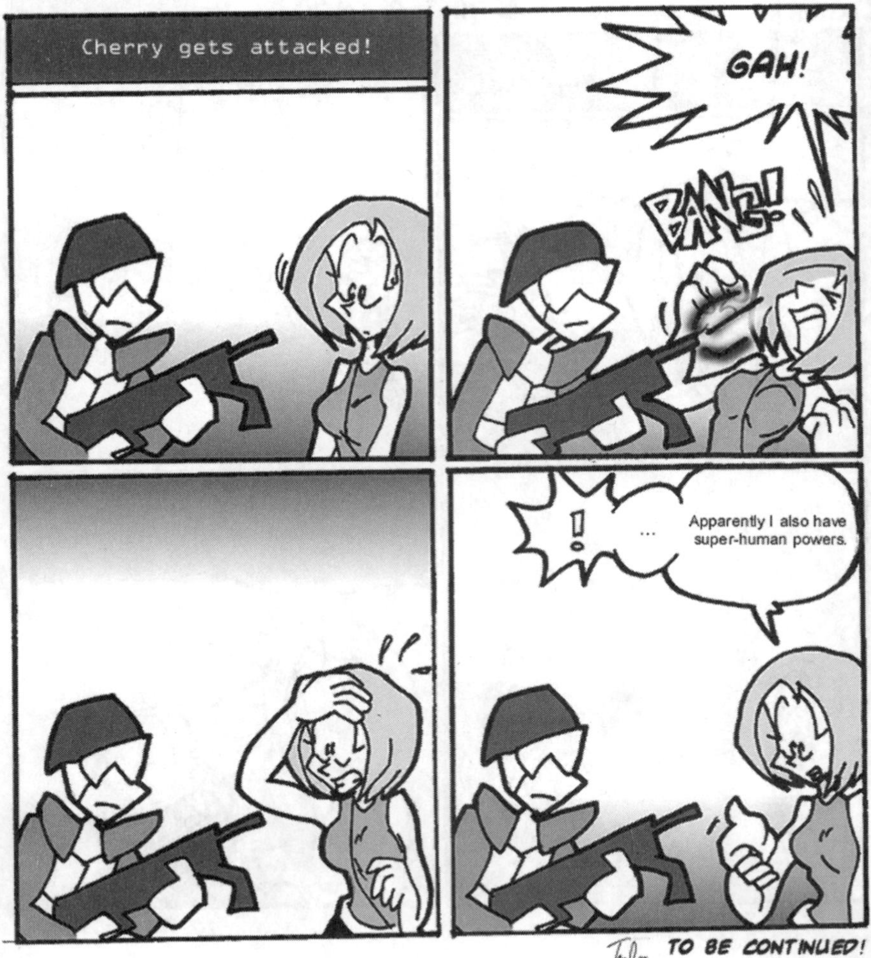
Cherry gets attacked!
GAH!
BANG!
!
...
Apparently I also have super-human powers.
TO BE CONTINUED!

RPG WORLD
ART/STORY BY IAN J.

"ATTACK ENVY"

#26

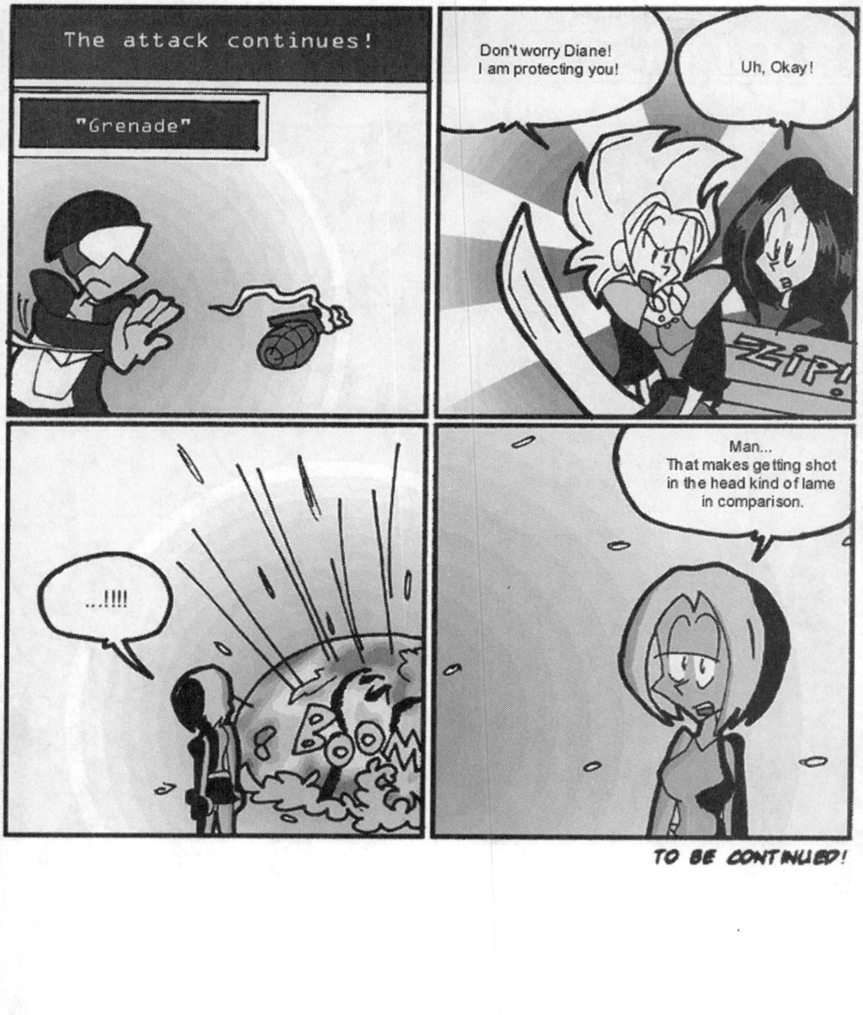
The attack continues!
"Grenade"
Don't worry Diane! I am protecting you!
Uh, Okay!
ZIP!
...!!!!
BOOM
Man... That makes getting shot in the head kind of lame in comparison.

TO BE CONTINUED!

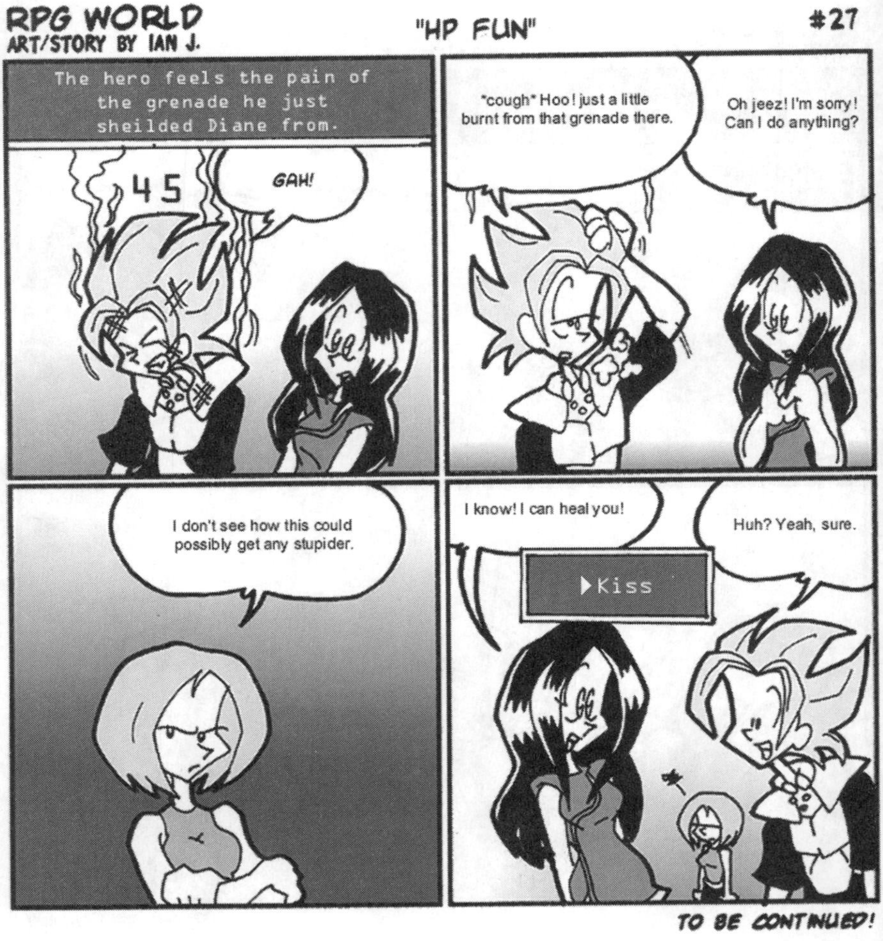
RPG WORLD
ART/STORY BY IAN J.
"HP FUN"
#27
The hero feels the pain of the grenade he just sheilded Diane from.
45
GAH!
cough Hoo! just a little burnt from that grenade there.
Oh jeez! I'm sorry! Can I do anything?
I don't see how this could possibly get any stupider.
I know! I can heal you!
Kiss
Huh? Yeah, sure.
TO BE CONTINUED!

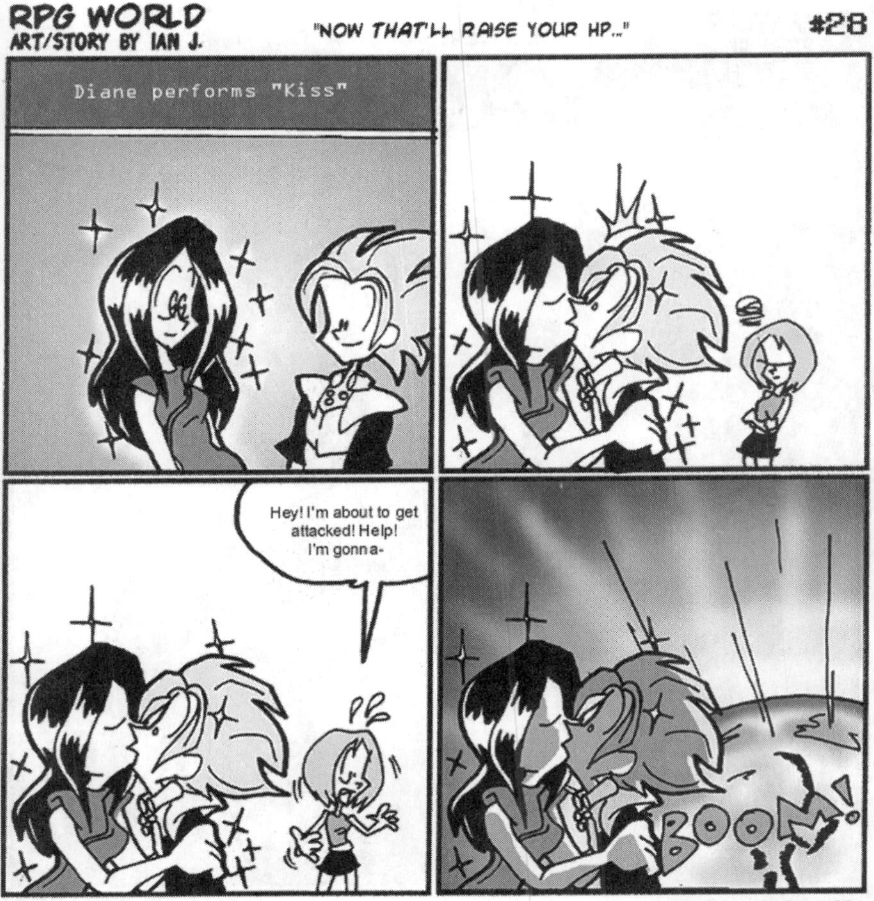
RPG WORLD
ART/STORY BY IAN J.
"NOW THAT'LL RAISE YOUR HP.."
#28
Diane performs "Kiss"
Hey! I'm about to get attacked! Help! I'm gonna-
BOOM!
TO BE CONTINUED!

RPG WORLD

ART/STORY BY IAN J.

"THIS IS A VERY LONG BATTLE, HUH?'

#29

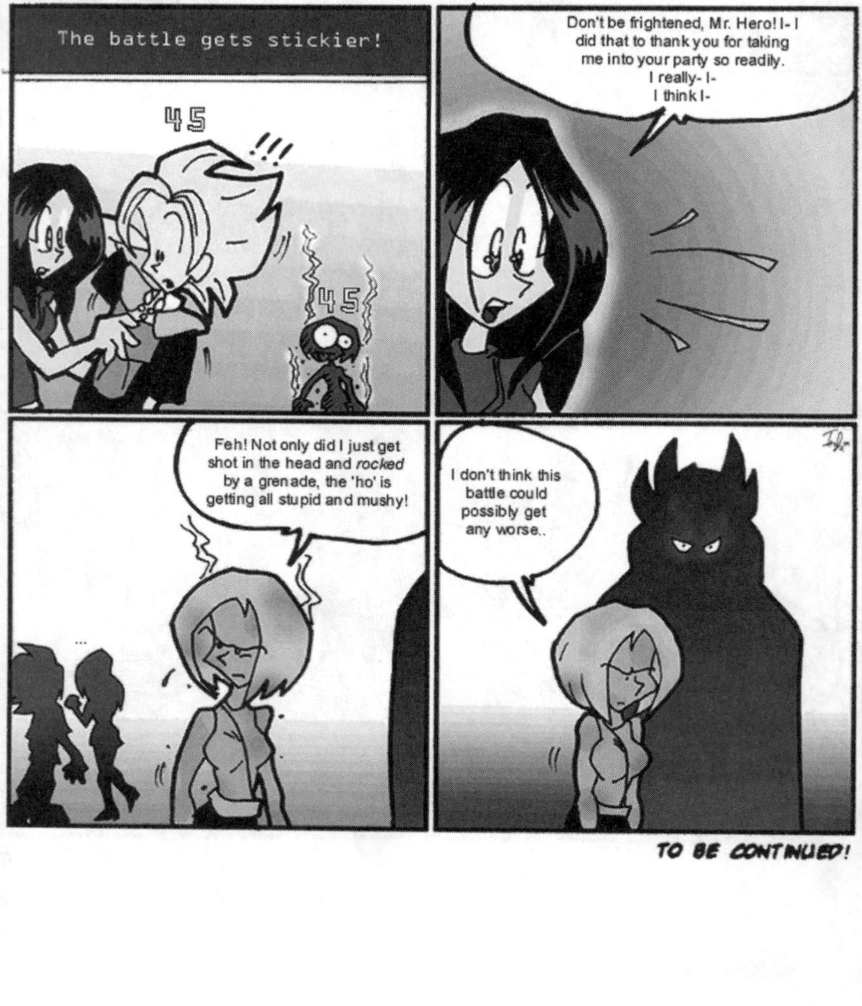
The battle gets stickier!
45
!!!
45
Don't be frightened, Mr. Hero! I- I did that to thank you for taking me into your party so readily. I really- I- I think I-
Feh! Not only did I just get shot in the head and *rocked* by a grenade, the 'ho' is getting all stupid and mushy!
...
I don't think this battle could possibly get any worse..

TO BE CONTINUED!

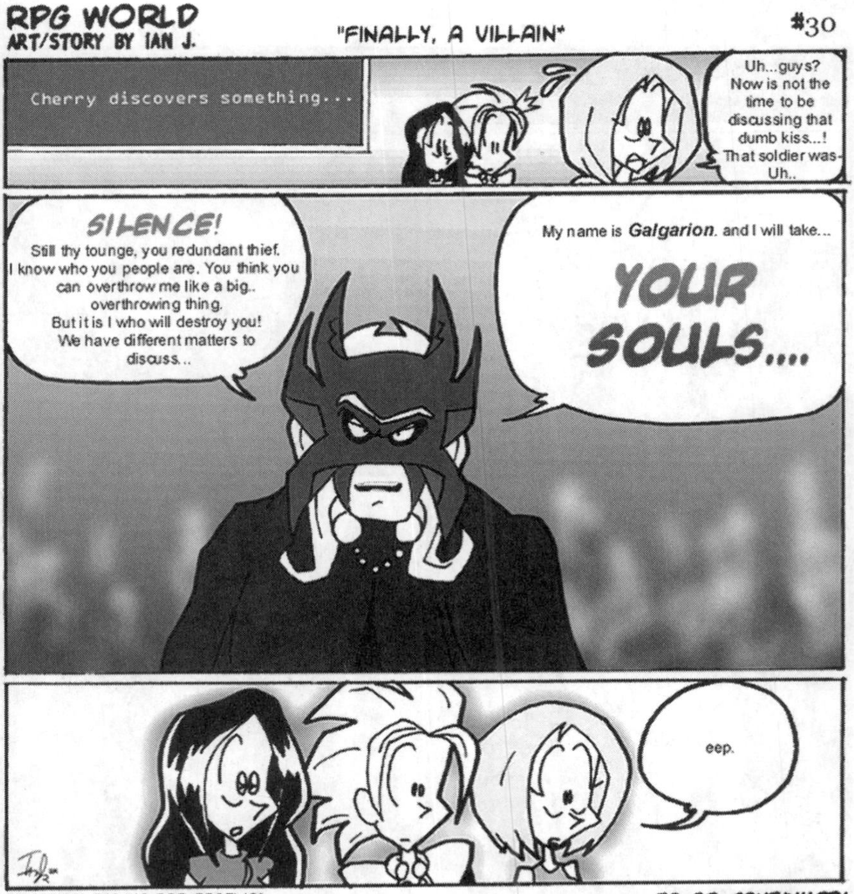
RPG WORLD
ART/STORY BY IAN J.
"FINALLY, A VILLAIN"
#30
Cherry discovers something...
Uh...guys? Now is not the time to be discussing that dumb kiss...! That soldier was- Uh..
SILENCE! Still thy tounge, you redundant thief. I know who you people are. You think you can overthrow me like a big.. overthrowing thing. But it is I who will destroy you! We have different matters to discuss...
My name is Galgarion. and I will take...
YOUR SOULS....
eep.
30 STRIPS! THANKS FOR READING!
TO BE CONTINUED!

RPG WORLD
ART/STORY BY IAN J.

"ENEMIES"

#31

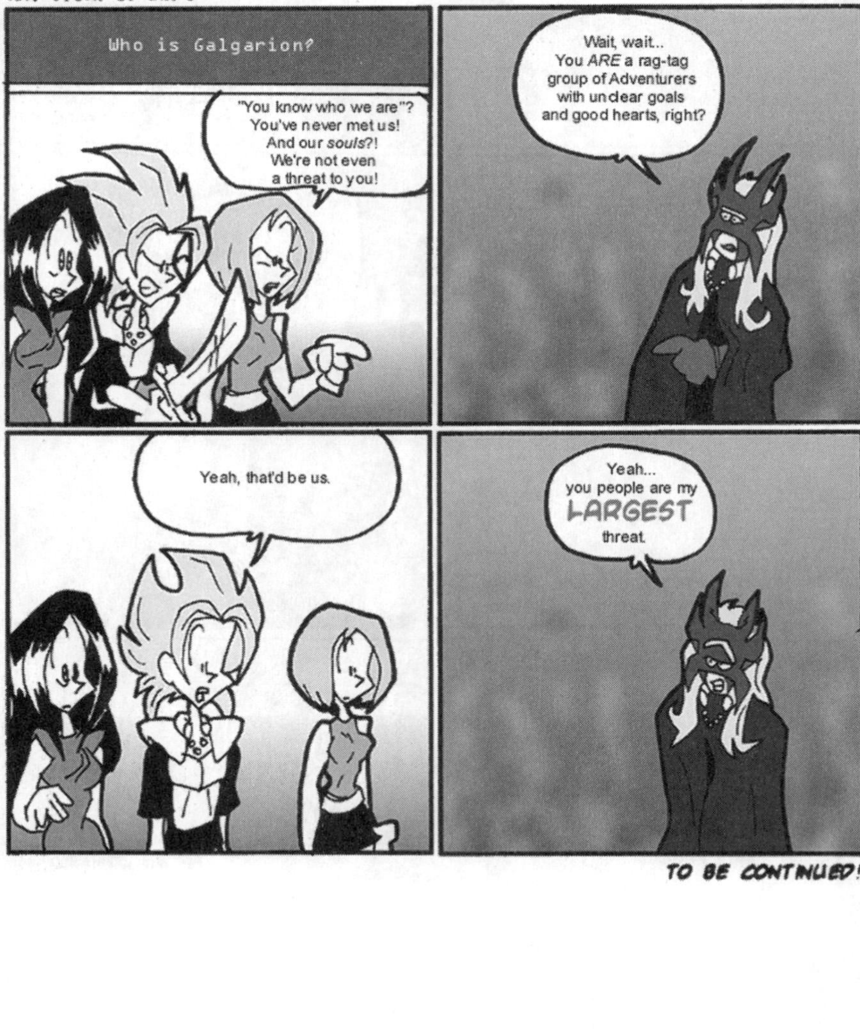
Who is Galgarion?
"You know who we are"? You've never met us! And our *souls*?! We're not even a threat to you!
Wait, wait... You *ARE* a rag-tag group of Adventurers with unclear goals and good hearts, right?
Yeah, that'd be us.
Yeah... you people are my LARGEST threat.

TO BE CONTINUED!

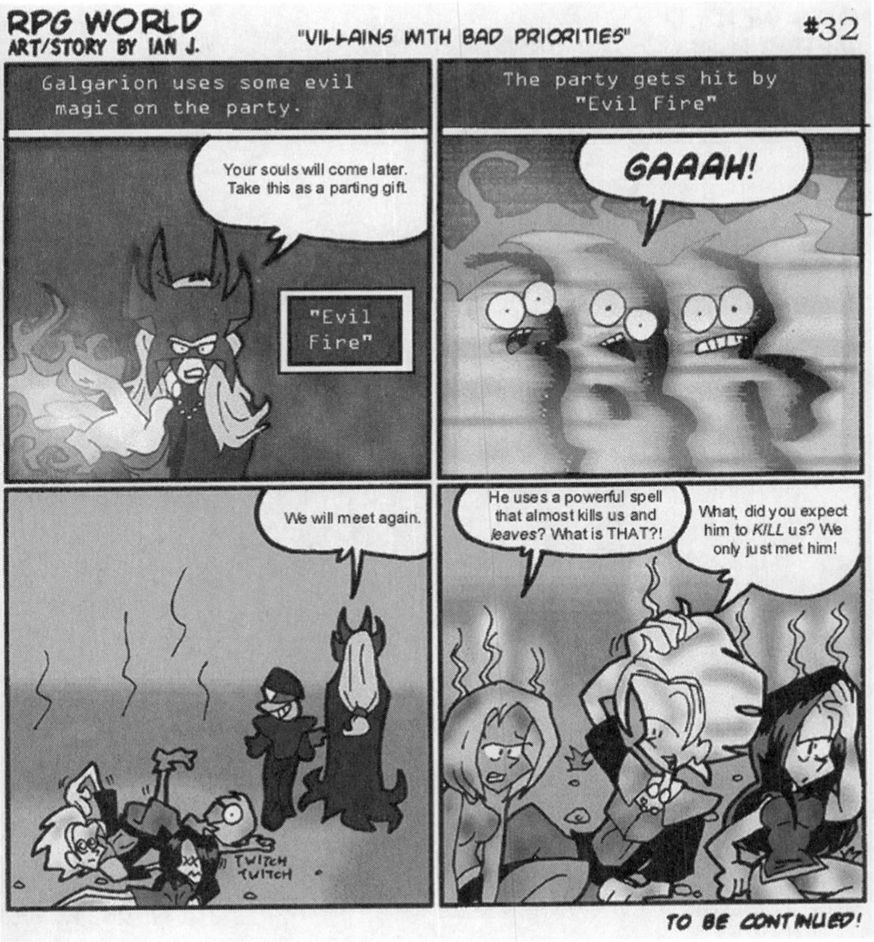
RPG WORLD
ART/STORY BY IAN J.
"VILLAINS WITH BAD PRIORITIES"
#32
Galgarion uses some evil magic on the party.
Your souls will come later. Take this as a parting gift.
"Evil Fire"
The party gets hit by "Evil Fire"
GAAAH!
We will meet again.
TWITCH TWITCH
He uses a powerful spell that almost kills us and *leaves*? What is THAT?!
What, did you expect him to *KILL* us? We only just met him!
TO BE CONTINUED!

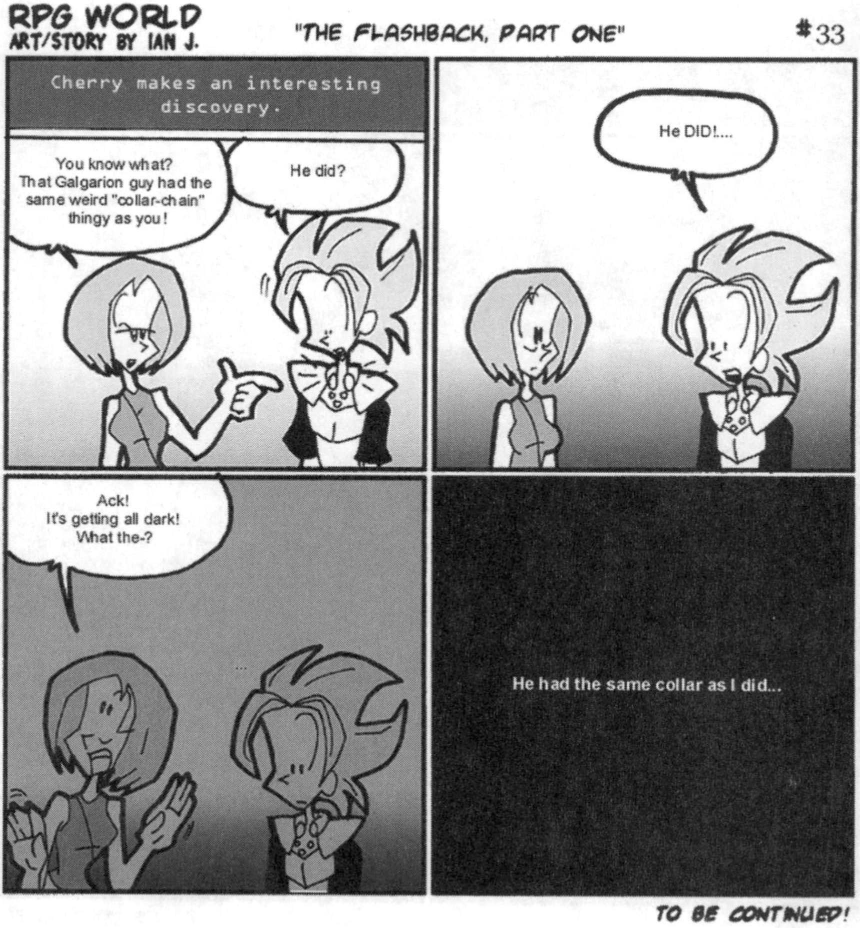
RPG WORLD
ART/STORY BY IAN J.
"THE FLASHBACK, PART ONE"
#33
Cherry makes an interesting discovery.
You know what? That Galgarion guy had the same weird "collar-chain" thingy as you!
He did?
He DID!...
Ack! It's getting all dark! What the-?
...
He had the same collar as I did...
TO BE CONTINUED!

RPG WORLD
ART/STORY BY IAN J.

"THE FLASHBACK, PART TWO"

#34

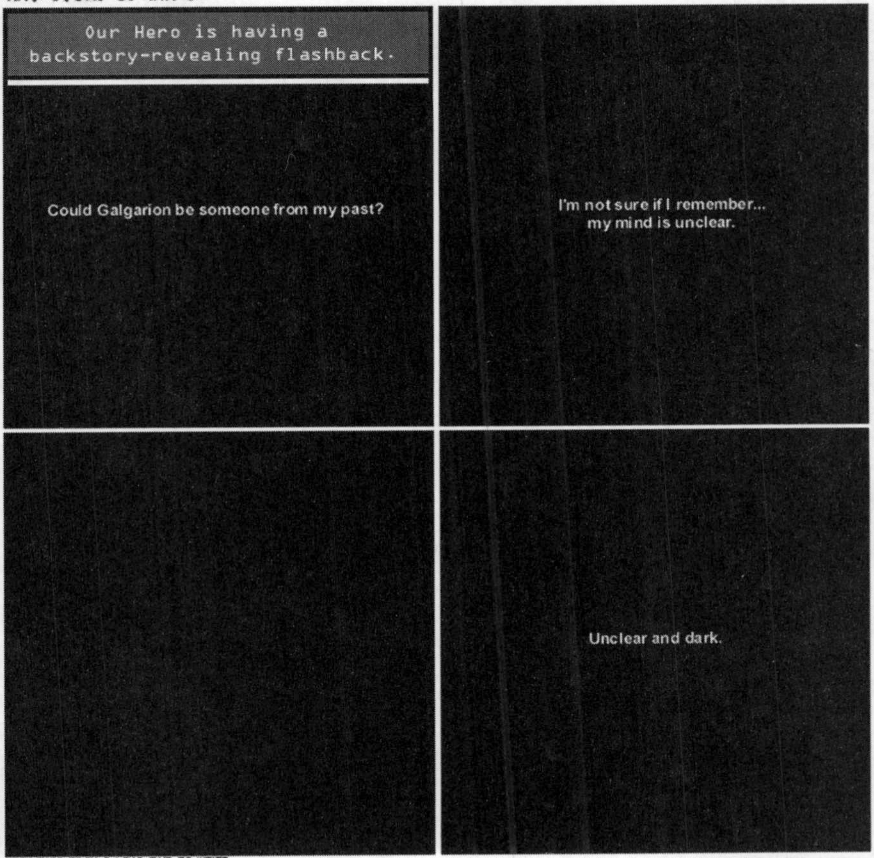
Our Hero is having a backstory-revealing flashback.
Could Galgarion be someone from my past?
I'm not sure if I remember... my mind is unclear.
Unclear and dark.

YEAH, THIS TOOK A LONG TIME TO WRITE.

TO BE CONTINUED!

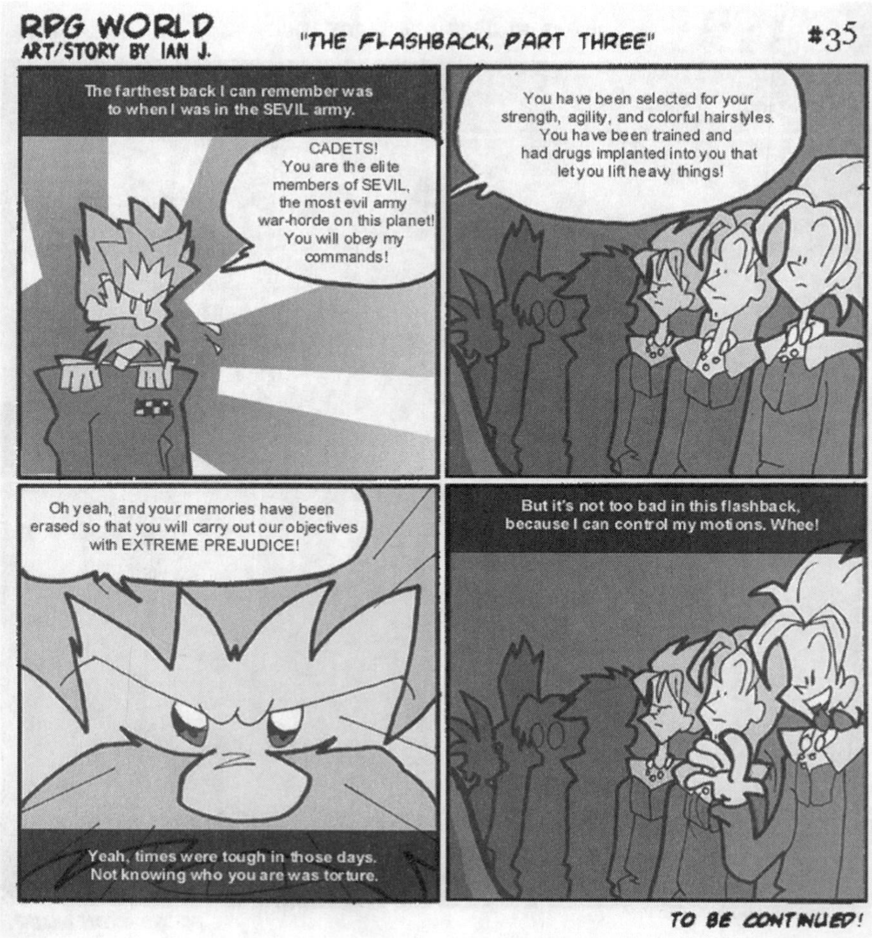
RPG WORLD
ART/STORY BY IAN J.
"THE FLASHBACK, PART THREE"
#35
The farthest back I can remember was to when I was in the SEVIL army.
CADETS! You are the elite members of SEVIL, the most evil army war-horde on this planet! You will obey my commands!
You have been selected for your strength, agility, and colorful hairstyles. You have been trained and had drugs implanted into you that let you lift heavy things!
Oh yeah, and your memories have been erased so that you will carry out our objectives with EXTREME PREJUDICE!
Yeah, times were tough in those days. Not knowing who you are was torture.
But it's not too bad in this flashback, because I can control my motions. Whee!
TO BE CONTINUED!

RPG WORLD
ART/STORY BY IAN J.

"CREATIVE LICENSE"

#36

One of our first missions was to raid and burn a village to find the legendary "Phoenix Book"
Wait.. wait.. no... we didn't burn the village... that would have been excessive...
..and needlessly violent..
..Oh what the heck.

TO BE CONTINUED!

RPG WORLD

ART/STORY BY IAN J.

"THE FLASHBACK, PART FIVE" #37

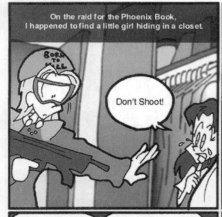

On the raid for the Phoenix Book,
I happened to find a little girl hiding in a closet.
Don't Shoot!
I don't know what it was, but I couldn't bring myself
to kill a little kid, even though I was ordered to.
So I reunited her with a bunch of escaped villagers.
c'mon...
Oh, thank you so much, Mister.. umm.. what's your name anyway?
Hey... I just realized... I don't *have* a name.
Don't worry, you'll always be *the hero* to me!
Aww... *cute*, huh?
Of course, I failed to kill her, so they kicked me out of SEVIL the next day.

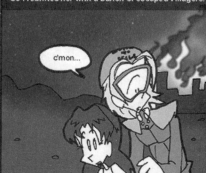

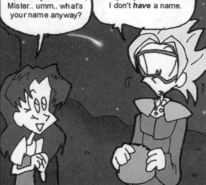

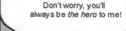

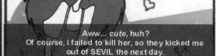

I GUARANTEE YOU WILL NEVER SEE THIS LITTLE GIRL AGAIN IN *RPG WORLD*.

TO BE CONTINUED!

RPG WORLD
ART/STORY BY IAN J.

"THE FLASHBACK PART SIX"

#38

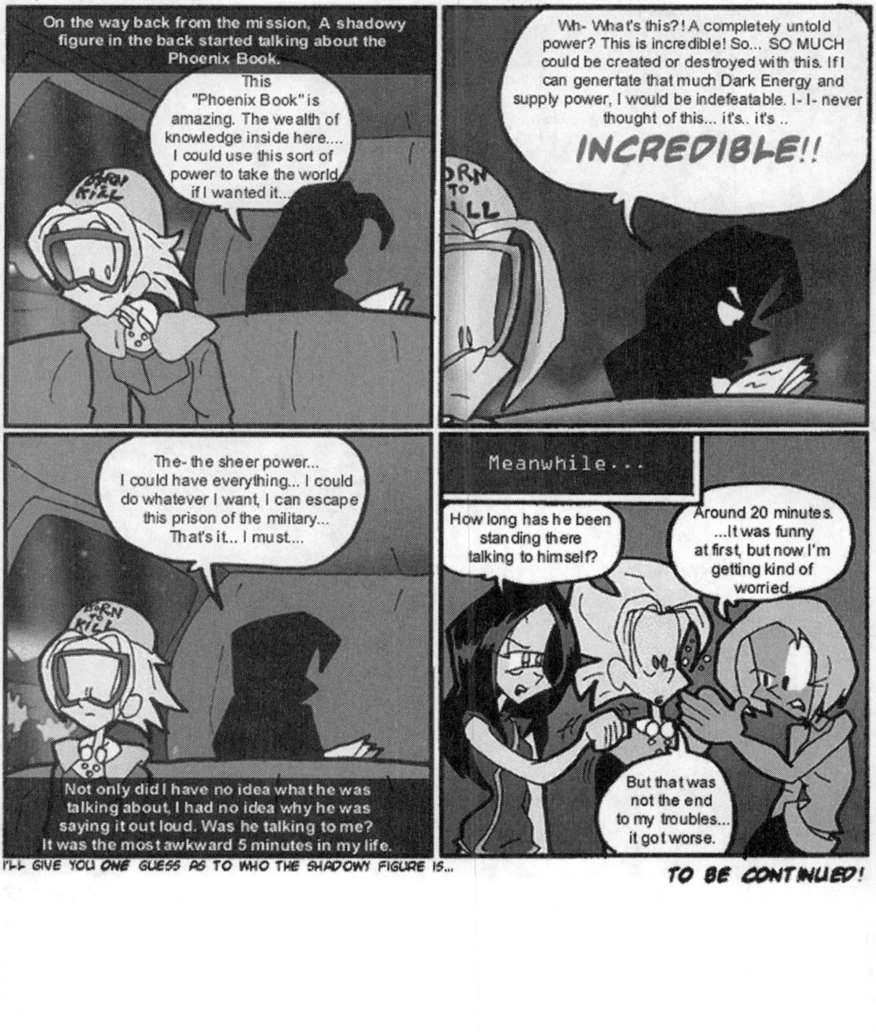
On the way back from the mission, A shadowy figure in the back started talking about the Phoenix Book.
This "Phoenix Book" is amazing. The wealth of knowledge inside here.... I could use this sort of power to take the world if I wanted it...
Wh- What's this?! A completely untold power? This is incredible! So... SO MUCH could be created or destroyed with this. If I can genertate that much Dark Energy and supply power, I would be indefeatable. I- I- never thought of this... it's.. it's ..
INCREDIBLE!!
The- the sheer power... I could have everything... I could do whatever I want, I can escape this prison of the military... That's it... I must....
Not only did I have no idea what he was talking about, I had no idea why he was saying it out loud. Was he talking to me? It was the most awkward 5 minutes in my life.
Meanwhile...
How long has he been standing there talking to himself?
Around 20 minutes. ...It was funny at first, but now I'm getting kind of worried.
But that was not the end to my troubles... it got worse.

I'LL GIVE YOU *ONE* GUESS AS TO WHO THE SHADOWY FIGURE IS...

TO BE CONTINUED!

RPG WORLD
ART/STORY BY IAN J.

"THE FLASHBACK, PART SEVEN"
(IT'LL BE OVER SOON, I PROMISE)

#39

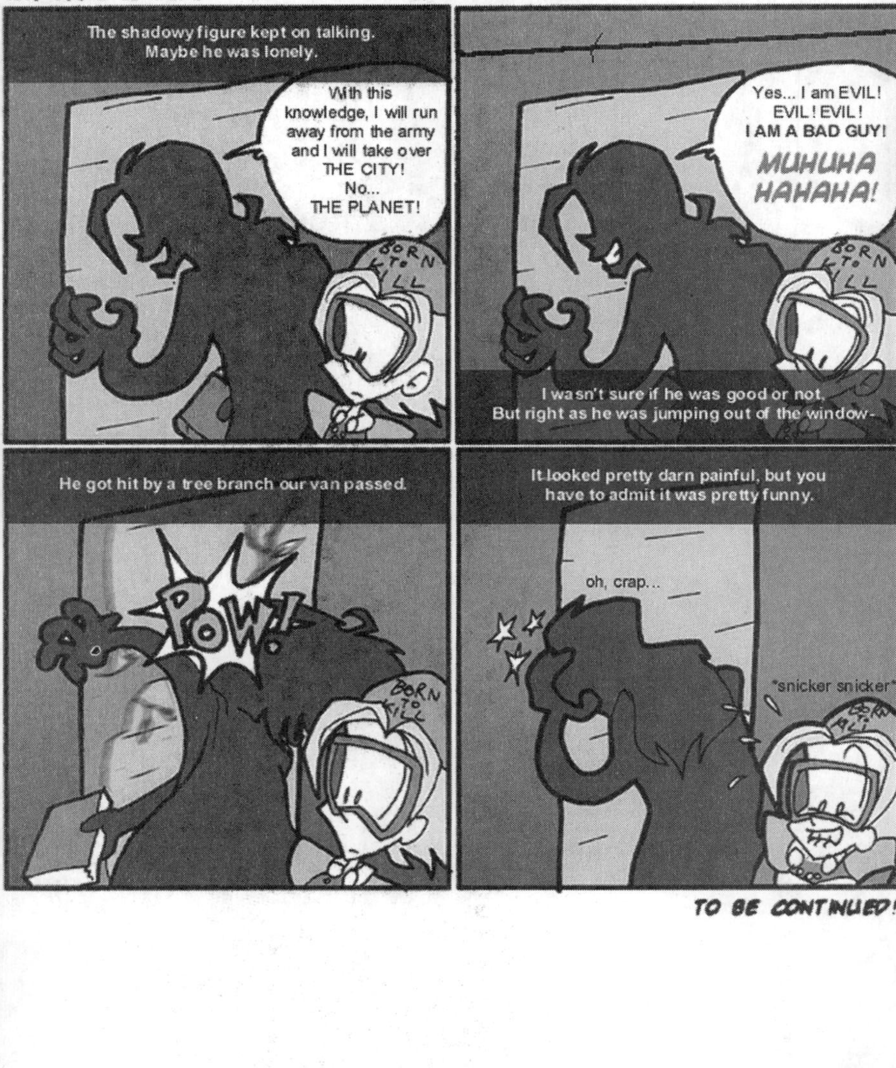

The shadowy figure kept on talking. Maybe he was lonely.
With this knowledge, I will run away from the army and I will take over THE CITY! No... THE PLANET!
BORN TO KILL
Yes... I am EVIL! EVIL! EVIL! I AM A BAD GUY!
MUHUHA HAHAHA!
BORN TO KILL
I wasn't sure if he was good or not. But right as he was jumping out of the window-
He got hit by a tree branch our van passed.
POW!!
BORN TO KILL
It looked pretty darn painful, but you have to admit it was pretty funny.
oh, crap...
snicker snicker

TO BE CONTINUED!

RPG WORLD
ART/STORY BY IAN J.

"THE FLASHBACK, PART EIGHT" #40

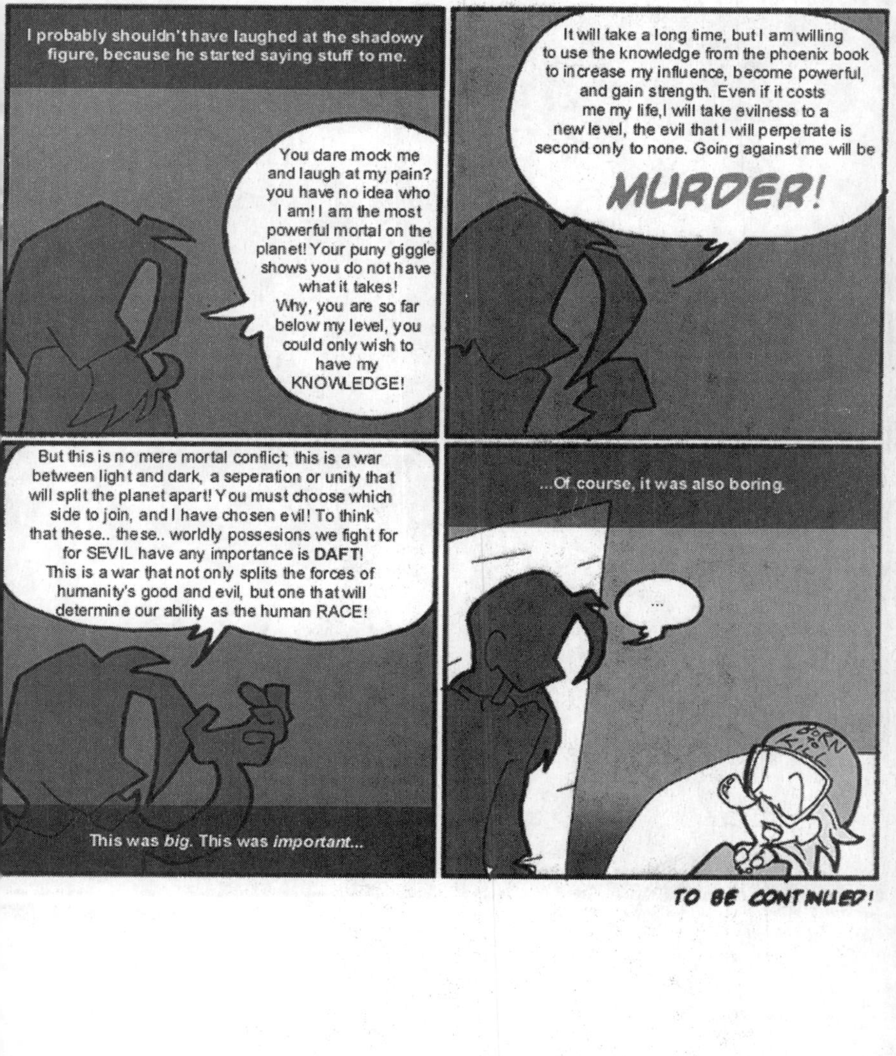

I probably shouldn't have laughed at the shadowy figure, because he started saying stuff to me.
You dare mock me and laugh at my pain? you have no idea who I am! I am the most powerful mortal on the planet! Your puny giggle shows you do not have what it takes! Why, you are so far below my level, you could only wish to have my KNOWLEDGE!
It will take a long time, but I am willing to use the knowledge from the phoenix book to increase my influence, become powerful, and gain strength. Even if it costs me my life,I will take evilness to a new level, the evil that I will perpetrate is second only to none. Going against me will be MURDER!
But this is no mere mortal conflict, this is a war between light and dark, a seperation or unity that will split the planet apart! You must choose which side to join, and I have chosen evil! To think that these.. these.. worldly possesions we fight for for SEVIL have any importance is DAFT! This is a war that not only splits the forces of humanity's good and evil, but one that will determine our ability as the human RACE!
This was big. This was important...
...Of course, it was also boring.
...

TO BE CONTINUED!

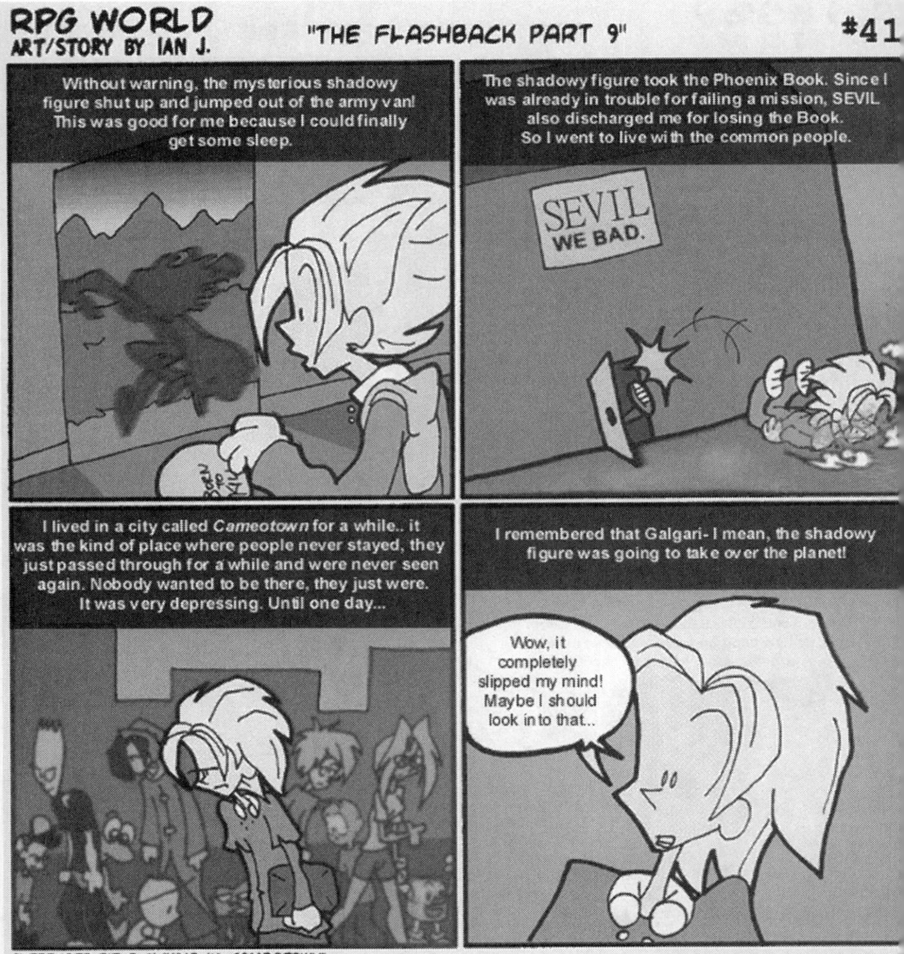
RPG WORLD
ART/STORY BY IAN J.
"THE FLASHBACK PART 9"
#41
Without warning, the mysterious shadowy figure shut up and jumped out of the army van! This was good for me because I could finally get some sleep.
The shadowy figure took the Phoenix Book. Since I was already in trouble for failing a mission, SEVIL also discharged me for losing the Book. So I went to live with the common people.
SEVIL
WE BAD.
I lived in a city called *Cameotown* for a while.. it was the kind of place where people never stayed, they just passed through for a while and were never seen again. Nobody wanted to be there, they just were. It was very depressing. Until one day...
I remembered that Galgari- I mean, the shadowy figure was going to take over the planet!
Wow, it completely slipped my mind! Maybe I should look into that...
ALTERNATE TITLE: "LIVING IN CAMEOTOWN"
TO BE CONTINUED

RPG WORLD
ART/STORY BY IAN J.

"THE FLASHBACK, PART 10"

#42

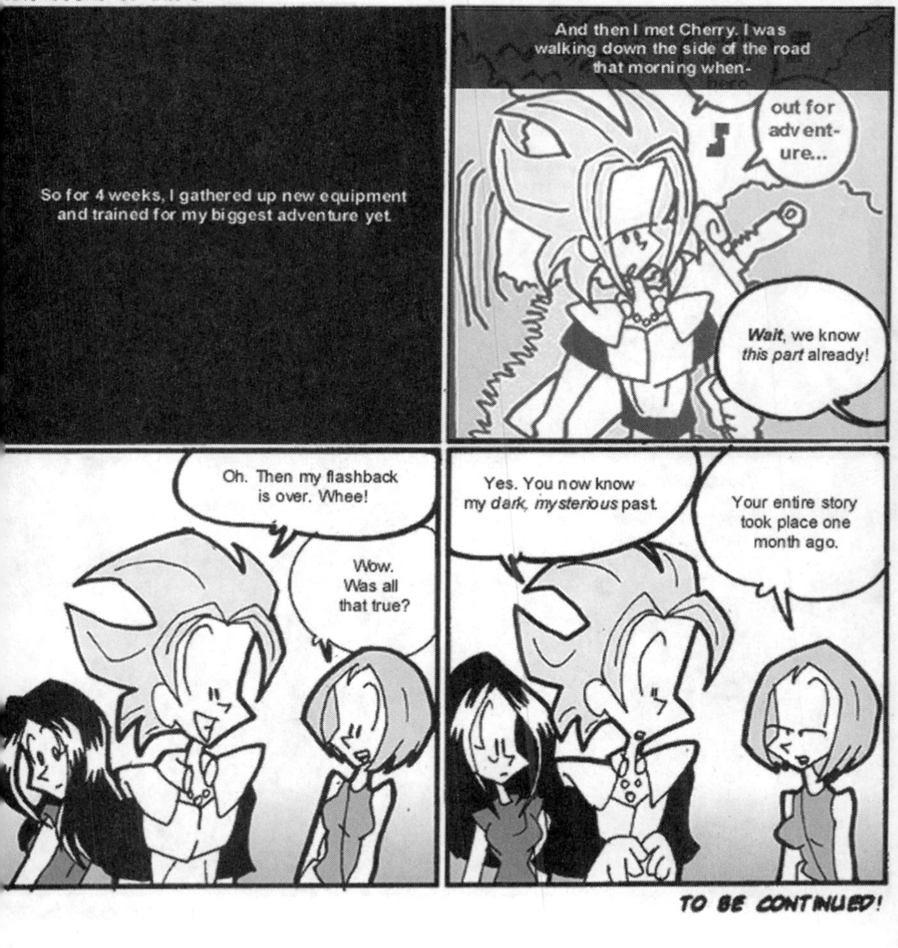

So for 4 weeks, I gathered up new equipment and trained for my biggest adventure yet.
And then I met Cherry. I was walking down the side of the road that morning when-
out for adv ent-ure...
Wait, we know *this part* already!
Oh. Then my flashback is over. Whee!
Wow. Was all that true?
Yes. You now know my *dark, mysterious* past.
Your entire story took place one month ago.

TO BE CONTINUED!

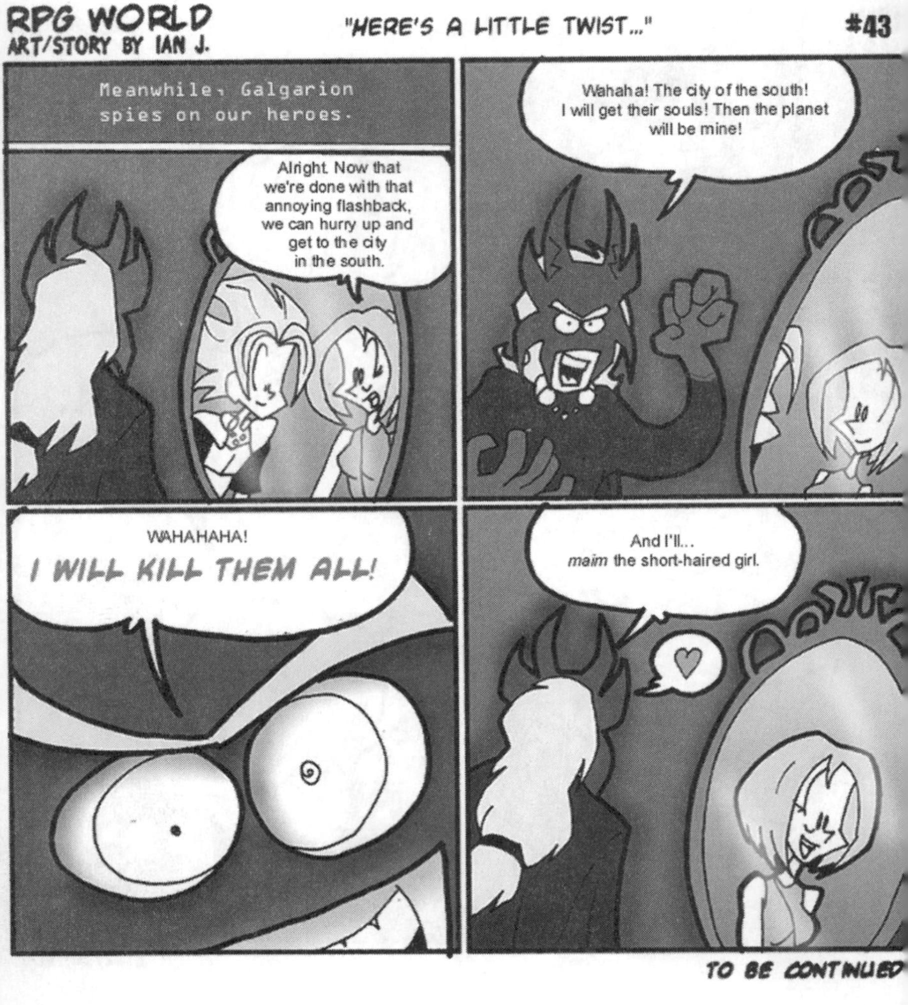
RPG WORLD
ART/STORY BY IAN J.
"HERE'S A LITTLE TWIST..."
#43
Meanwhile, Galgarion spies on our heroes.
Alright. Now that we're done with that annoying flashback, we can hurry up and get to the city in the south.
Wahaha! The city of the south! I will get their souls! Then the planet will be mine!
WAHAHAHA!
I WILL KILL THEM ALL!
And I'll... *maim* the short-haired girl.
TO BE CONTINUED

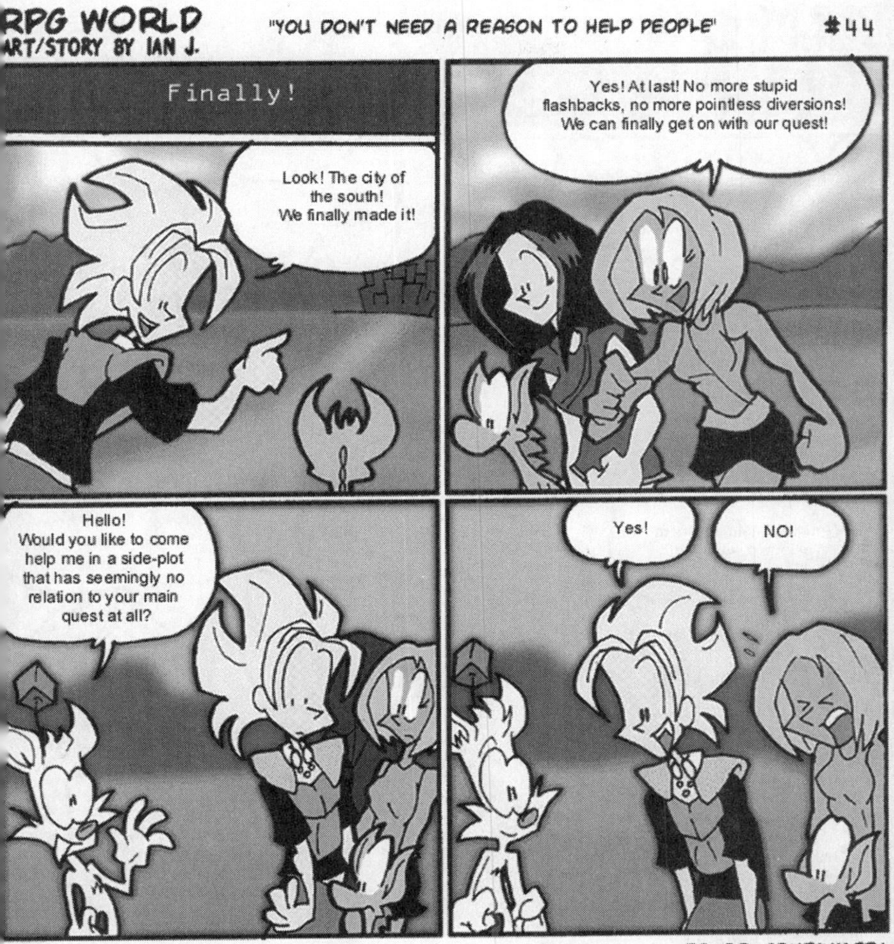
RPG WORLD
ART/STORY BY IAN J.
"YOU DON'T NEED A REASON TO HELP PEOPLE"
#44
Finally!
Look! The city of the south! We finally made it!
Yes! At last! No more stupid flashbacks, no more pointless diversions! We can finally get on with our quest!
Hello! Would you like to come help me in a side-plot that has seemingly no relation to your main quest at all?
Yes!
NO!
TO BE CONTINUED!

RPG WORLD
ART/STORY BY IAN J.

"WIGGLEBOTTOM"

#45

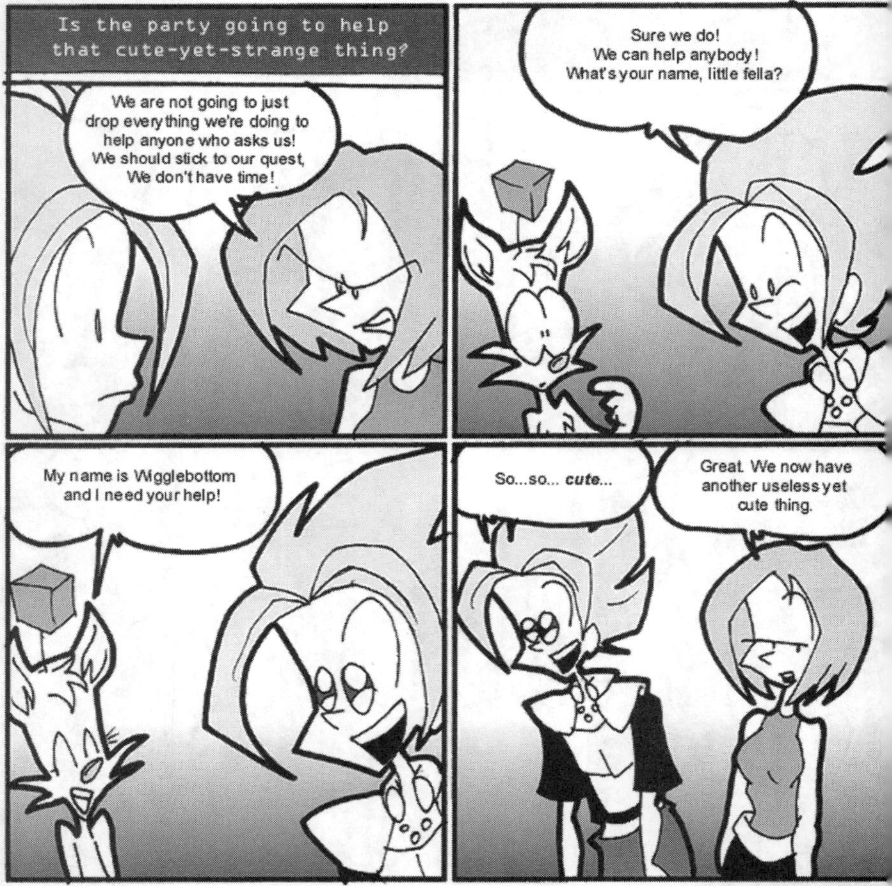
Is the party going to help that cute-yet-strange thing?
We are not going to just drop everything we're doing to help anyone who asks us! We should stick to our quest, We don't have time!
Sure we do! We can help anybody! What's your name, little fella?
My name is Wigglebottom and I need your help!
So...so... *cute*...
Great. We now have another useless yet cute thing.

TO BE CONTINUED!

RPG WORLD
ART/STORY BY IAN J.

"...YOU *DO* NEED A REASON TO HELP PEOPLE."

#46

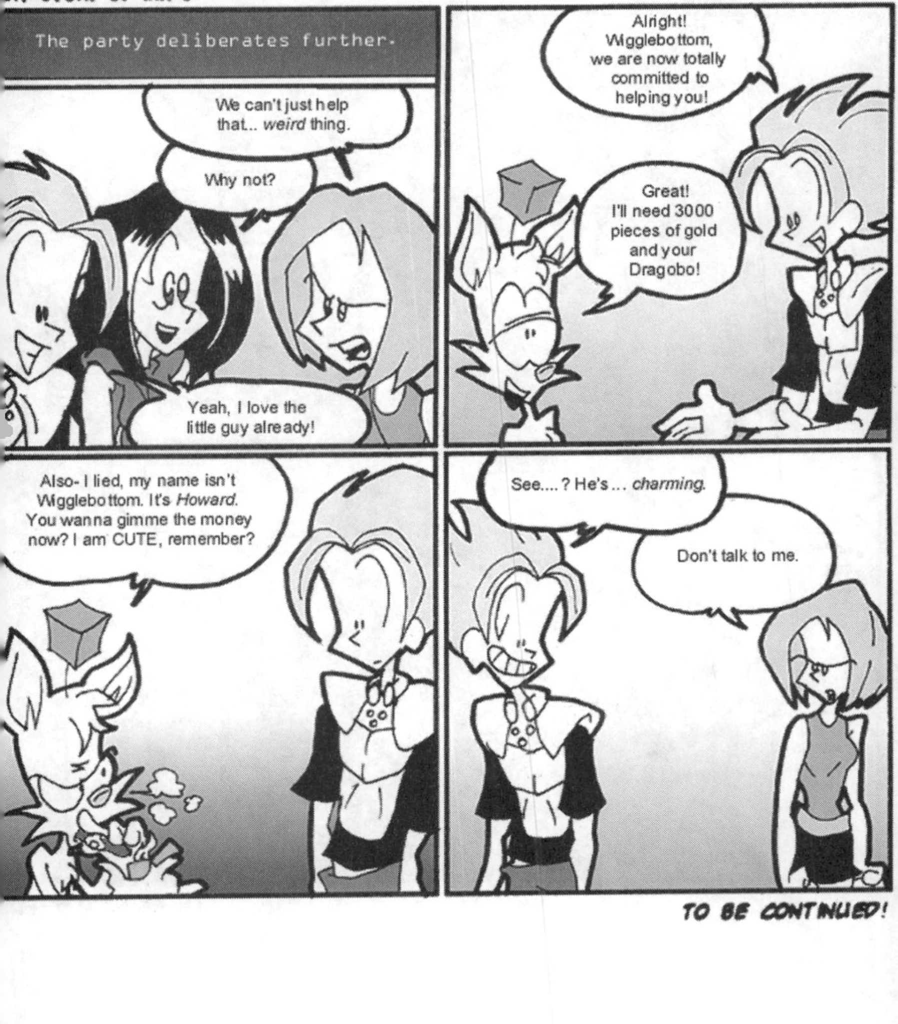

The party deliberates further.
We can't just help that... *weird* thing.
Why not?
Yeah, I love the little guy already!
Alright! Wigglebottom, we are now totally committed to helping you!
Great! I'll need 3000 pieces of gold and your Dragobo!
Also- I lied, my name isn't Wigglebottom. It's *Howard.* You wanna gimme the money now? I am CUTE, remember?
See....? He's... *charming.*
Don't talk to me.

TO BE CONTINUED!

RPG WORLD
ART/STORY BY IAN J.

"THE NEGOTIATOR"

#47

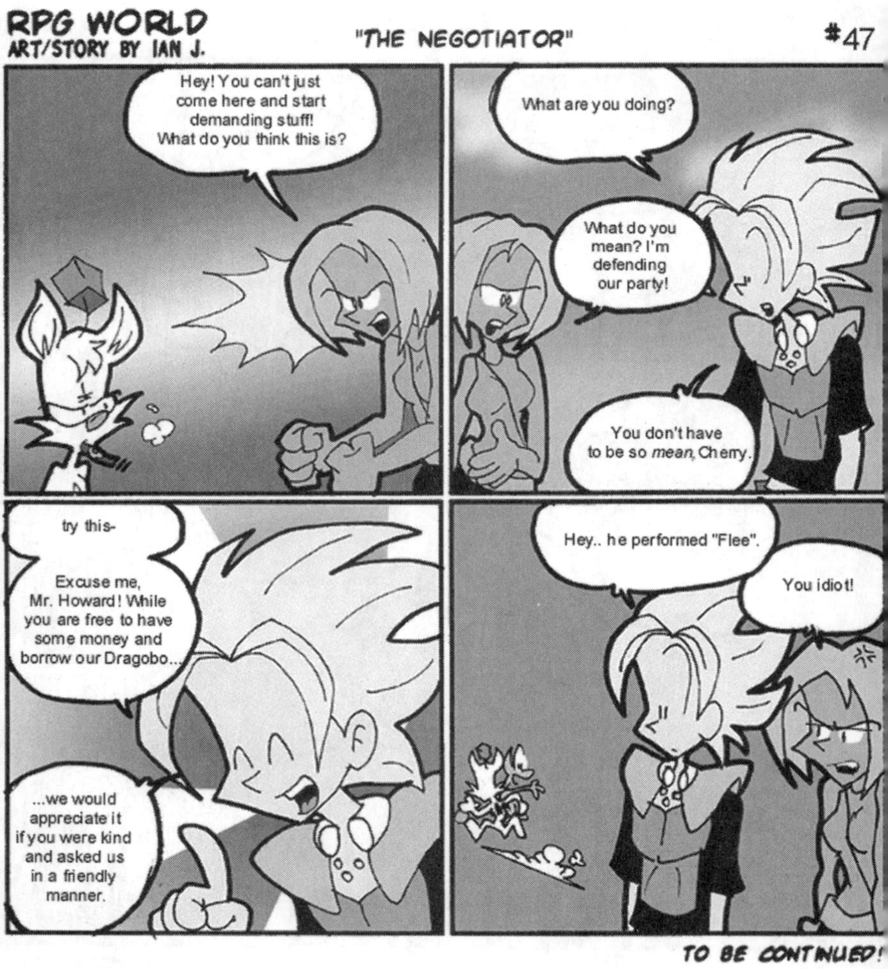

Hey! You can't just come here and start demanding stuff! What do you think this is?
What are you doing?
What do you mean? I'm defending our party!
You don't have to be so *mean*, Cherry.
try this-
Excuse me, Mr. Howard! While you are free to have some money and borrow our Dragobo...
...we would appreciate it if you were kind and asked us in a friendly manner.
Hey.. he performed "Flee".
You idiot!

TO BE CONTINUED!

RPG WORLD
ART/STORY BY IAN J.

"EVIL PLOT...FOR LOVE"

#48

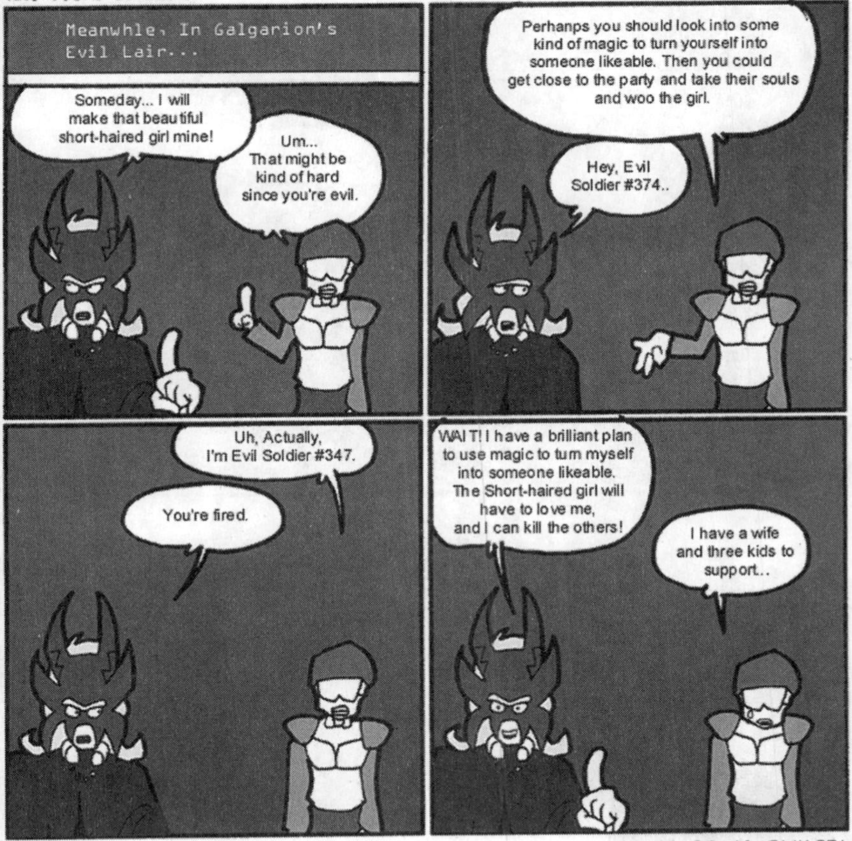
Meanwhle, In Galgarion's Evil Lair...
Someday... I will make that beautiful short-haired girl mine!
Um... That might be kind of hard since you're evil.
Perhanps you should look into some kind of magic to turn yourself into someone likeable. Then you could get close to the party and take their souls and woo the girl.
Hey, Evil Soldier #374..
Uh, Actually, I'm Evil Soldier #347.
You're fired.
WAIT! I have a brilliant plan to use magic to turn myself into someone likeable. The Short-haired girl will have to love me, and I can kill the others!
I have a wife and three kids to support...

TO BE CONTINUED!

RPG WORLD
ART/STORY BY IAN J.

"ACTIVE TIME EVENT"

#49

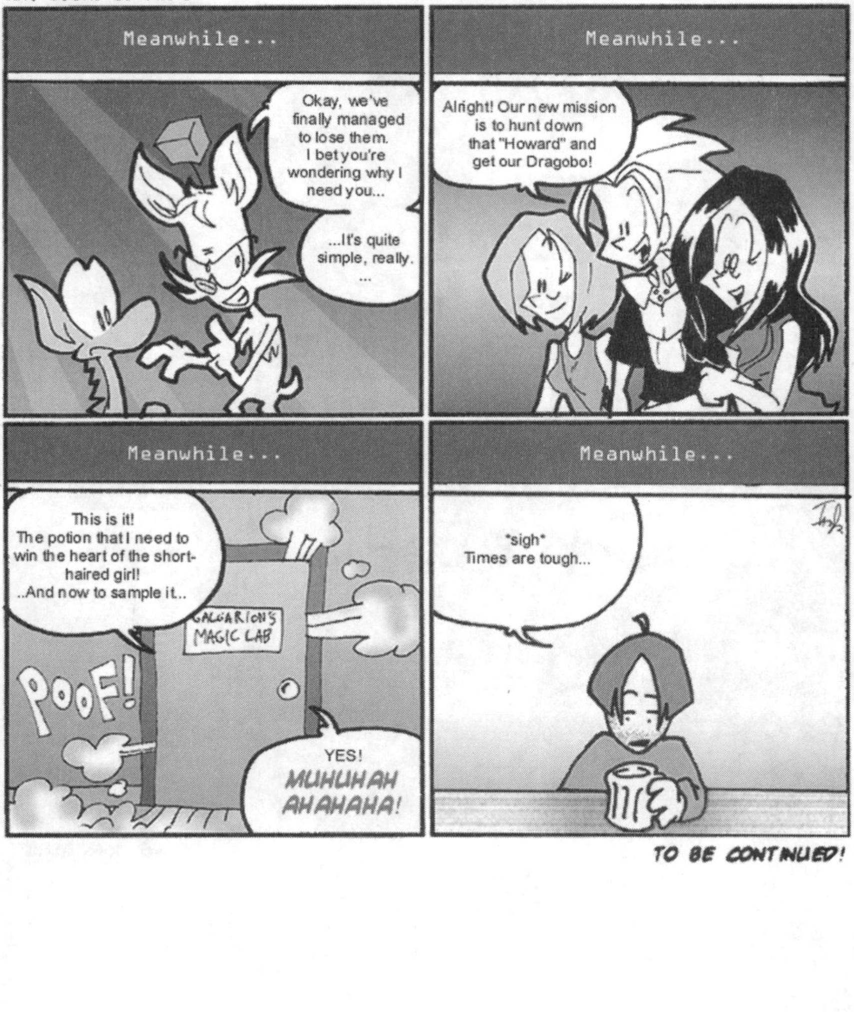
Meanwhile...
Okay, we've finally managed to lose them. I bet you're wondering why I need you...
...It's quite simple, really.
...
Meanwhile...
Alright! Our new mission is to hunt down that "Howard" and get our Dragobo!
Meanwhile...
This is it! The potion that I need to win the heart of the short-haired girl! ..And now to sample it...
GALGARION'S MAGIC LAB
POOF!
YES!
MUHUHAH AHAHAHA!
Meanwhile...
sigh Times are tough...

TO BE CONTINUED!

RPG WORLD
ART/STORY BY IAN J.

AN RPG WORLD SUPER-SPECIAL:
"BOSS ENCOUNTER!"

#50!

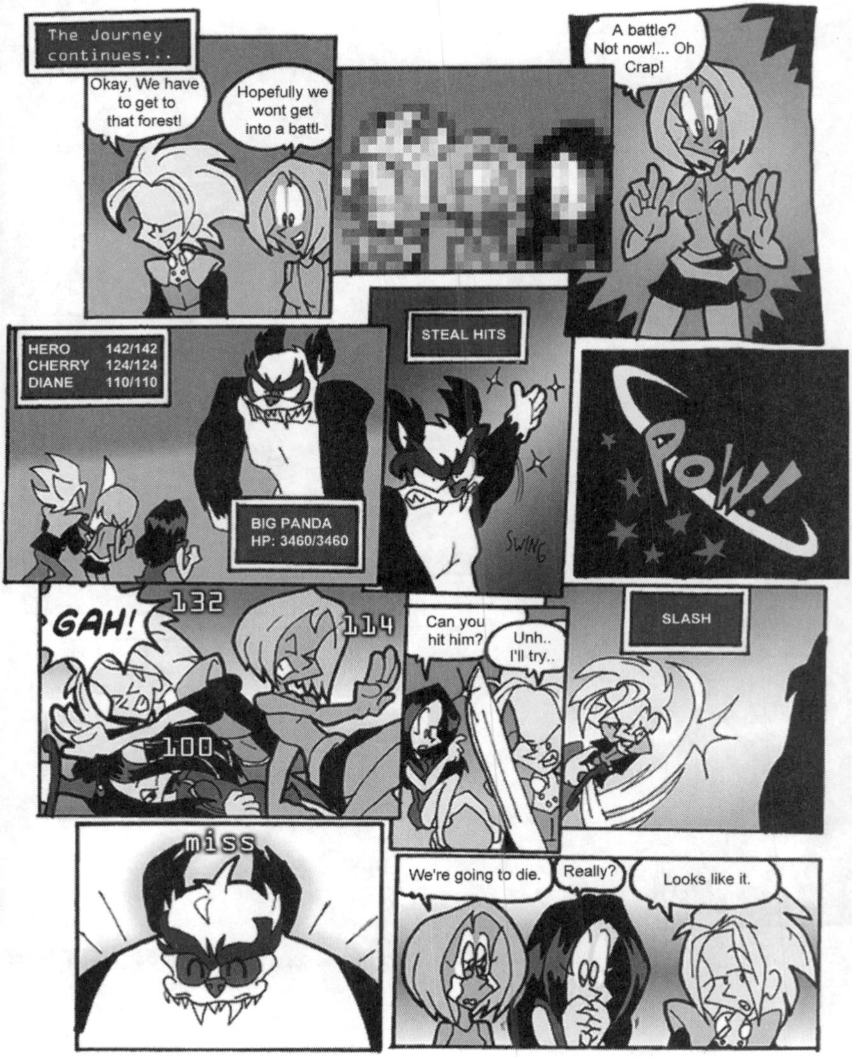

The Journey continues...
Okay, We have to get to that forest!
Hopefully we wont get into a batt!-
A battle? Not now!... Oh Crap!
HERO 142/142
CHERRY 124/124
DIANE 110/110
BIG PANDA
HP: 3460/3460
STEAL HITS
SWING
POW!
GAH!
132
114
100
Can you hit him?
Unh.. I'll try..
SLASH
miss
We're going to die.
Really?
Looks like it.

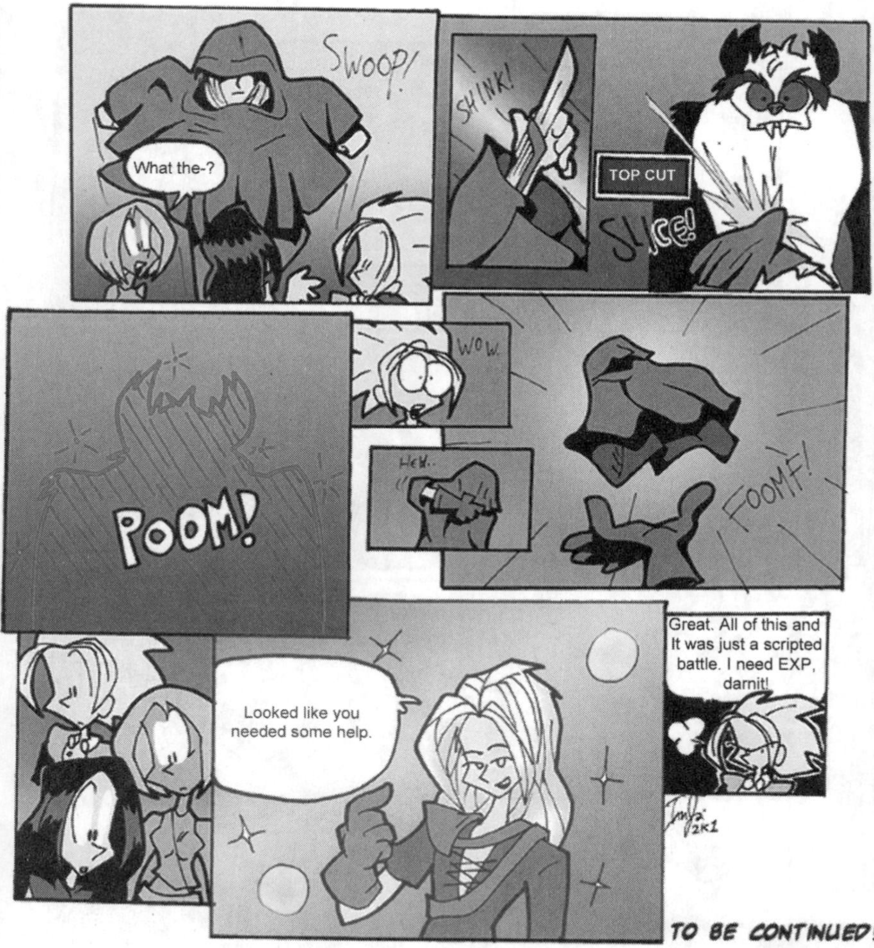
What the-?
SWOOP!
SHINK!
TOP CUT
POOM!
WOW.
HEH..
FOOMF!
Looked like you needed some help.
Great. All of this and It was just a scripted battle. I need EXP, darnit!

TO BE CONTINUED!

RPG WORLD "HAZING THE NEW GUY" #51

ART/STORY BY IAN J.

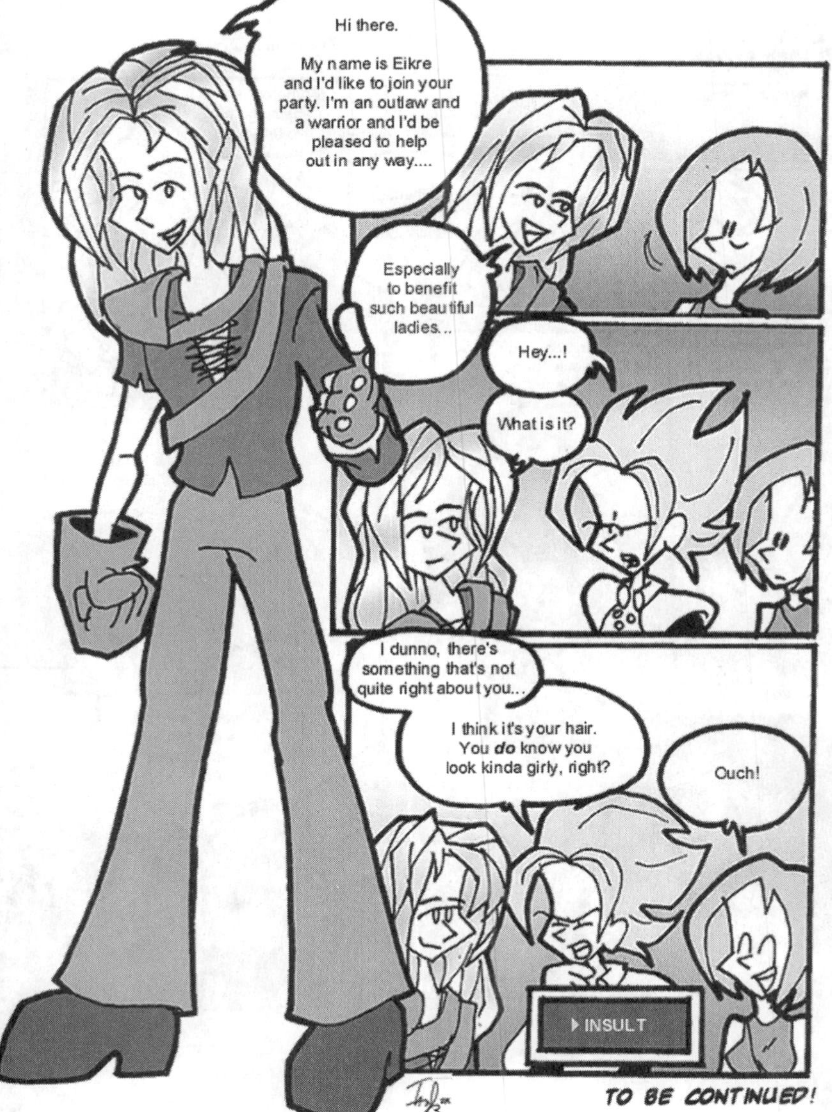
Hi there.
My name is Eikre and I'd like to join your party. I'm an outlaw and a warrior and I'd be pleased to help out in any way....
Especially to benefit such beautiful ladies...
Hey...!
What is it?
I dunno, there's something that's not quite right about you...
I think it's your hair. You *do* know you look kinda girly, right?
Ouch!
▸ INSULT
TO BE CONTINUED!

RPG WORLD

ART/STORY BY IAN J.

"LONG OVERDUE EXPLANATION" #52

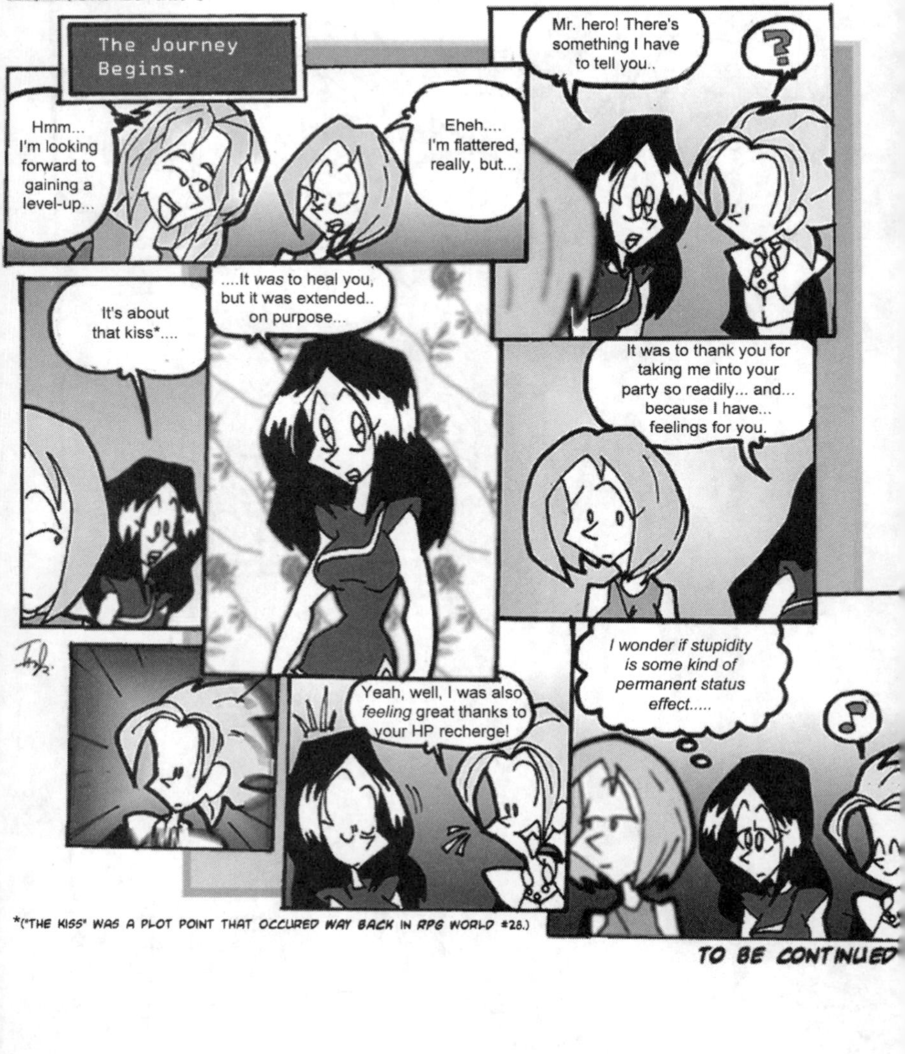

The Journey Begins.
Hmm... I'm looking forward to gaining a level-up...
Eheh.... I'm flattered, really, but...
Mr. hero! There's something I have to tell you..
?
It's about that kiss*....
....It *was* to heal you, but it was extended.. on purpose...
It was to thank you for taking me into your party so readily... and... because I have... feelings for you.
Yeah, well, I was also *feeling* great thanks to your HP recherge!
I wonder if stupidity is some kind of permanent status effect.....

*("THE KISS" WAS A PLOT POINT THAT OCCURED *WAY BACK* IN *RPG WORLD* #28.)

TO BE CONTINUED

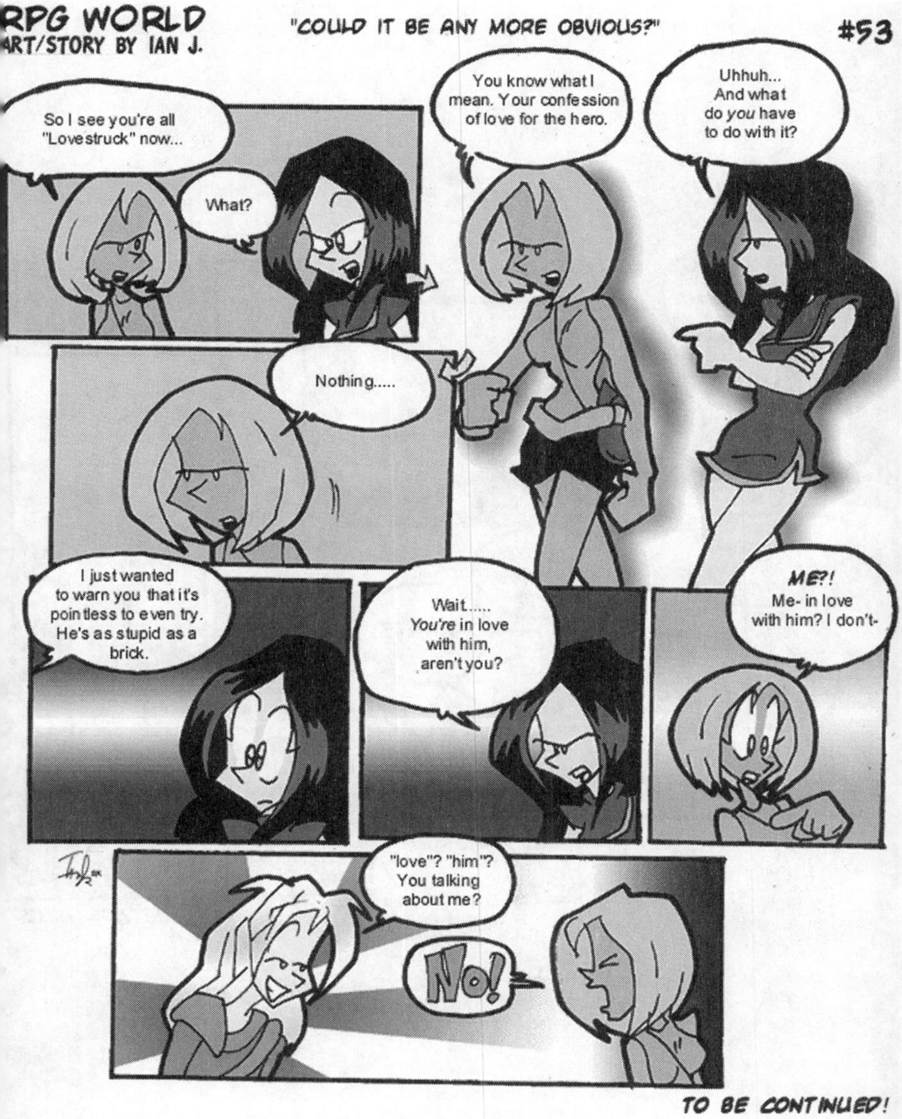
RPG WORLD
ART/STORY BY IAN J.
"COULD IT BE ANY MORE OBVIOUS?"
#53
So I see you're all "Lovestruck" now...
What?
You know what I mean. Your confession of love for the hero.
Uhhuh... And what do *you* have to do with it?
Nothing.....
I just wanted to warn you that it's pointless to even try. He's as stupid as a brick.
Wait..... *You're* in love with him, aren't you?
ME?! Me- in love with him? I don't-
"love"? "him"? You talking about me?
NO!
TO BE CONTINUED!

RPG WORLD
ART/STORY BY IAN J.

"I DON'T WANNA"

#54

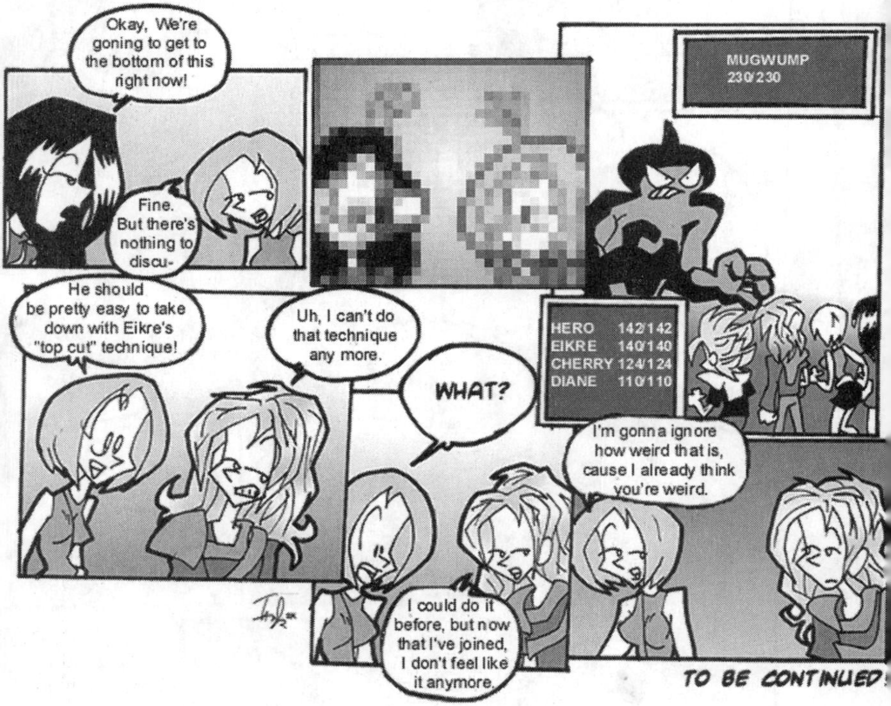

RPG WORLD

ART/STORY BY IAN J.

"WHOOPS!"

#55

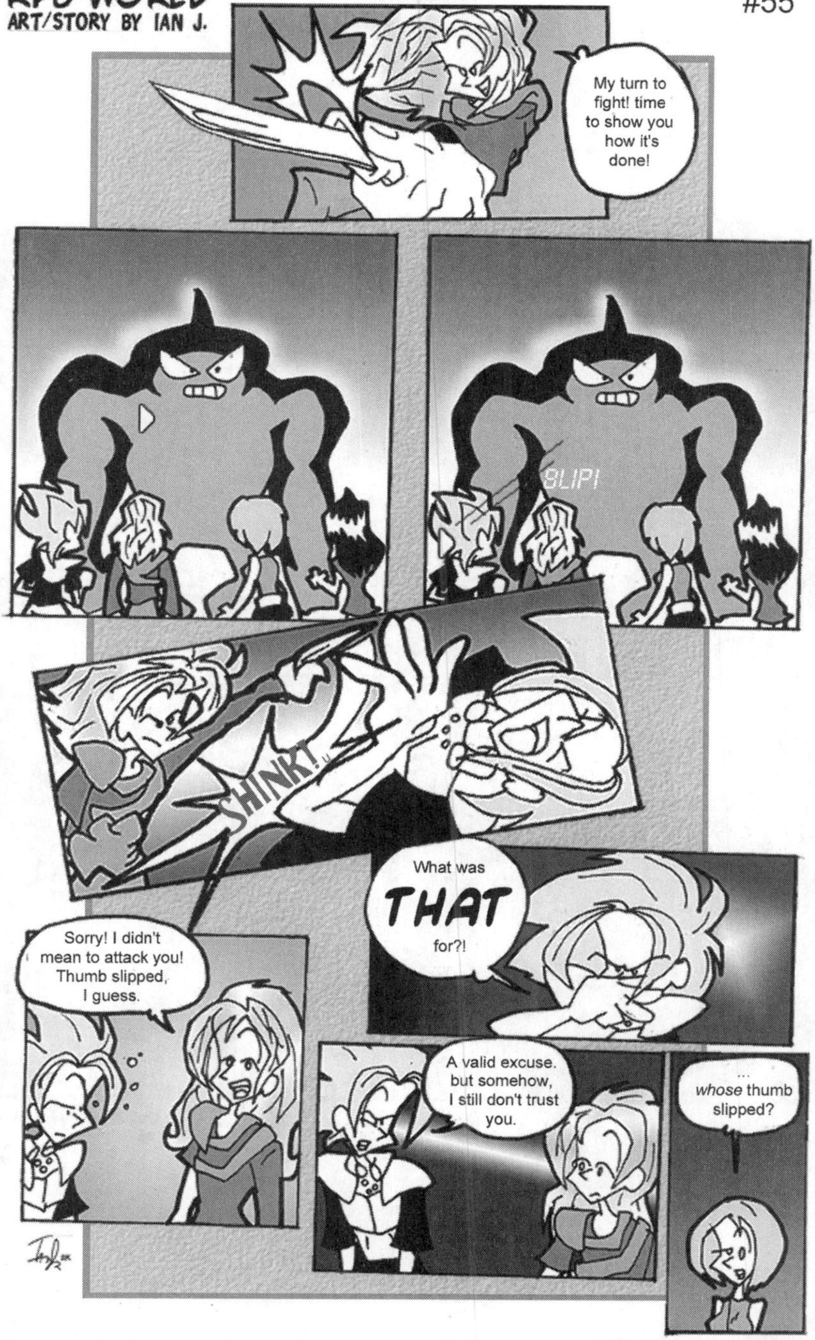
My turn to fight! time to show you how it's done!
SLIP!
SHINK!
What was THAT for?!
Sorry! I didn't mean to attack you! Thumb slipped, I guess.
A valid excuse. but somehow, I still don't trust you.
... *whose* thumb slipped?

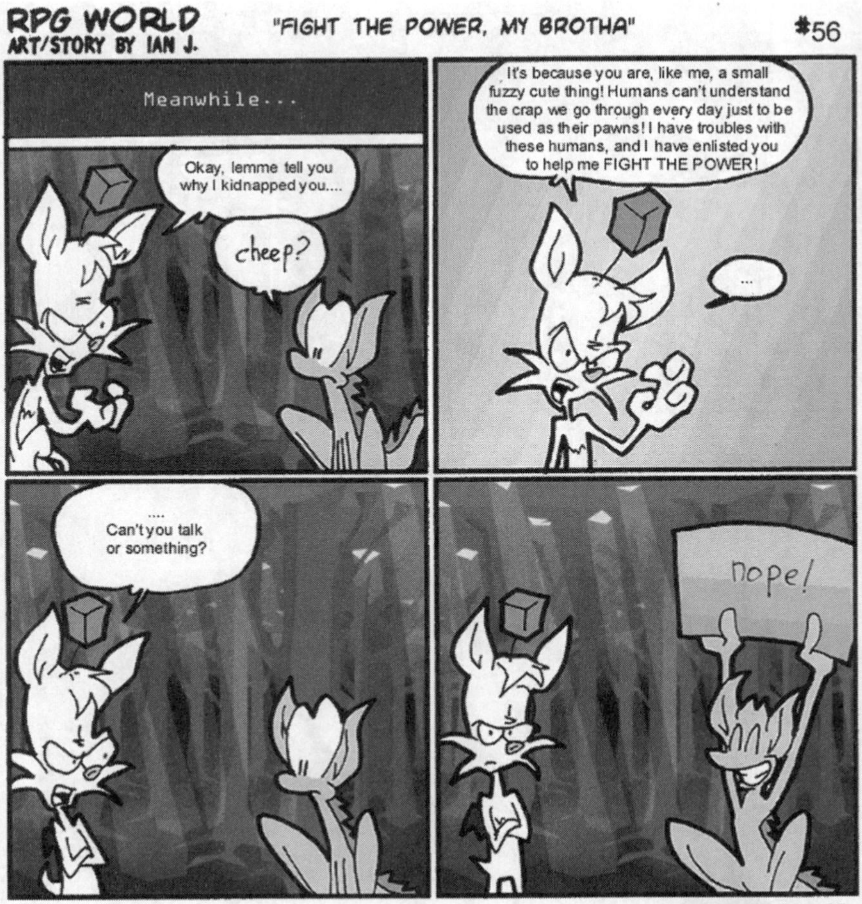
RPG WORLD
ART/STORY BY IAN J.
"FIGHT THE POWER, MY BROTHA"
#56
Meanwhile...
Okay, lemme tell you why I kidnapped you....
cheep?
It's because you are, like me, a small fuzzy cute thing! Humans can't understand the crap we go through every day just to be used as their pawns! I have troubles with these humans, and I have enlisted you to help me FIGHT THE POWER!
...
.... Can't you talk or something?
nope!
TO BE CONTINUED!

RPG WORLD
ART/STORY BY IAN J.

"I HAD TO SAY IT EVENTUALLY..."

#57

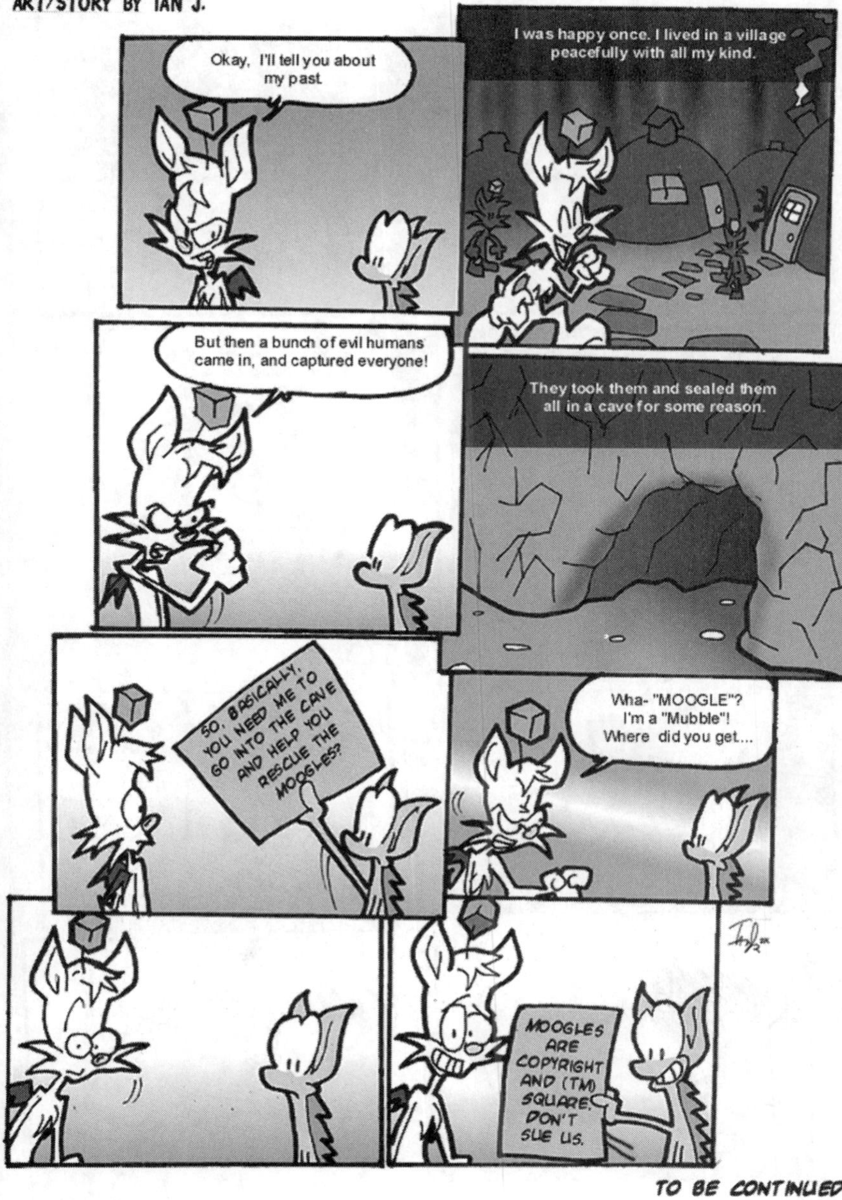

Okay, I'll tell you about my past.
I was happy once. I lived in a village peacefully with all my kind.
But then a bunch of evil humans came in, and captured everyone!
They took them and sealed them all in a cave for some reason.
SO, BASICALLY, YOU NEED ME TO GO INTO THE CAVE AND HELP YOU RESCUE THE MOOGLES?
Wha- "MOOGLE"? I'm a "Mubble"! Where did you get....
MOOGLES ARE COPYRIGHT AND (TM) SQUARE. DON'T SUE US.

TO BE CONTINUED!

RPG WORLD

ART/STORY BY IAN J.

"IT'S TRUE, IT'S TRUE."

#58

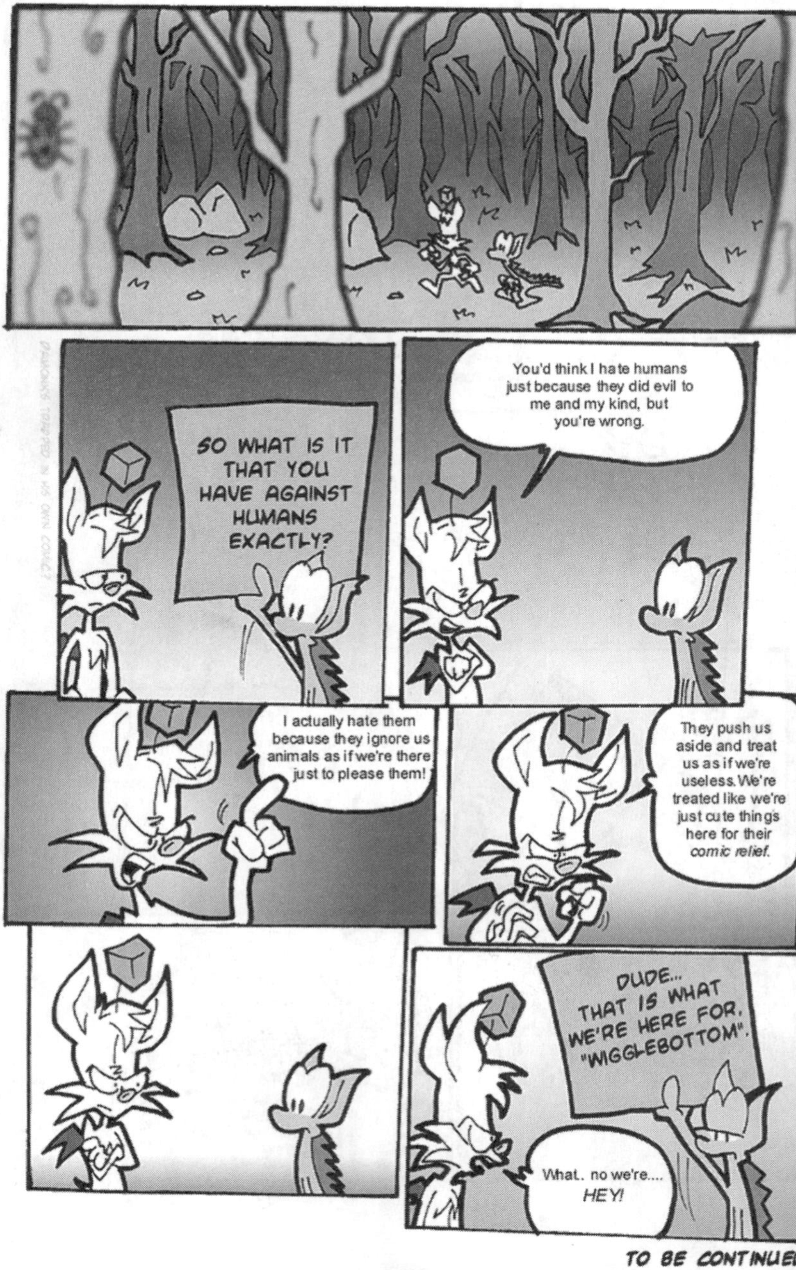

SO WHAT IS IT THAT YOU HAVE AGAINST HUMANS EXACTLY?
You'd think I hate humans just because they did evil to me and my kind, but you're wrong.
I actually hate them because they ignore us animals as if we're there just to please them!
They push us aside and treat us as if we're useless. We're treated like we're just cute things here for their *comic relief*.
DUDE... THAT IS WHAT WE'RE HERE FOR, "WIGGLEBOTTOM".
What.. no we're.... *HEY!*

TO BE CONTINUED!

RPG WORLD
ART/STORY BY IAN J.

"MORE FORESHADOWING"

#59

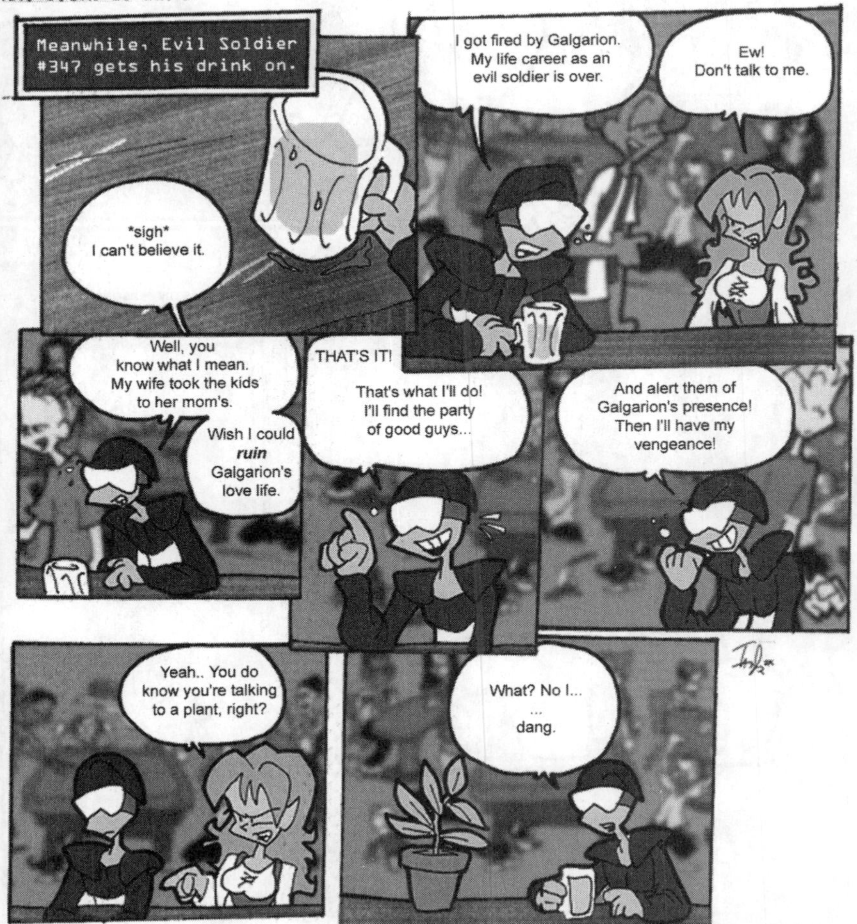
Meanwhile, Evil Soldier #347 gets his drink on.
sigh I can't believe it.
I got fired by Galgarion. My life career as an evil soldier is over.
Ew! Don't talk to me.
Well, you know what I mean. My wife took the kids to her mom's.
Wish I could ***ruin*** Galgarion's love life.
THAT'S IT!
That's what I'll do! I'll find the party of good guys...
And alert them of Galgarion's presence! Then I'll have my vengeance!
Yeah.. You do know you're talking to a plant, right?
What? No I...
...
dang.

TO BE CONTINUED!

RPG WORLD
ART/STORY BY IAN J.

"MOVING THE PLOT ALONG"

#60

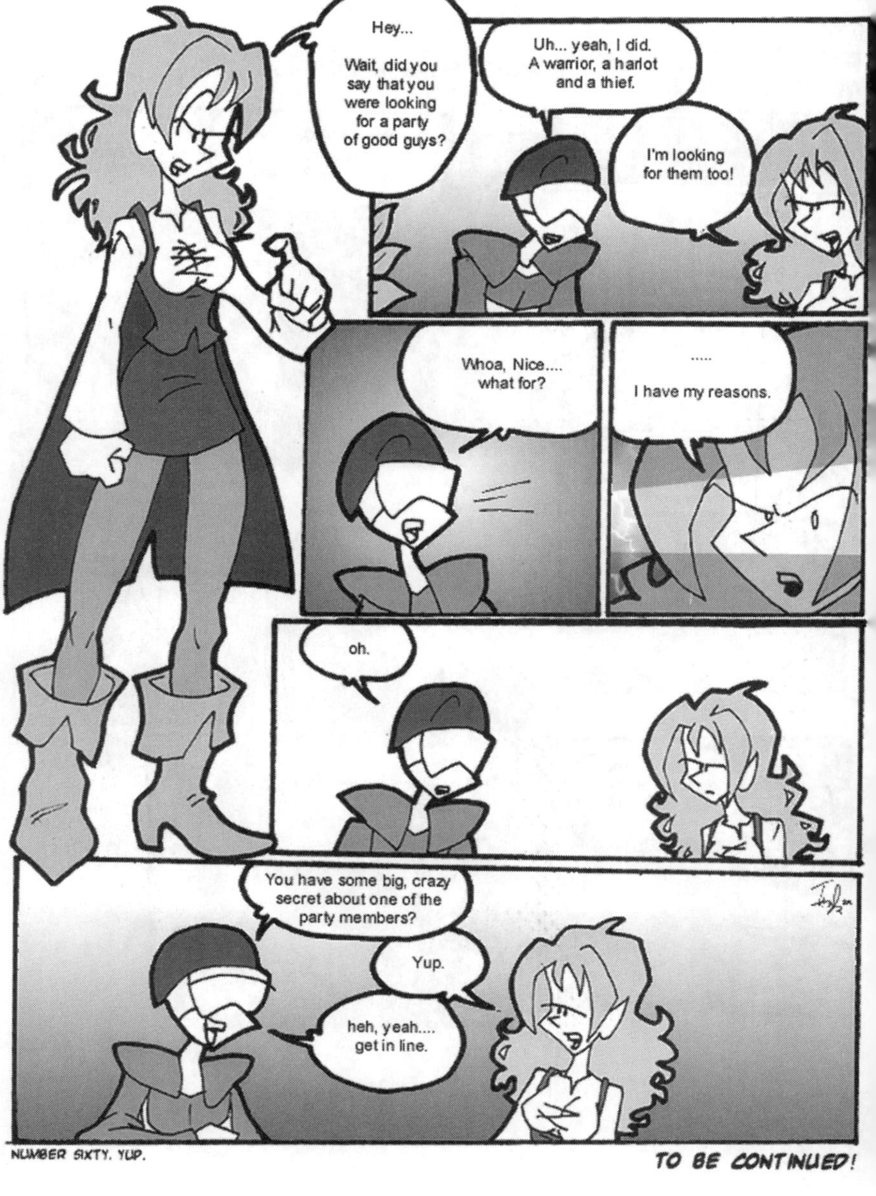

Hey...
Wait, did you say that you were looking for a party of good guys?
Uh... yeah, I did. A warrior, a harlot and a thief.
I'm looking for them too!
Whoa, Nice.... what for?
.....
I have my reasons.
oh.
You have some big, crazy secret about one of the party members?
Yup.
heh, yeah.... get in line.

NUMBER SIXTY. YUP.

TO BE CONTINUED!

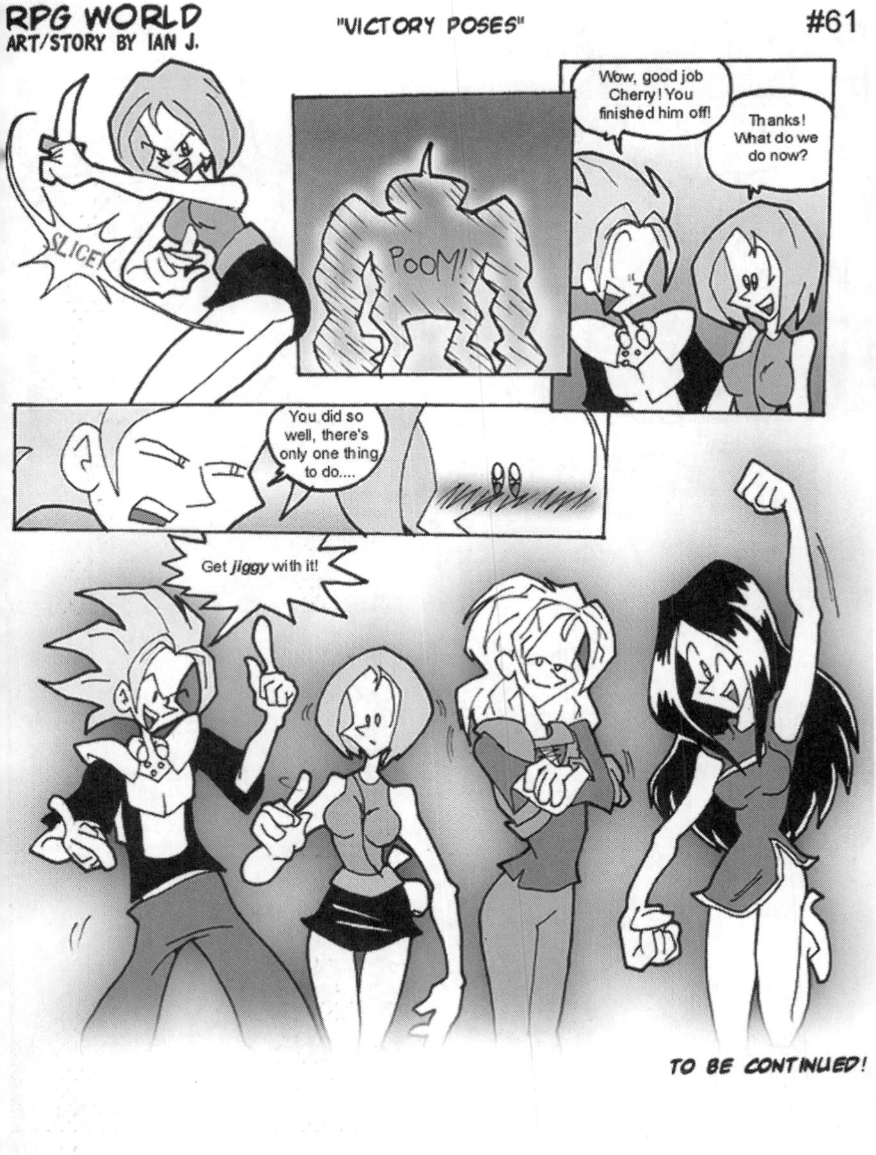
RPG WORLD
ART/STORY BY IAN J.
"VICTORY POSES"
#61
SLICE!
POOM!
Wow, good job Cherry! You finished him off!
Thanks! What do we do now?
You did so well, there's only one thing to do....
Get *jiggy* with it!
TO BE CONTINUED!

RPG WORLD

ART/STORY BY IAN J. "MORE SUBTLE FORESHADOWING" #62

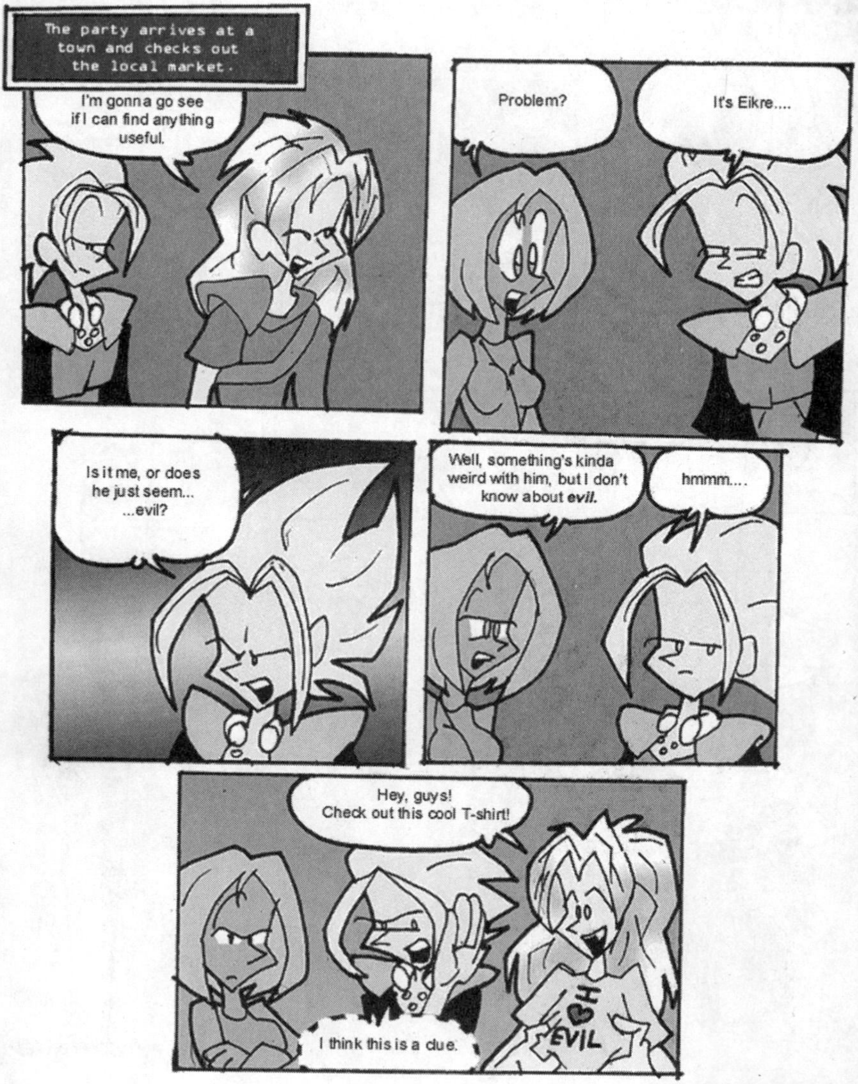
The party arrives at a town and checks out the local market.
I'm gonna go see if I can find anything useful.
Problem?
It's Eikre....
Is it me, or does he just seem... ...evil?
Well, something's kinda weird with him, but I don't know about *evil.*
hmmm....
Hey, guys! Check out this cool T-shirt!
EVIL
I think this is a clue.

TO BE CONTINUED!

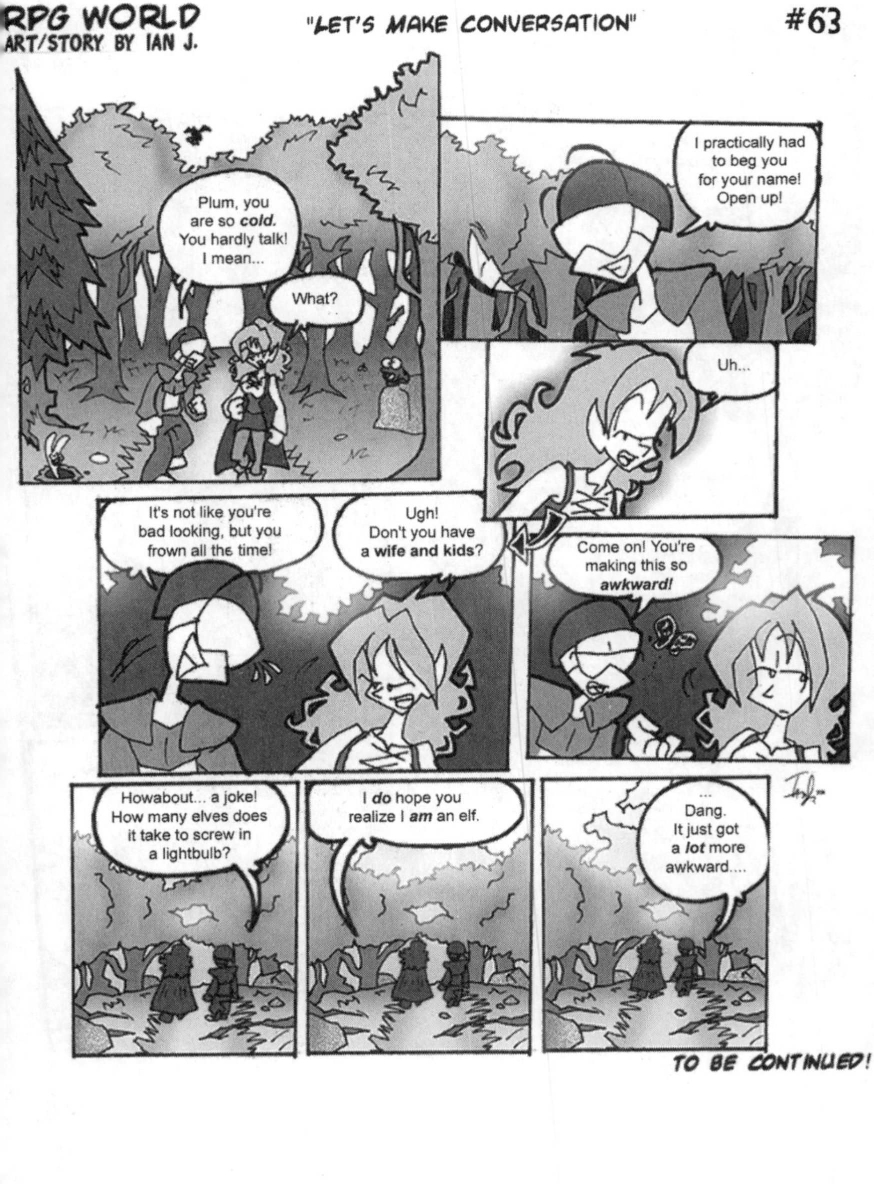

RPG WORLD
ART/STORY BY IAN J.
"LET'S MAKE CONVERSATION"
#63
Plum, you are so *cold.* You hardly talk! I mean...
What?
I practically had to beg you for your name! Open up!
Uh...
It's not like you're bad looking, but you frown all the time!
Ugh! Don't you have a **wife and kids**?
Come on! You're making this so ***awkward!***
Howabout... a joke! How many elves does it take to screw in a lightbulb?
I ***do*** hope you realize I ***am*** an elf.
... Dang. It just got a ***lot*** more awkward....
TO BE CONTINUED!

RPG WORLD
ART/STORY BY IAN J.

"FRIENDLY CONVERSATION"

#64

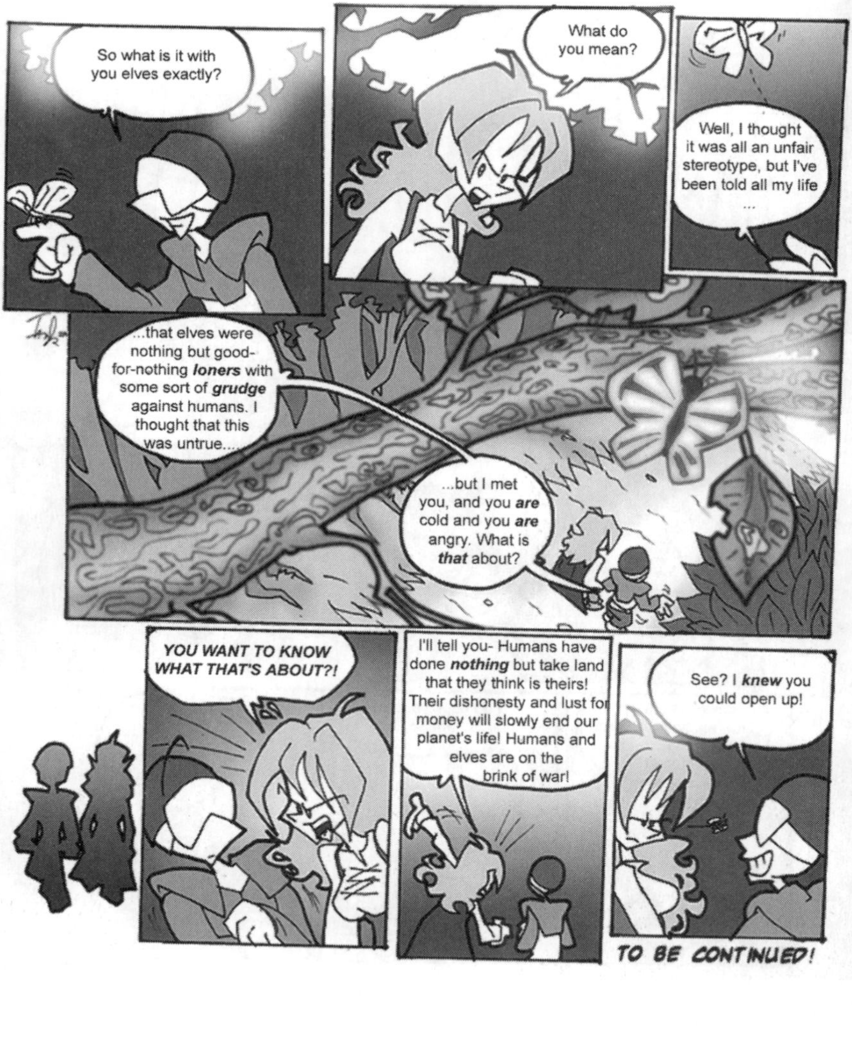

So what is it with you elves exactly?
What do you mean?
Well, I thought it was all an unfair stereotype, but I've been told all my life ...
...that elves were nothing but good-for-nothing ***loners*** with some sort of ***grudge*** against humans. I thought that this was untrue....
...but I met you, and you ***are*** cold and you ***are*** angry. What is ***that*** about?
YOU WANT TO KNOW WHAT THAT'S ABOUT?!
I'll tell you- Humans have done ***nothing*** but take land that they think is theirs! Their dishonesty and lust for money will slowly end our planet's life! Humans and elves are on the brink of war!
See? I ***knew*** you could open up!
TO BE CONTINUED!

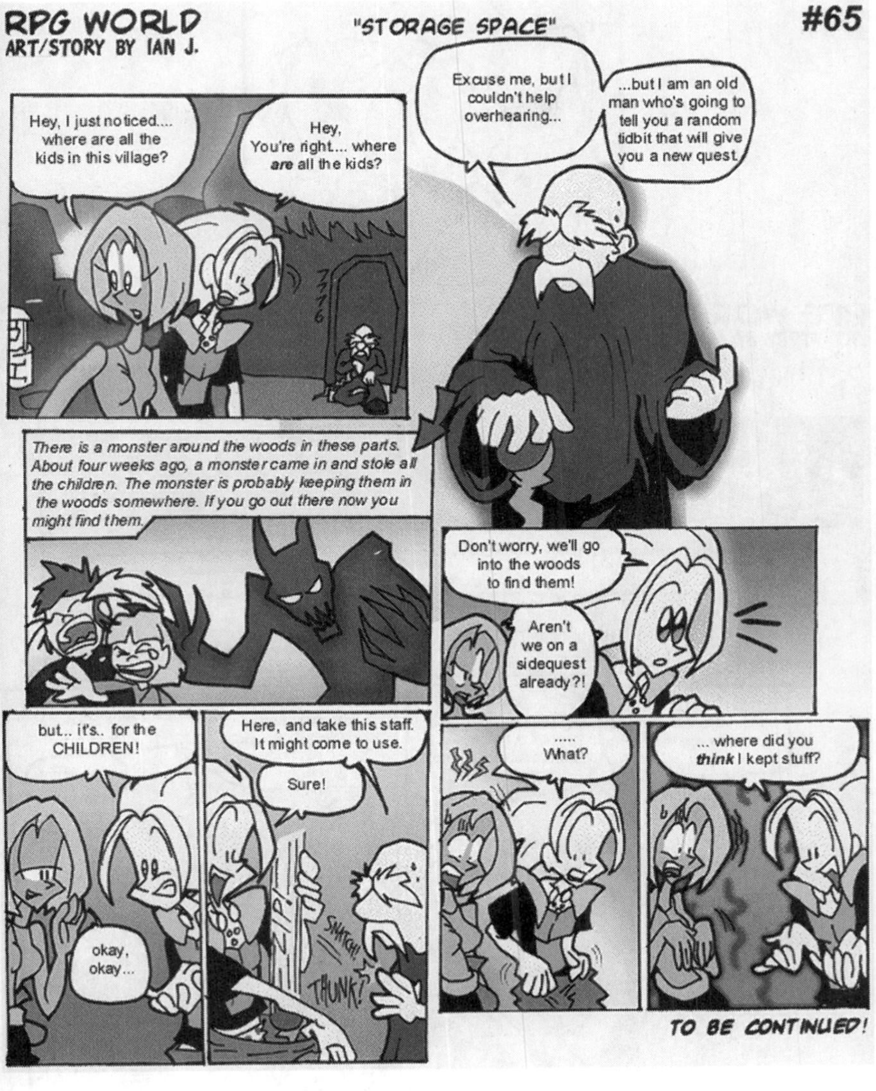
RPG WORLD
ART/STORY BY IAN J.
"STORAGE SPACE"
#65
Hey, I just noticed.... where are all the kids in this village?
Hey, You're right.... where *are* all the kids?
Excuse me, but I couldn't help overhearing...
...but I am an old man who's going to tell you a random tidbit that will give you a new quest.
There is a monster around the woods in these parts. About four weeks ago, a monster came in and stole all the children. The monster is probably keeping them in the woods somewhere. If you go out there now you might find them.
Don't worry, we'll go into the woods to find them!
Aren't we on a sidequest already?!
but... it's.. for the CHILDREN!
okay, okay...
Here, and take this staff. It might come to use.
Sure!
SNATCH!
THUNK!
..... What?
... where did you **think** I kept stuff?
TO BE CONTINUED!

RPG WORLD
ART/STORY BY IAN J. "SAVE POINT" #66

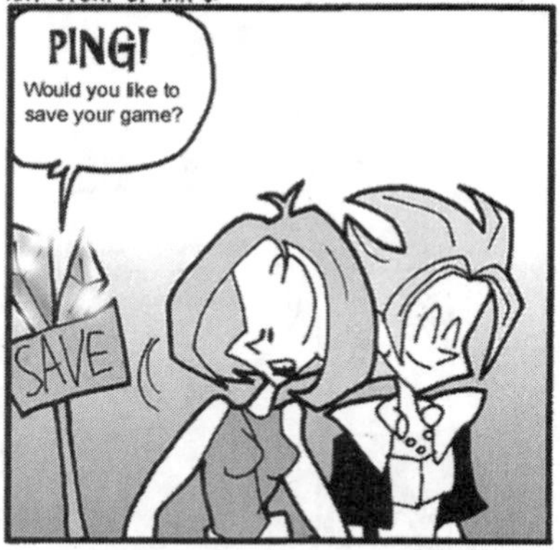
PING!
Would you like to save your game?
SAVE

"Gah! Is this some sort of monster?"

RPG WORLD
ART/STORY BY IAN J. "SAVED BY THE BELL" #67

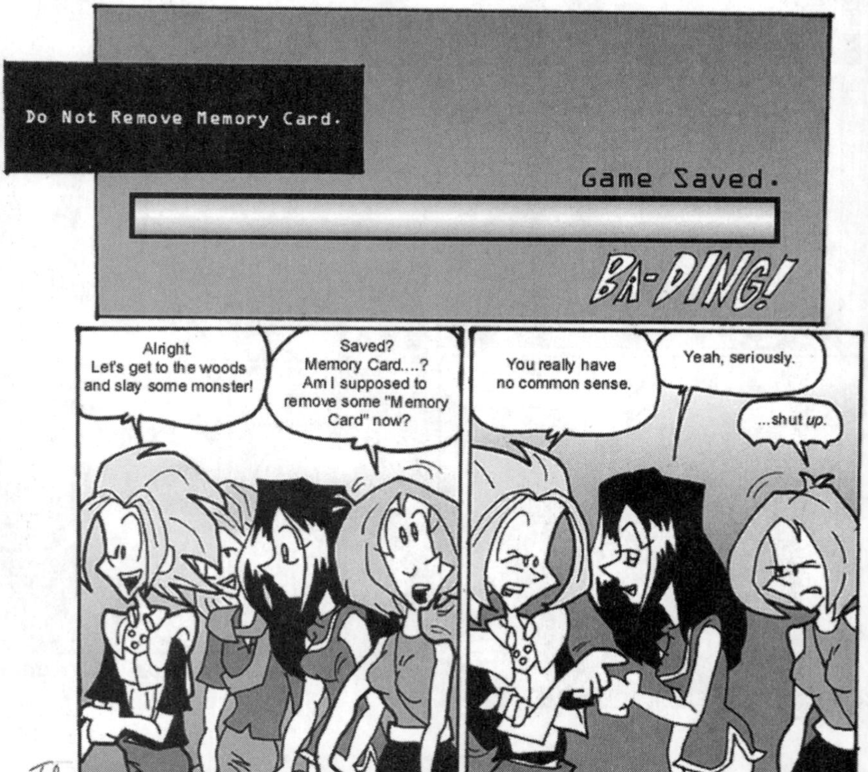
Do Not Remove Memory Card.
Game Saved.
BA-DING!
Alright. Let's get to the woods and slay some monster!
Saved? Memory Card....? Am I supposed to remove some "Memory Card" now?
You really have no common sense.
Yeah, seriously.
...shut *up*.

TO BE CONTINUED!

RPG WORLD
ART/STORY BY IAN J.

"PARTY REFORM"

#68

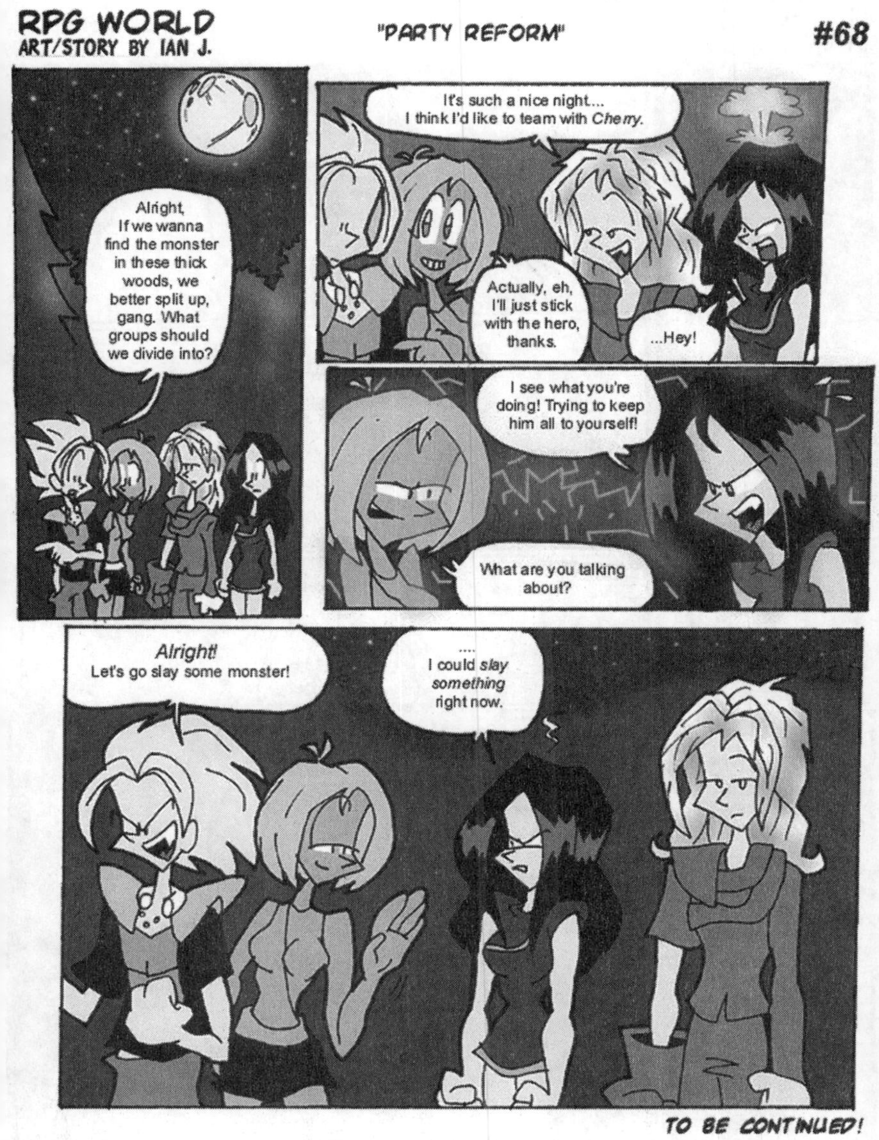

Alright, If we wanna find the monster in these thick woods, we better split up, gang. What groups should we divide into?
It's such a nice night... I think I'd like to team with *Cherry*.
Actually, eh, I'll just stick with the hero, thanks.
...Hey!
I see what you're doing! Trying to keep him all to yourself!
What are you talking about?
Alright! Let's go slay some monster!
.... I could *slay something* right now.

TO BE CONTINUED!

RPG WORLD

ART/STORY BY IAN J.

"CONFESSION"

#69

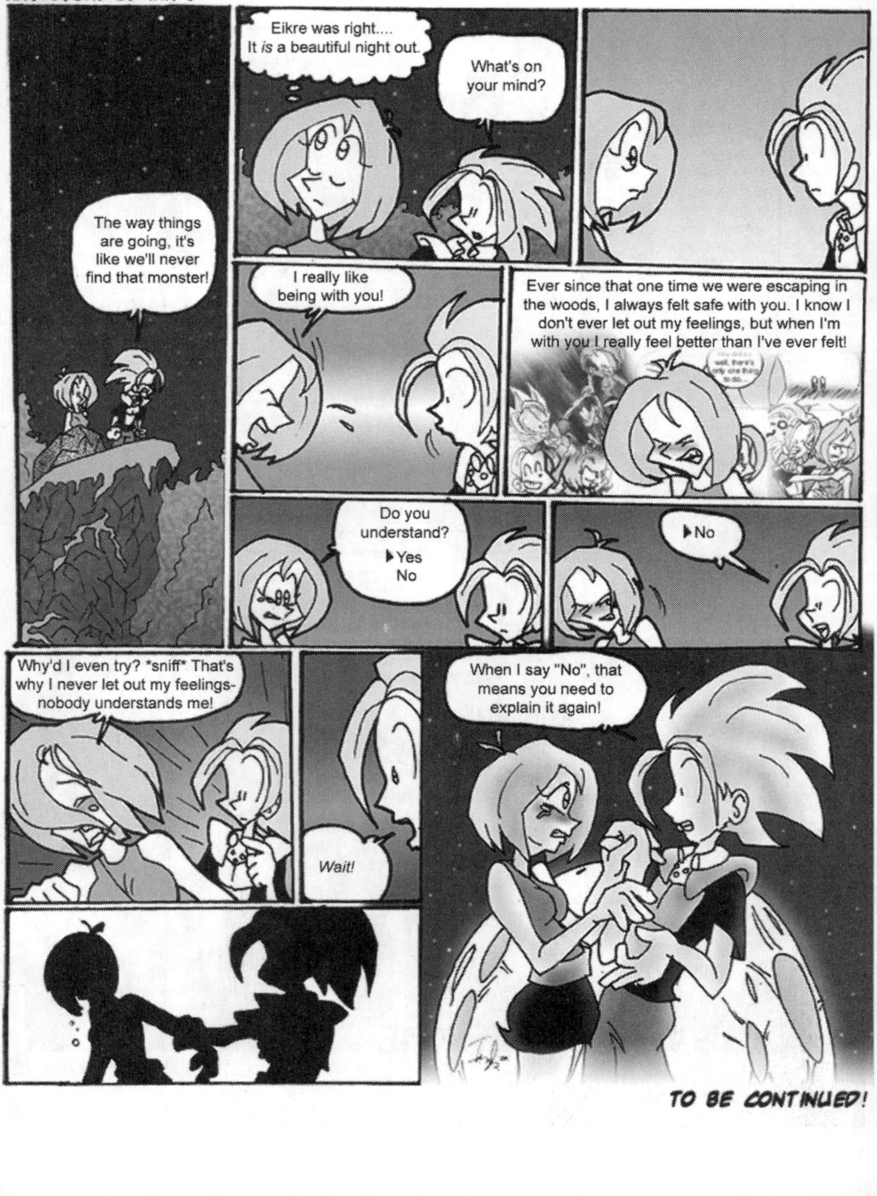

Eikre was right.... It *is* a beautiful night out.
What's on your mind?
The way things are going, it's like we'll never find that monster!
I really like being with you!
Ever since that one time we were escaping in the woods, I always felt safe with you. I know I don't ever let out my feelings, but when I'm with you I really feel better than I've ever felt!
Do you understand?
▶Yes
No
▶No
Why'd I even try? *sniff* That's why I never let out my feelings- nobody understands me!
Wait!
When I say "No", that means you need to explain it again!

TO BE CONTINUED!

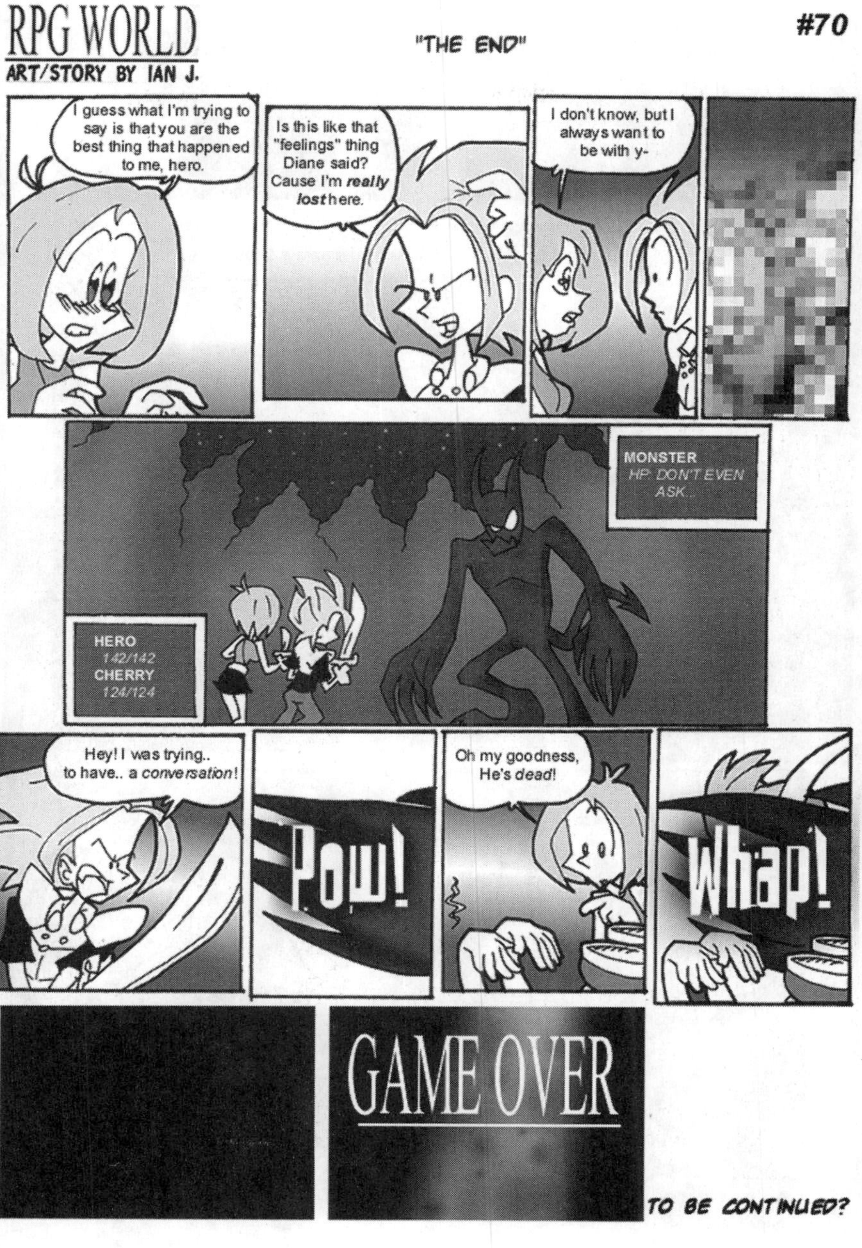
RPG WORLD
ART/STORY BY IAN J.
"THE END"
#70
I guess what I'm trying to say is that you are the best thing that happened to me, hero.
Is this like that "feelings" thing Diane said? Cause I'm really lost here.
I don't know, but I always want to be with y-
MONSTER
HP: DON'T EVEN ASK...
HERO
142/142
CHERRY
124/124
Hey! I was trying.. to have.. a conversation!
Pow!
Oh my goodness, He's dead!
Whap!
GAME OVER
TO BE CONTINUED?

TO BE CONTINUED!

RPG WORLD

ART/STORY BY IAN J.

"CONFESSION, ROUND TWO"

#72

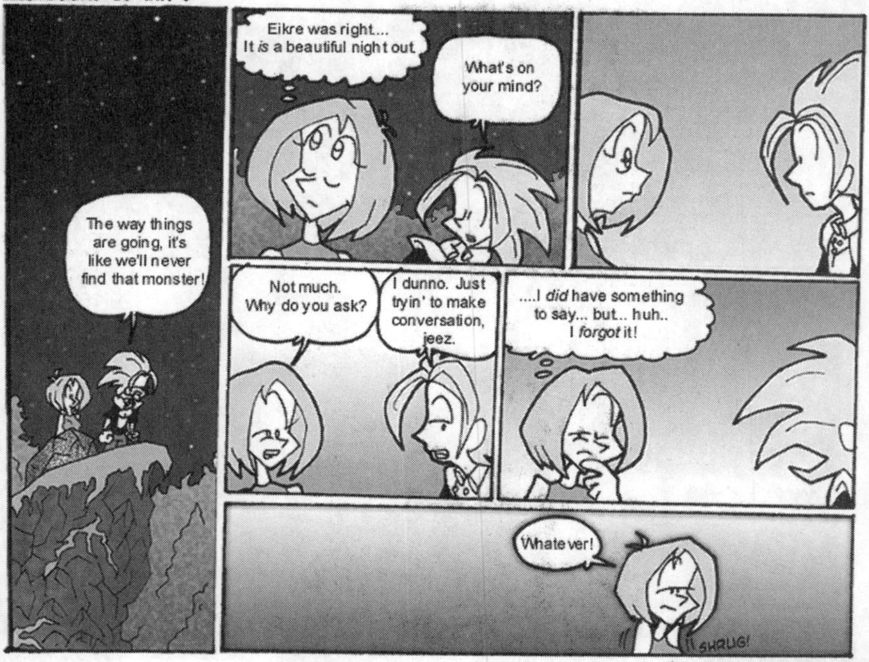

The way things are going, it's like we'll never find that monster!
Eikre was right.... It *is* a beautiful night out.
What's on your mind?
Not much. Why do you ask?
I dunno. Just tryin' to make conversation, jeez.
....I *did* have something to say... but... huh.. I *forgot* it!
Whatever!
SHRUG!

TO BE CONTINUED!

RPG WORLD

ART/STORY BY IAN J.

"DRAGOBO'S MYSTERIOUS DUNGEON: PART ONE"

#73

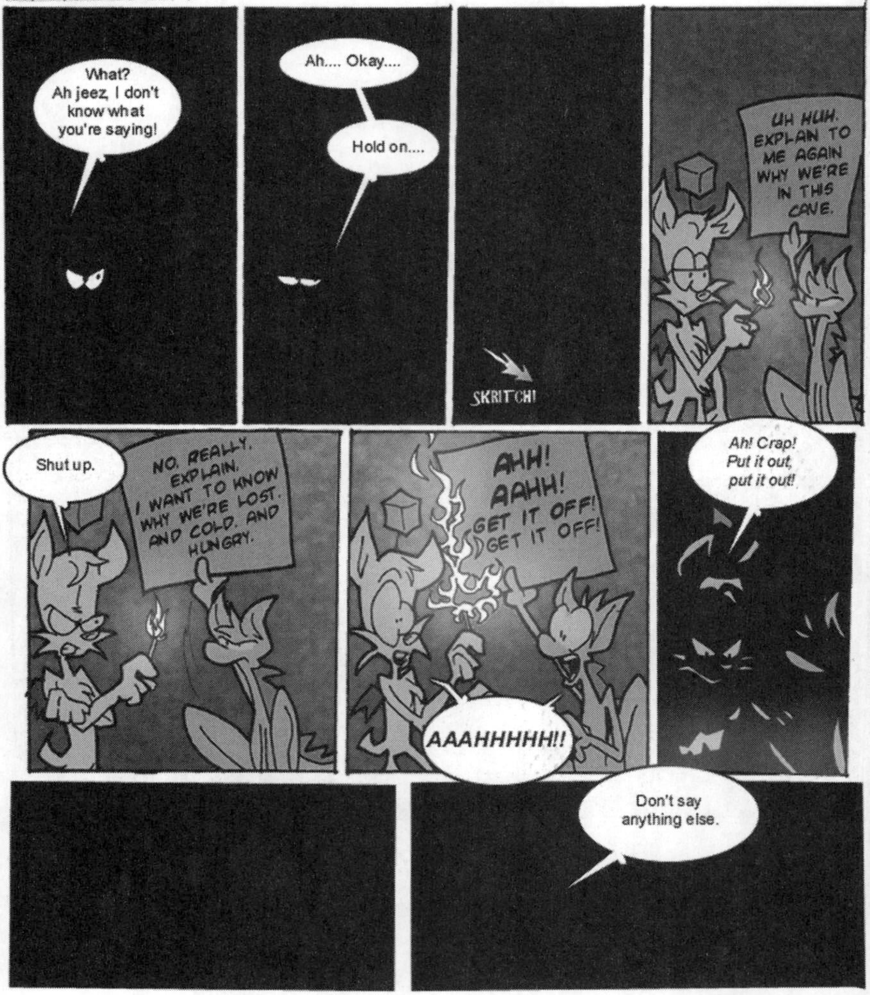
What? Ah jeez, I don't know what you're saying!
Ah.... Okay....
Hold on....
SKRITCH!
UH HUH. EXPLAIN TO ME AGAIN WHY WE'RE IN THIS CAVE.
Shut up.
NO, REALLY. EXPLAIN. I WANT TO KNOW WHY WE'RE LOST. AND COLD. AND HUNGRY.
AHH! AAHH! GET IT OFF! GET IT OFF!
AAAHHHHH!!
Ah! Crap! Put it out, put it out!
Don't say anything else.

TO BE CONTINUED!

RPG WORLD
BY WEBRUNNER

#74

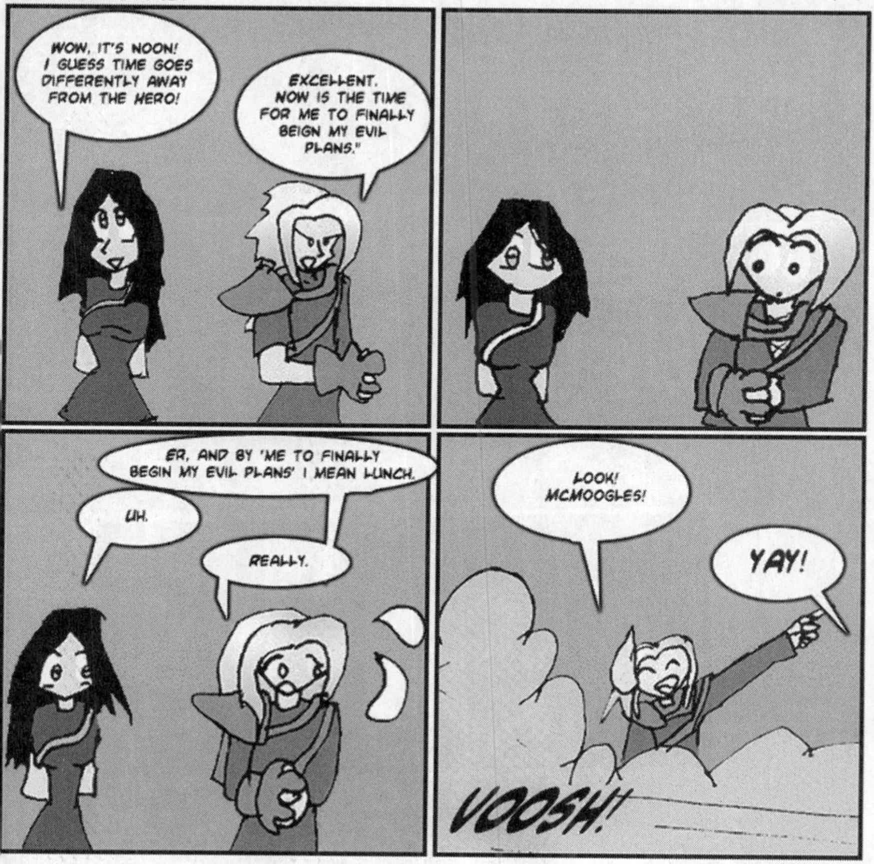

WOW, IT'S NOON! I GUESS TIME GOES DIFFERENTLY AWAY FROM THE HERO!
EXCELLENT. NOW IS THE TIME FOR ME TO FINALLY BEIGN MY EVIL PLANS."
ER, AND BY 'ME TO FINALLY BEGIN MY EVIL PLANS' I MEAN LUNCH.
UH.
REALLY.
LOOK! MCMOOGLES!
YAY!
VOOSH!

TO BE CONTINUED!

RPG WORLD

ART/STORY BY IAN J.

DRAGOBO'S MYSTERIOUS DUNGEON PART TWO:
"WHO GETS THE CREDIT?"

#75

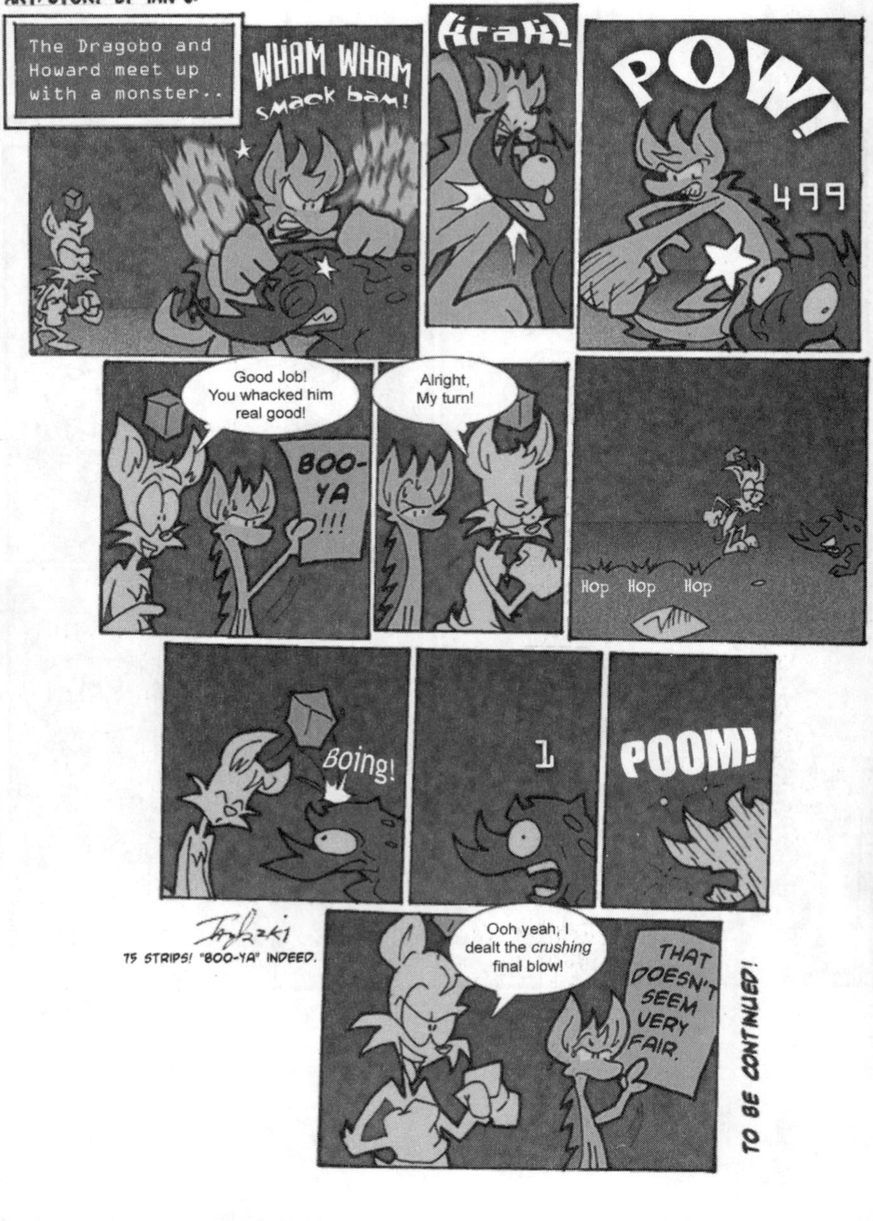

The Dragobo and Howard meet up with a monster..
WHAM WHAM
smack bam!
KRAK!
POW!
499
Good Job! You whacked him real good!
BOO-YA!!!
Alright, My turn!
Hop Hop Hop
Boing!
1
POOM!
75 STRIPS! "BOO-YA" INDEED.
Ooh yeah, I dealt the *crushing* final blow!
THAT DOESN'T SEEM VERY FAIR.
TO BE CONTINUED!

RPG WORLD

ART/STORY BY IAN J.

DRAGOBO'S MYSTERIOUS DUNGEON: PART THREE

#76

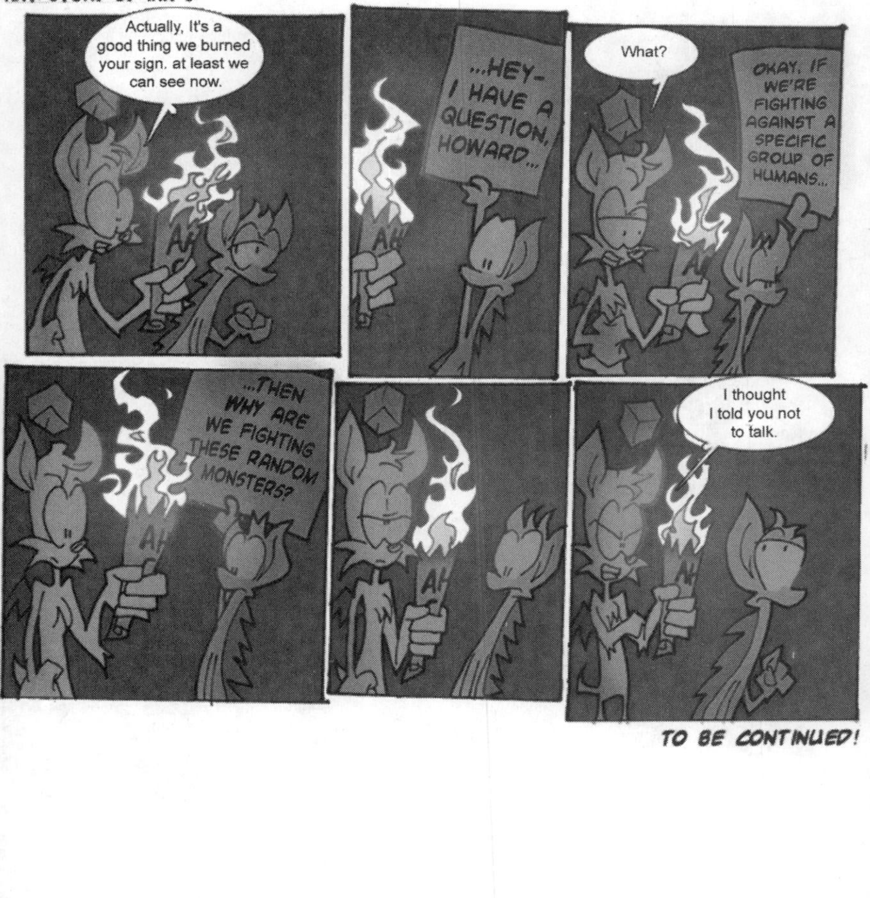

Actually, It's a good thing we burned your sign. at least we can see now.
...HEY- I HAVE A QUESTION, HOWARD...
What?
OKAY. IF WE'RE FIGHTING AGAINST A SPECIFIC GROUP OF HUMANS...
...THEN WHY ARE WE FIGHTING THESE RANDOM MONSTERS?
I thought I told you not to talk.

TO BE CONTINUED!

RPG WORLD

ART/STORY BY IAN J.

"DRAGOBO'S MYSTERIOUS DUNGEON PART 4"

#77

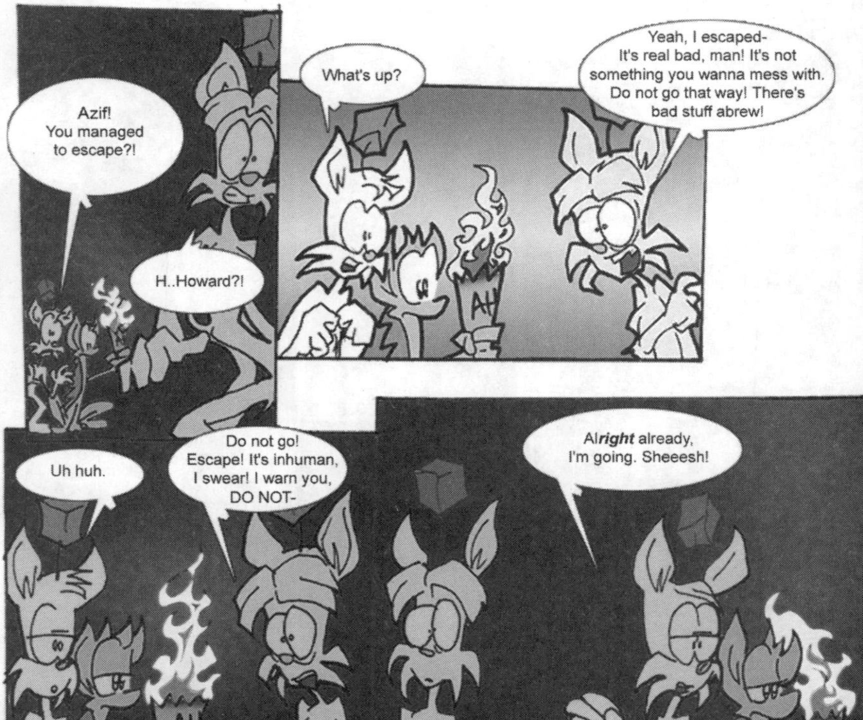
Azif! You managed to escape?!
H..Howard?!
What's up?
Yeah, I escaped- It's real bad, man! It's not something you wanna mess with. Do not go that way! There's bad stuff abrew!
AH
Uh huh.
Do not go! Escape! It's inhuman, I swear! I warn you, DO NOT-
AH
Al*right* already, I'm going. Sheeesh!
AH

TO BE CONTINUED!

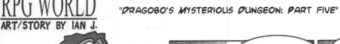

RPG WORLD

ART/STORY BY IAN J.

"DRAGOBO'S MYSTERIOUS DUNGEON: PART FIVE"

#78

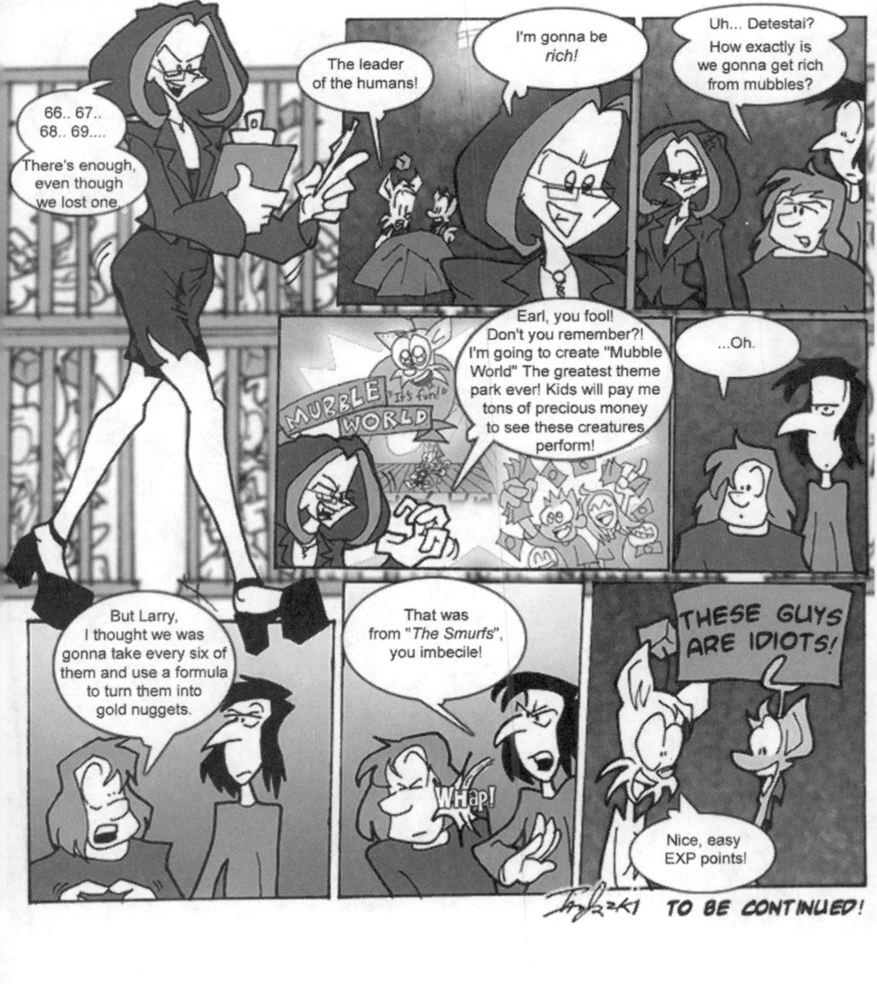

66.. 67.. 68.. 69....
There's enough, even though we lost one.
The leader of the humans!
I'm gonna be *rich!*
Uh... Detestai? How exactly is we gonna get rich from mubbles?
MUBBLE WORLD
It's fun!
Earl, you fool! Don't you remember?! I'm going to create "Mubble World" The greatest theme park ever! Kids will pay me tons of precious money to see these creatures perform!
...Oh.
But Larry, I thought we was gonna take every six of them and use a formula to turn them into gold nuggets.
That was from "*The Smurfs*", you imbecile!
WHap!
THESE GUYS ARE IDIOTS!
Nice, easy EXP points!
TO BE CONTINUED!

RPG WORLD

ART/STORY BY IAN J.

"DRAGOBO'S MYSTERIOUS DUNGEON: PART SIX"

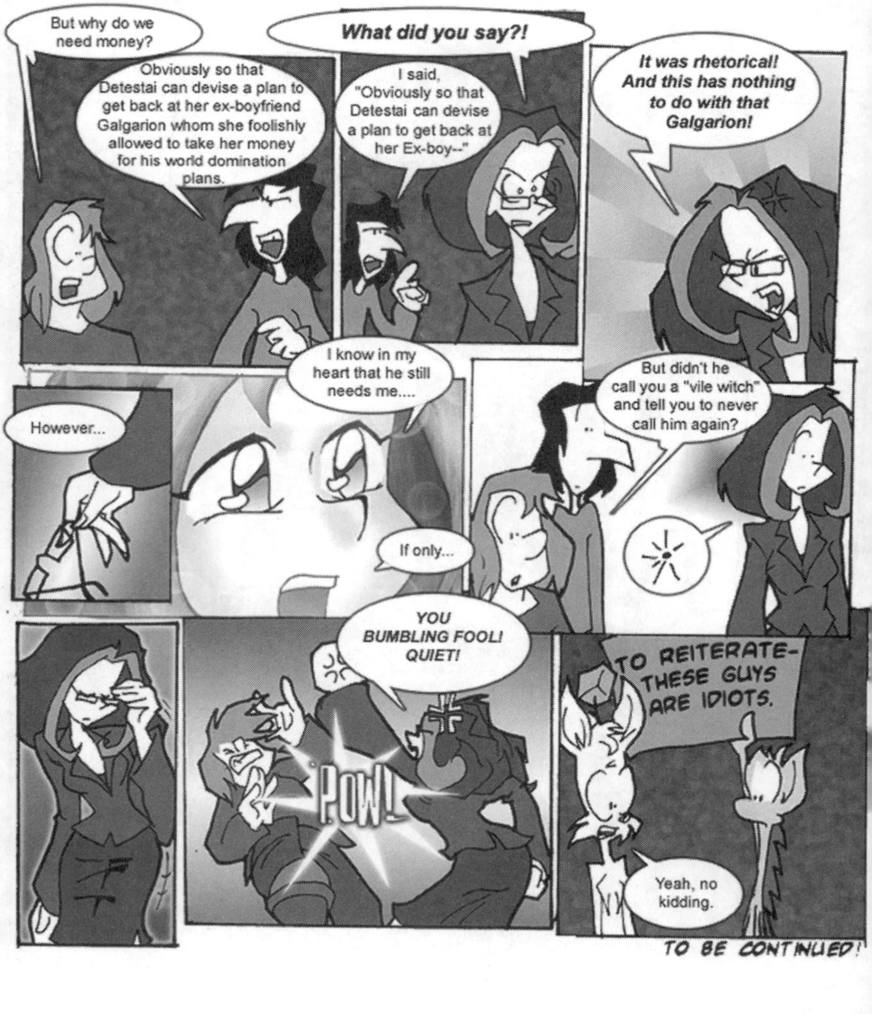
But why do we need money?
Obviously so that Detestai can devise a plan to get back at her ex-boyfriend Galgarion whom she foolishly allowed to take her money for his world domination plans.
What did you say?!
I said, "Obviously so that Detestai can devise a plan to get back at her Ex-boy--"
It was rhetorical! And this has nothing to do with that Galgarion!
However...
I know in my heart that he still needs me....
If only...
But didn't he call you a "vile witch" and tell you to never call him again?
YOU BUMBLING FOOL! QUIET!
POW!
TO REITERATE- THESE GUYS ARE IDIOTS.
Yeah, no kidding.

TO BE CONTINUED!

RPG WORLD

ART/STORY BY IAN J.

"DRAGOBO'S MYSTERIOUS DUNGEON PART SEVEN"

#80

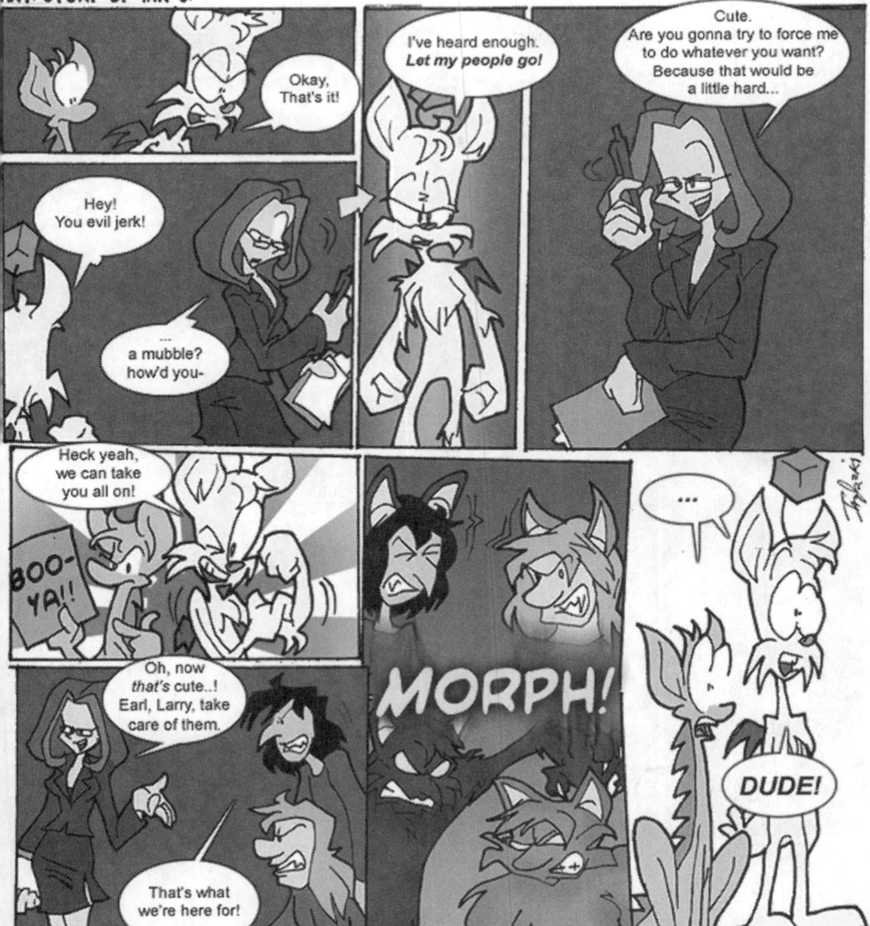
Okay,
That's it!
Hey!
You evil jerk!
...
a mubble?
how'd you-
I've heard enough.
Let my people go!
Cute.
Are you gonna try to force me to do whatever you want? Because that would be a little hard...
Heck yeah, we can take you all on!
BOO-YA!!
Oh, now *that's* cute..! Earl, Larry, take care of them.
That's what we're here for!
MORPH!
...
DUDE!

TO BE CONTINUED!

RPG WORLD

"DRAGOBO'S MYSTERIOUS DUNGEON: PART EIGHT" #81

ART/STORY BY IAN J.

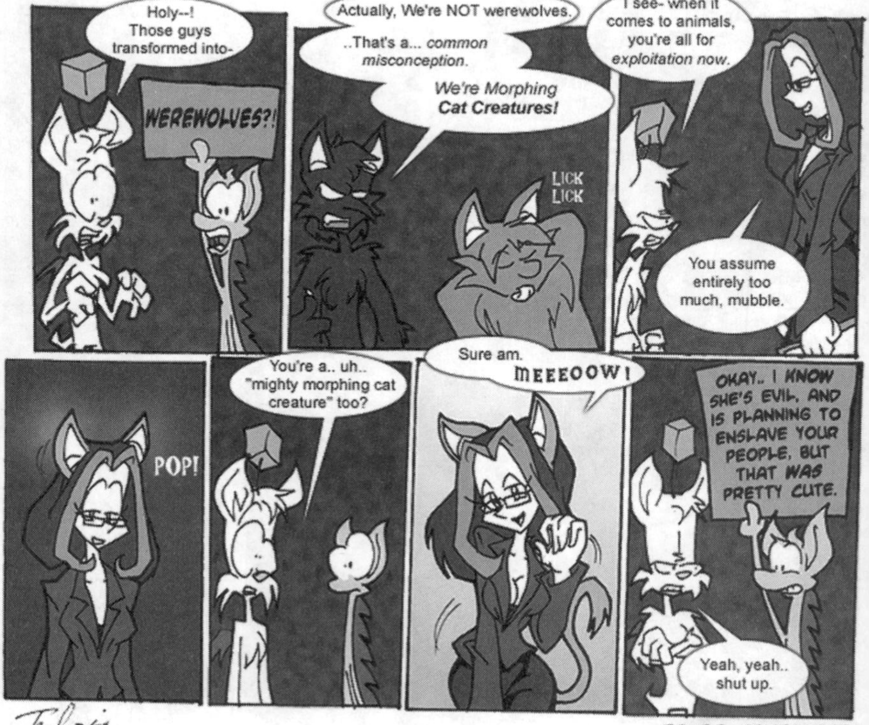
Holy--! Those guys transformed into-
WEREWOLVES?!
Actually, We're NOT werewolves.
..That's a... *common misconception*.
We're Morphing **Cat Creatures!**
LICK LICK
I see- when it comes to animals, you're all for *exploitation now*.
You assume entirely too much, mubble.
POP!
You're a.. uh.. "mighty morphing cat creature" too?
Sure am.
MEEEOOW!
OKAY.. I KNOW SHE'S EVIL, AND IS PLANNING TO ENSLAVE YOUR PEOPLE, BUT THAT *WAS* PRETTY CUTE.
Yeah, yeah.. shut up.

TO BE CONTINUED!

RPG WORLD

"DRAGOBO'S MYSTERIOUS DUNGEON: PART NINE" #82

ART/STORY BY IAN J.

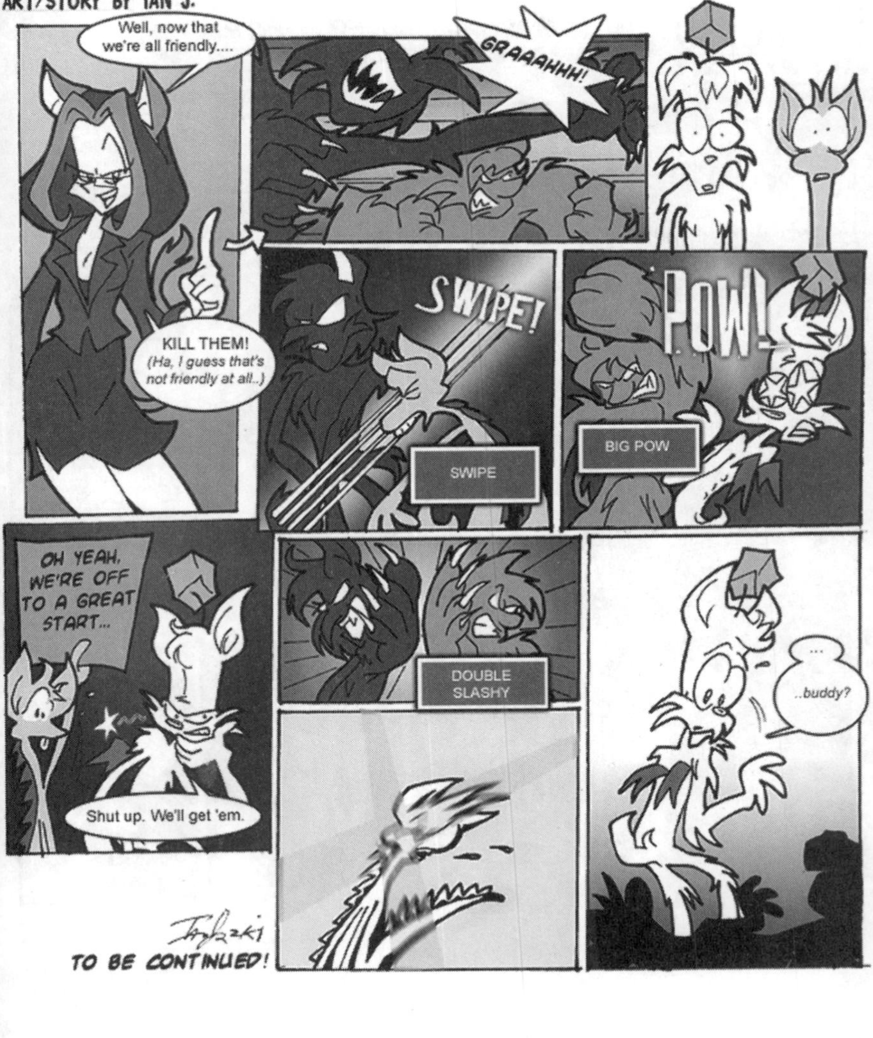

Well, now that we're all friendly....
KILL THEM!
(Ha, I guess that's not friendly at all..)
GRAAAHHH!
SWIPE!
SWIPE
POW!
BIG POW
OH YEAH, WE'RE OFF TO A GREAT START...
Shut up. We'll get 'em.
DOUBLE SLASHY
...
..buddy?

TO BE CONTINUED!

RPG WORLD

ART/STORY BY IAN J.

RPG WORLD SUPER SPECIAL: "DRAGOBO'S MYSTERIOUS DUNGEON PART TEN"

#83

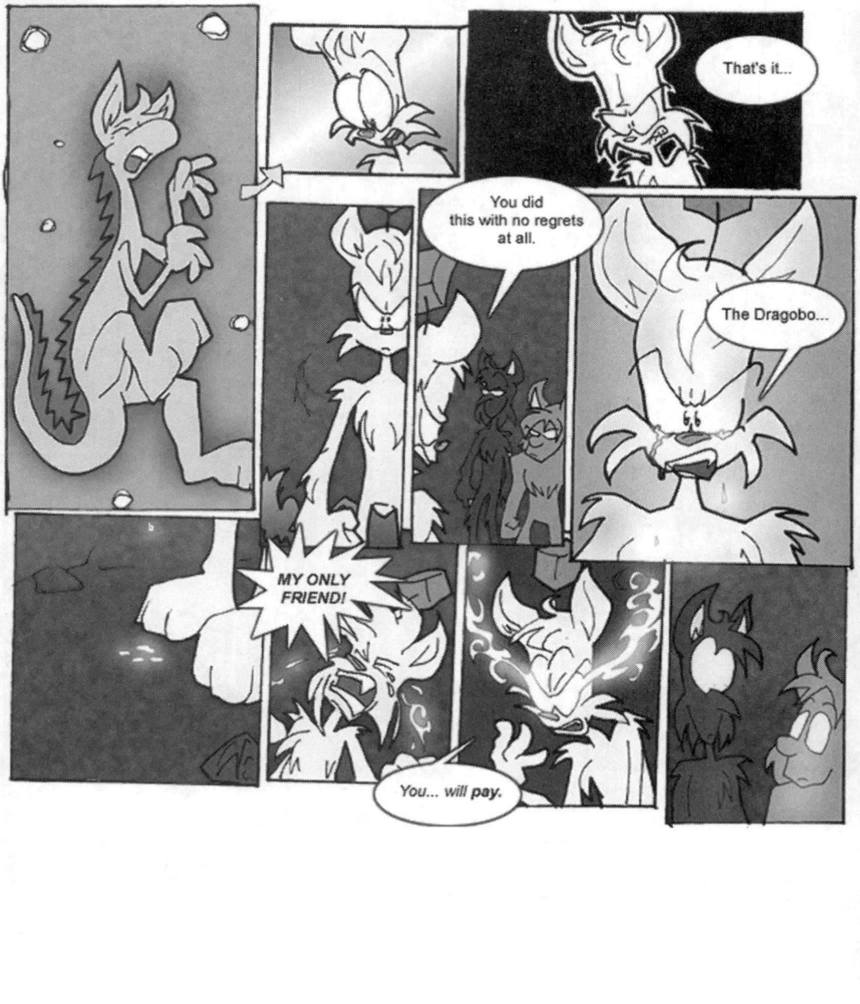
That's it...
You did this with no regrets at all.
The Dragobo...
MY ONLY FRIEND!
You... will pay.

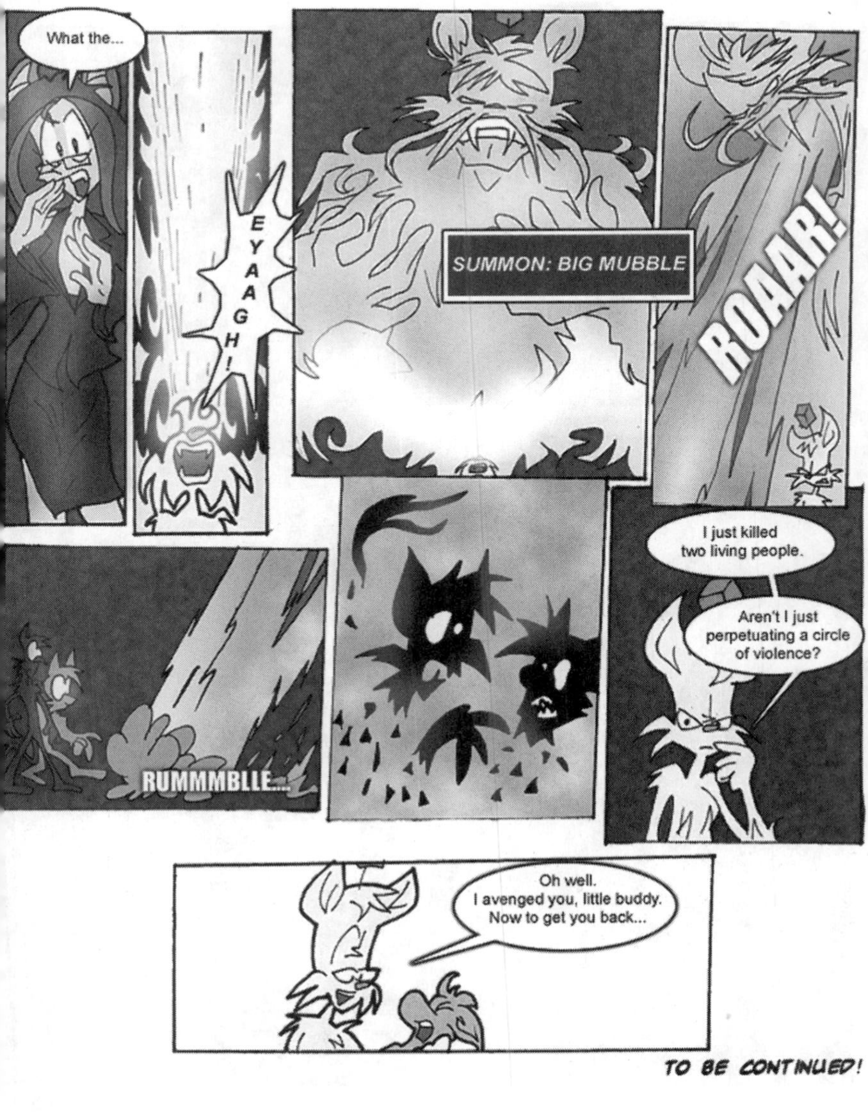

What the...
EYAAGH!
SUMMON: BIG MUBBLE
ROAAR!
RUMMMBLLE...
I just killed two living people.
Aren't I just perpetuating a circle of violence?
Oh well. I avenged you, little buddy. Now to get you back...

TO BE CONTINUED!

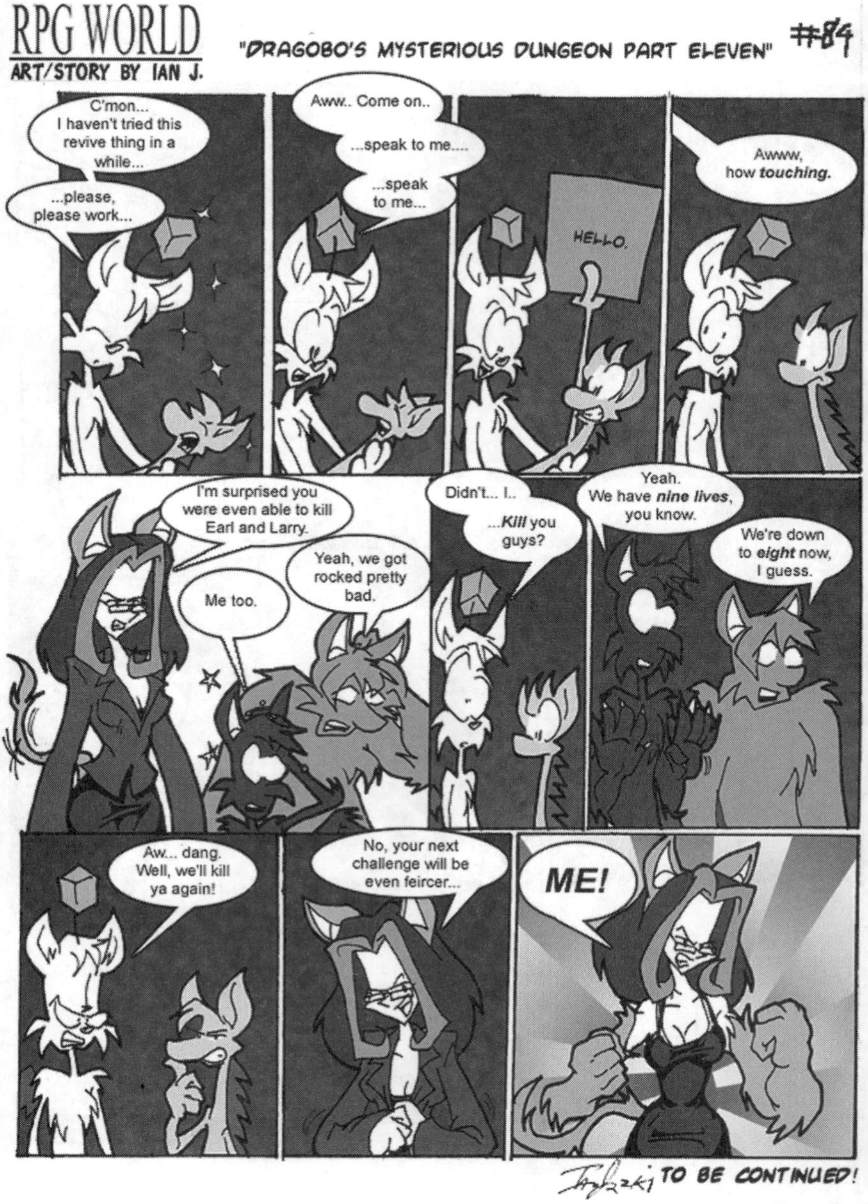
RPG WORLD
ART/STORY BY IAN J.
"DRAGOBO'S MYSTERIOUS DUNGEON PART ELEVEN"
#84
C'mon... I haven't tried this revive thing in a while...
...please, please work...
Aww.. Come on..
...speak to me....
...speak to me...
HELLO.
Awww, how *touching.*
I'm surprised you were even able to kill Earl and Larry.
Me too.
Yeah, we got rocked pretty bad.
Didn't... I..
...*Kill* you guys?
Yeah. We have *nine lives*, you know.
We're down to *eight* now, I guess.
Aw... dang. Well, we'll kill ya again!
No, your next challenge will be even feircer...
ME!
TO BE CONTINUED!

RPG WORLD

"DRAGOBO'S MYSTERIOUS DUNGEON PART TWELVE"

#85

ART/STORY BY IAN J.

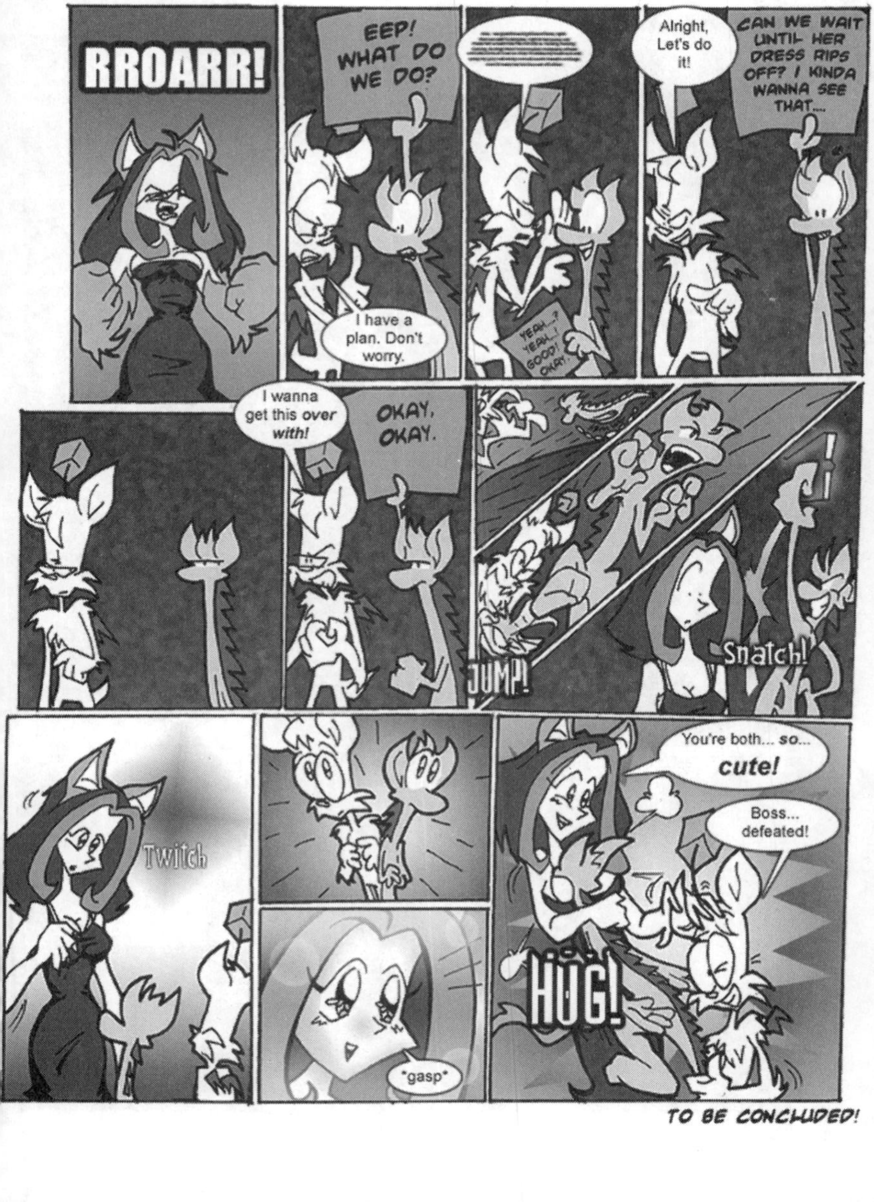

RROARR!
EEP! WHAT DO WE DO?
I have a plan. Don't worry.
YEAH...? YEAH...! GOOD! OKAY.
Alright, Let's do it!
CAN WE WAIT UNTIL HER DRESS RIPS OFF? I KINDA WANNA SEE THAT....
I wanna get this over with!
OKAY, OKAY.
JUMP!
Snatch!
!
Twitch
gasp
You're both... so... cute!
Boss... defeated!
HUG!

TO BE CONCLUDED!

RPG WORLD

"DRAGOBO'S MYSTERIOUS DUNGEON PART THIRTEEN"

#86

ART/STORY BY IAN J.

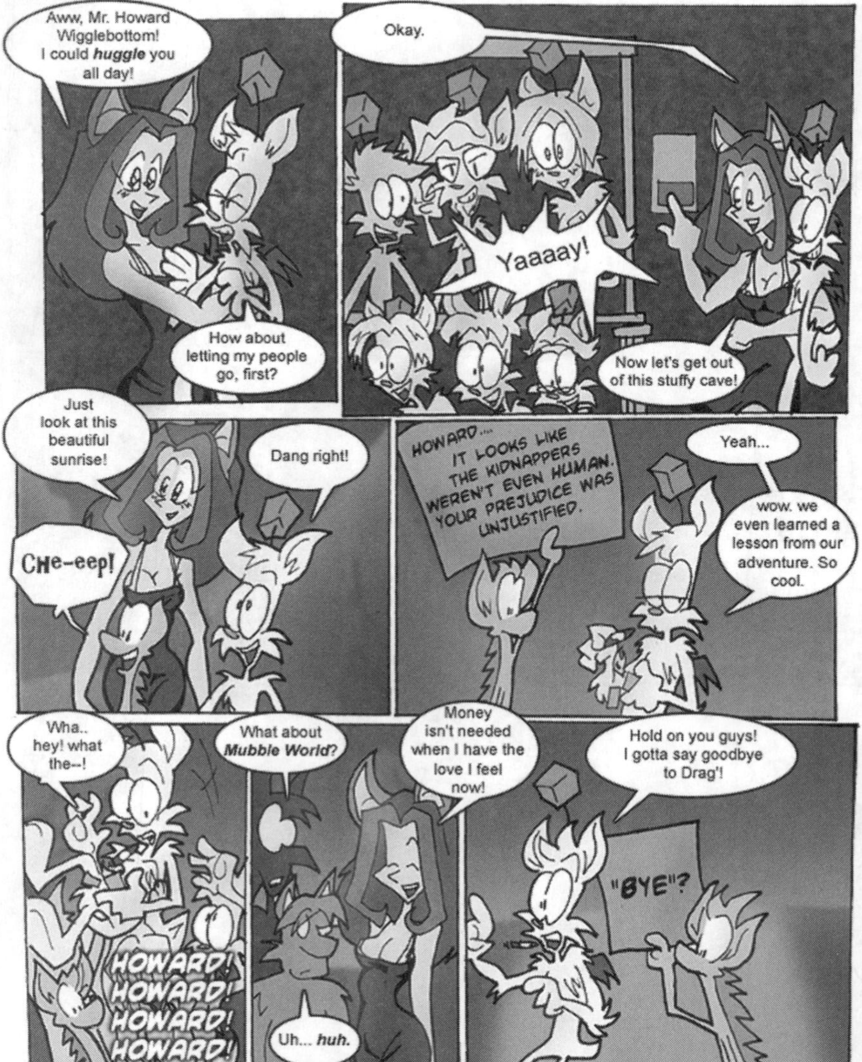

Aww, Mr. Howard Wigglebottom! I could *huggle* you all day!
How about letting my people go, first?
Okay.
Yaaaay!
Now let's get out of this stuffy cave!
Just look at this beautiful sunrise!
Dang right!
CHe-eep!
HOWARD... IT LOOKS LIKE THE KIDNAPPERS WEREN'T EVEN HUMAN. YOUR PREJUDICE WAS UNJUSTIFIED.
Yeah...
wow. we even learned a lesson from our adventure. So cool.
Wha.. hey! what the--!
HOWARD! HOWARD! HOWARD! HOWARD!
What about *Mubble World*?
Money isn't needed when I have the love I feel now!
Uh... *huh.*
Hold on you guys! I gotta say goodbye to Drag'!
"BYE"?

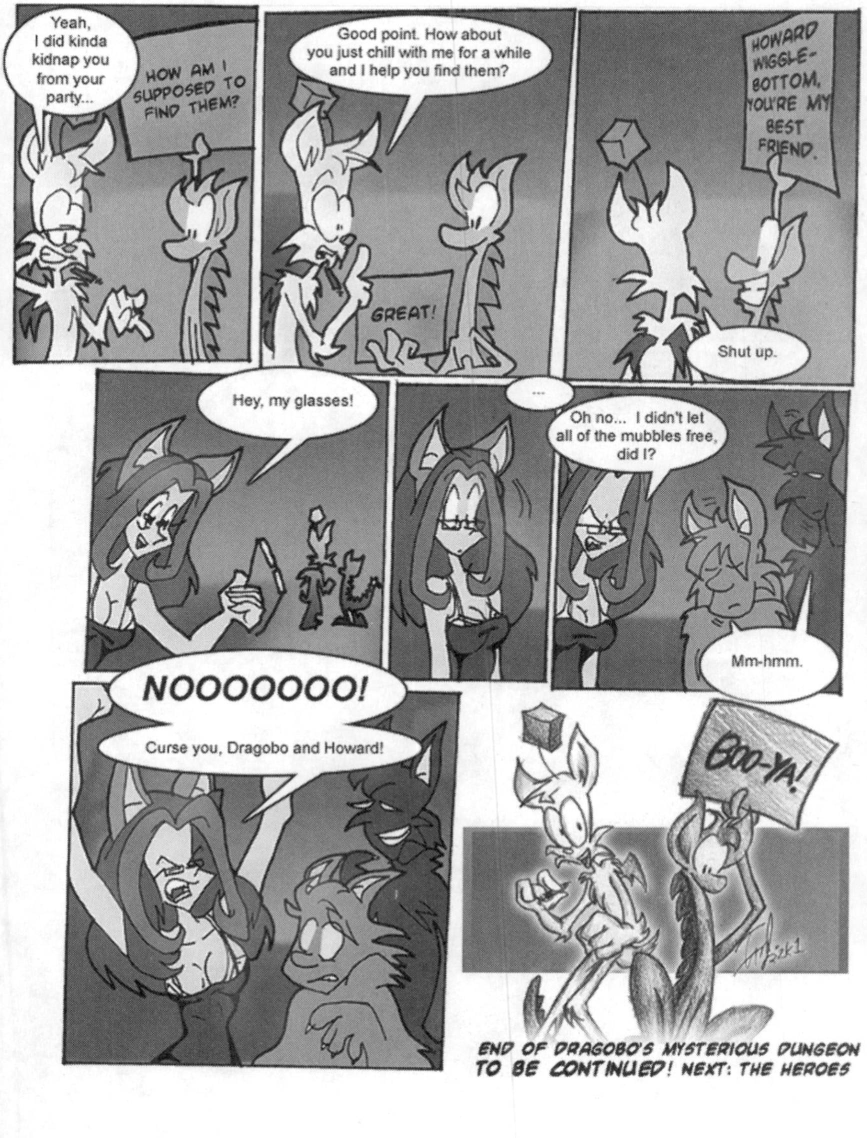
Yeah, I did kinda kidnap you from your party...
HOW AM I SUPPOSED TO FIND THEM?
Good point. How about you just chill with me for a while and I help you find them?
GREAT!
HOWARD WIGGLE-BOTTOM, YOU'RE MY BEST FRIEND.
Shut up.
Hey, my glasses!
...
Oh no... I didn't let all of the mubbles free, did I?
Mm-hmm.
NOOOOOOO!
Curse you, Dragobo and Howard!
BOO-YA!

END OF DRAGOBO'S MYSTERIOUS DUNGEON
TO BE CONTINUED! NEXT: THE HEROES

RPG WORLD

ART/STORY BY IAN J.

"RETURN TO NORMALCY"

#87

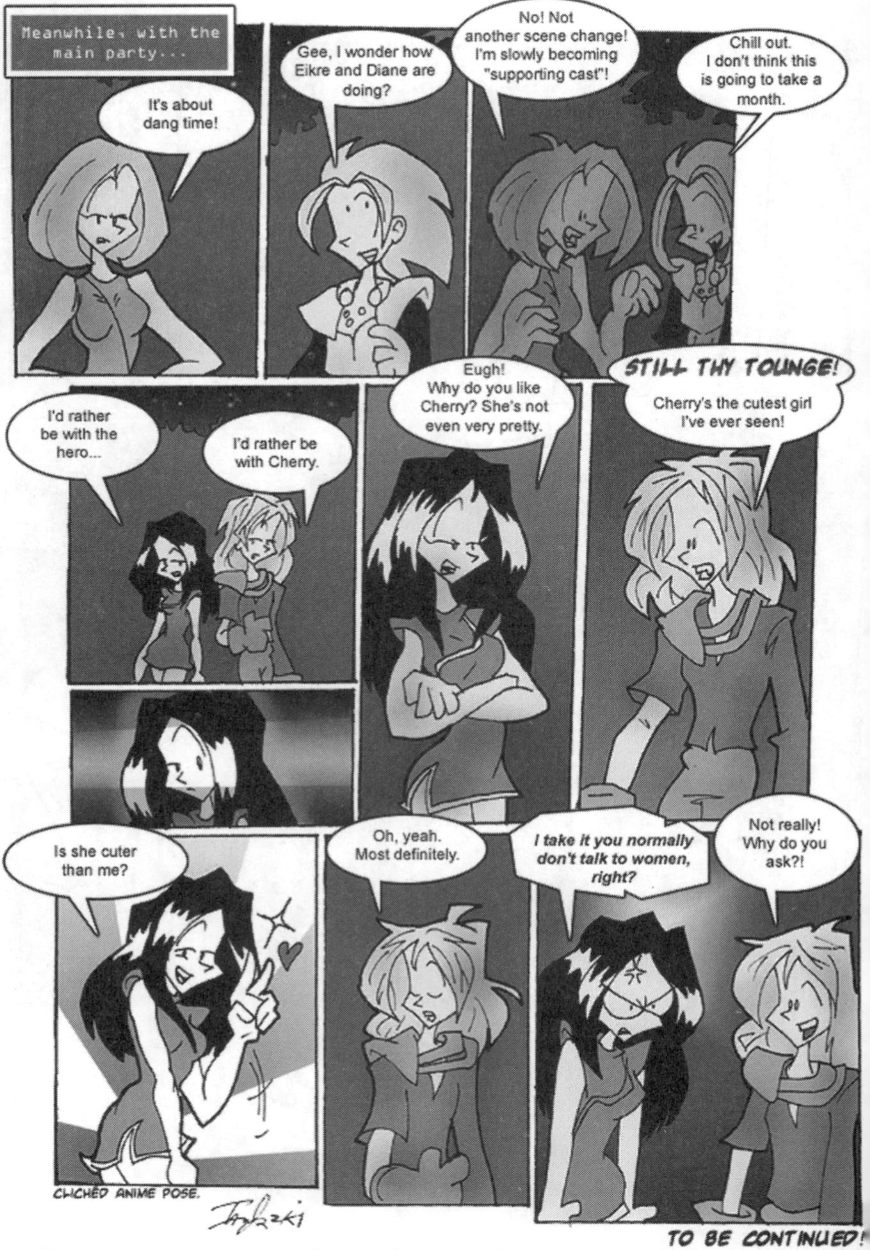
Meanwhile, with the main party...
It's about dang time!
Gee, I wonder how Eikre and Diane are doing?
No! Not another scene change! I'm slowly becoming "supporting cast"!
Chill out. I don't think this is going to take a month.
I'd rather be with the hero...
I'd rather be with Cherry.
Eugh! Why do you like Cherry? She's not even very pretty.
STILL THY TOUNGE!
Cherry's the cutest girl I've ever seen!
Is she cuter than me?
CLICHED ANIME POSE.
Oh, yeah. Most definitely.
I take it you normally don't talk to women, right?
Not really! Why do you ask?!
TO BE CONTINUED!

RPG WORLD

"INSTINCT"

#88

ART/STORY BY IAN J.

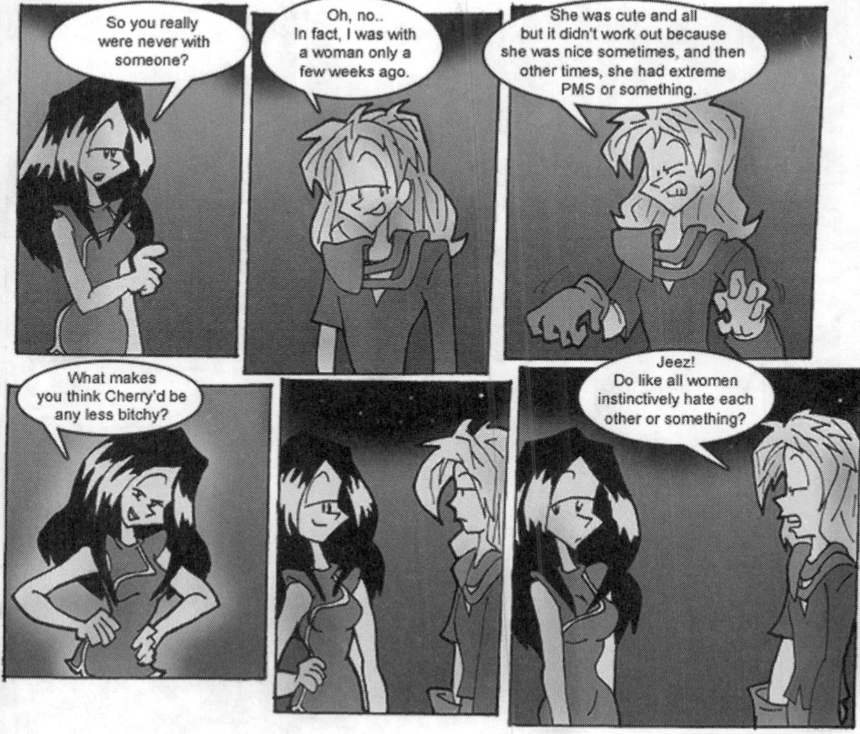
So you really were never with someone?
Oh, no..
In fact, I was with a woman only a few weeks ago.
She was cute and all but it didn't work out because she was nice sometimes, and then other times, she had extreme PMS or something.
What makes you think Cherry'd be any less bitchy?
Jeez!
Do like all women instinctively hate each other or something?

TO BE CONTINUED!

RPG WORLD

ART/STORY BY IAN J.

"HARLOTRY"

#89

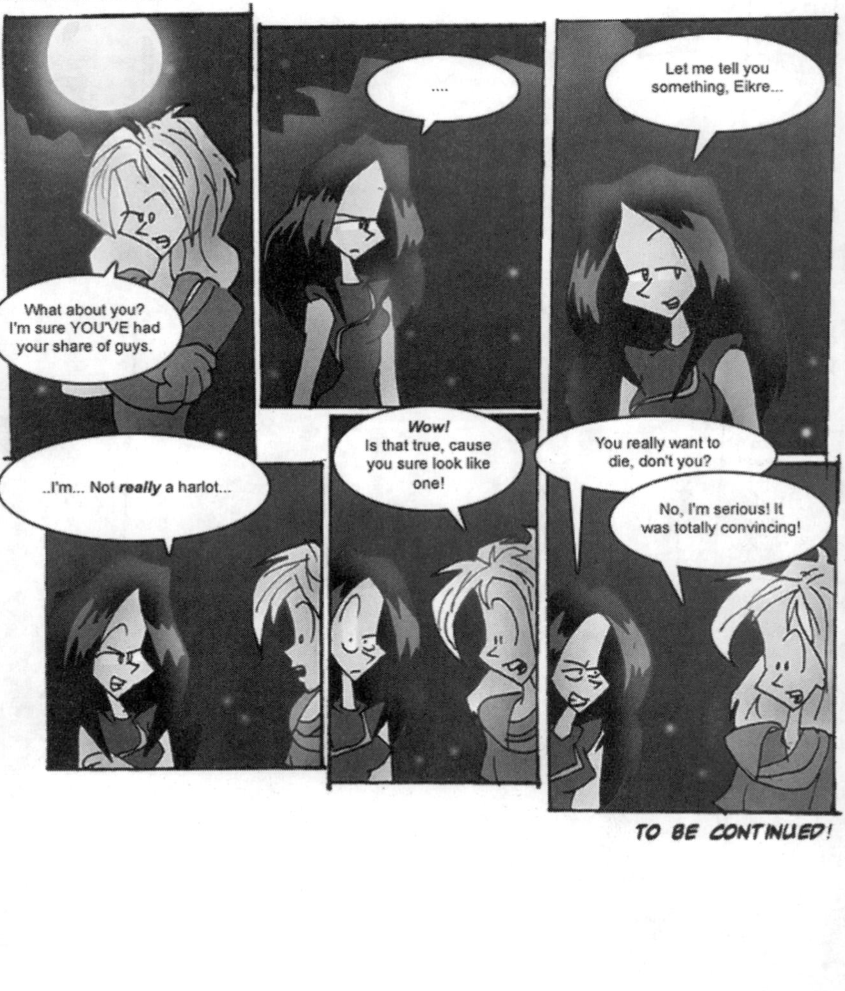
What about you? I'm sure YOU'VE had your share of guys.
....
Let me tell you something, Eikre...
..I'm... Not *really* a harlot...
Wow! Is that true, cause you sure look like one!
You really want to die, don't you?
No, I'm serious! It was totally convincing!

TO BE CONTINUED!

RPG WORLD

"HARLOTRY PART TWO" #90

ART/STORY BY IAN J.

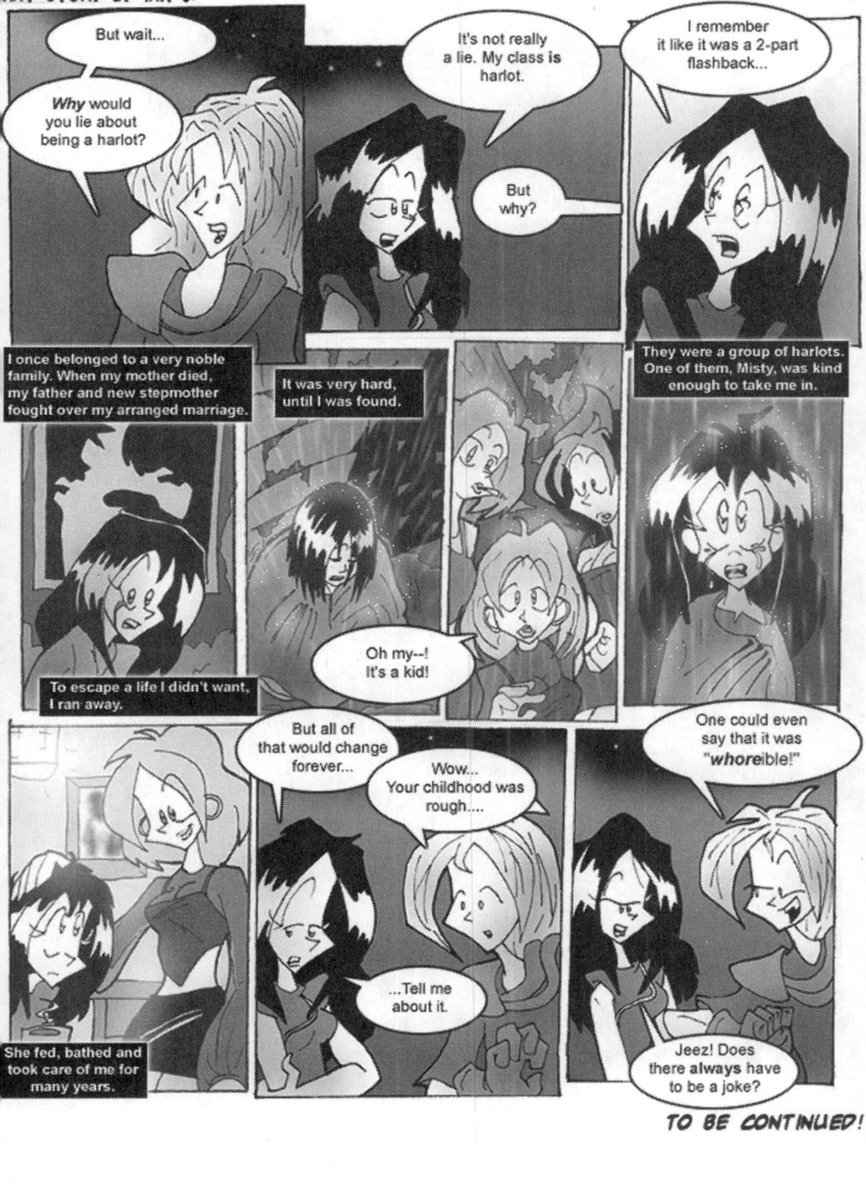

But wait...
Why would you lie about being a harlot?
It's not really a lie. My class is harlot.
But why?
I remember it like it was a 2-part flashback...
I once belonged to a very noble family. When my mother died, my father and new stepmother fought over my arranged marriage.
To escape a life I didn't want, I ran away.
It was very hard, until I was found.
Oh my--! It's a kid!
They were a group of harlots. One of them, Misty, was kind enough to take me in.
She fed, bathed and took care of me for many years.
But all of that would change forever...
Wow... Your childhood was rough....
...Tell me about it.
One could even say that it was "**whore**ible!"
Jeez! Does there **always** have to be a joke?

TO BE CONTINUED!

RPG WORLD

ART/STORY BY IAN J.

"HARLOTRY PART THREE"

#91

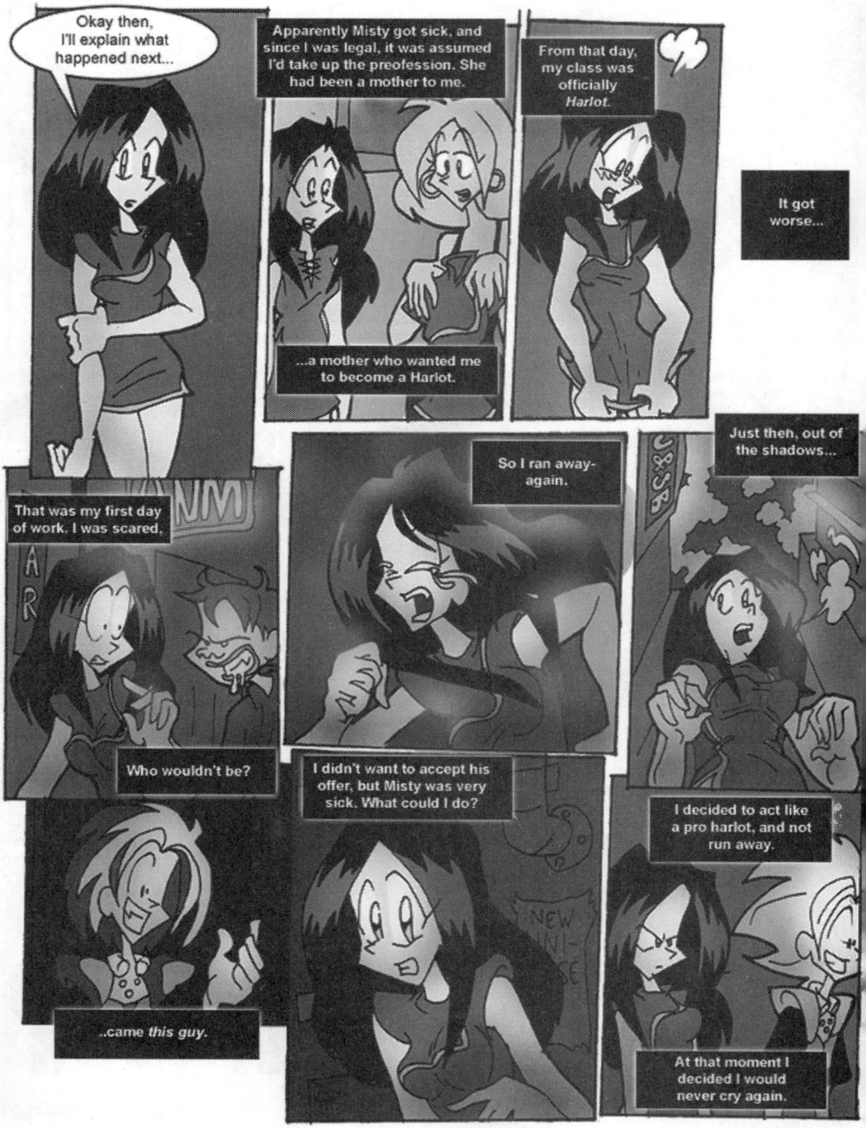

Okay then, I'll explain what happened next...
Apparently Misty got sick, and since I was legal, it was assumed I'd take up the preofession. She had been a mother to me.
...a mother who wanted me to become a Harlot.
From that day, my class was officially *Harlot.*
It got worse...
That was my first day of work. I was scared.
Who wouldn't be?
So I ran away- again.
Just then, out of the shadows...
..came *this guy.*
I didn't want to accept his offer, but Misty was very sick. What could I do?
I decided to act like a pro harlot, and not run away.
At that moment I decided I would never cry again.

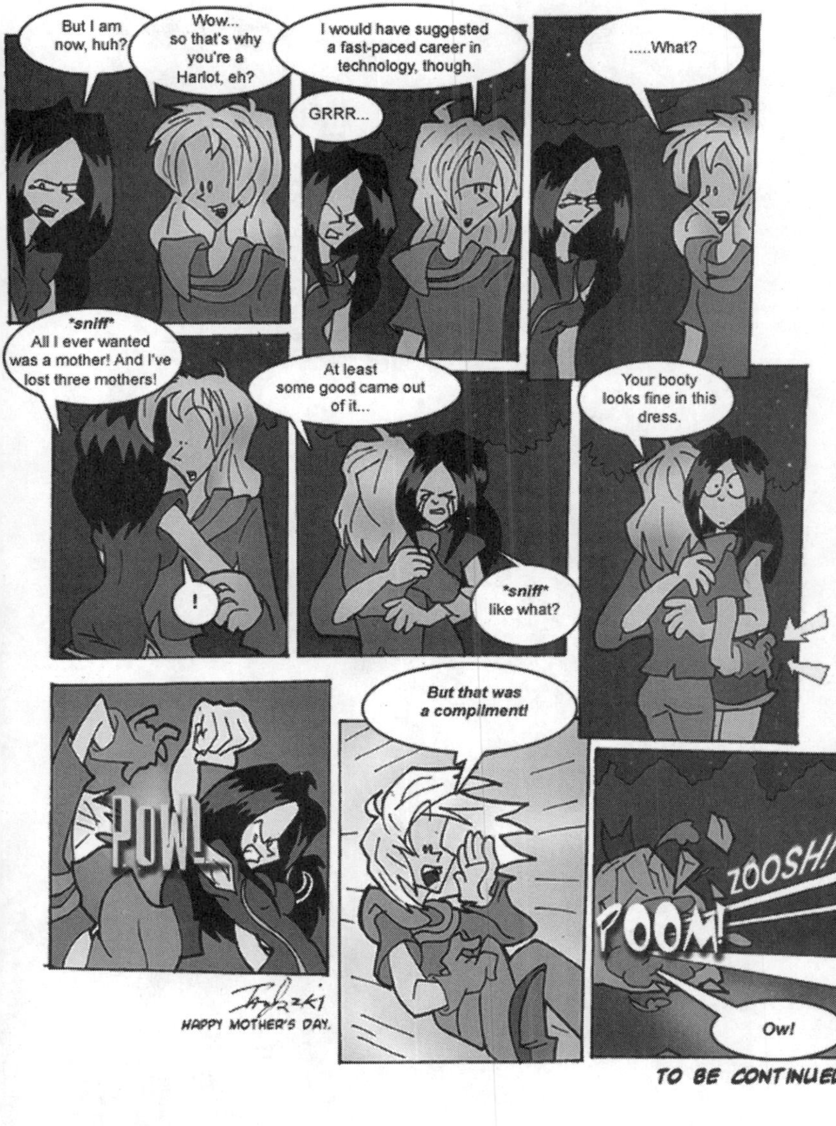
But I am now, huh?
Wow... so that's why you're a Harlot, eh?
I would have suggested a fast-paced career in technology, though.
GRRR...
.....What?
sniff All I ever wanted was a mother! And I've lost three mothers!
!
At least some good came out of it...
sniff like what?
Your booty looks fine in this dress.
POW!
But that was a compilment!
ZOOSH!
POOM!
Ow!

HAPPY MOTHER'S DAY.

TO BE CONTINUED!

RPG WORLD

ART/STORY BY IAN J.

"THE MONSTER"

#92

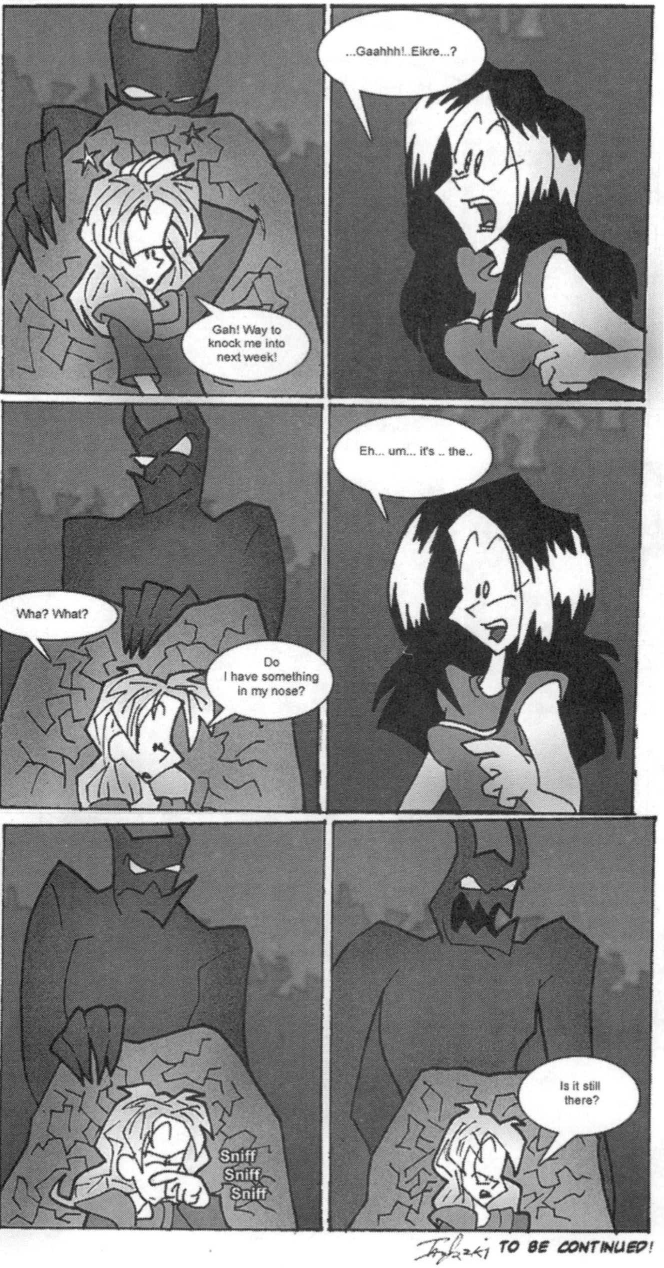

Gah! Way to knock me into next week!
...Gaahhh!..Eikre...?
Wha? What?
Do I have something in my nose?
Eh... um... it's .. the..
Sniff
Sniff
Sniff
Is it still there?

TO BE CONTINUED!

RPG WORLD

ART/STORY BY IAN J.

"BACK TO HERO AND CHERRY"

#93

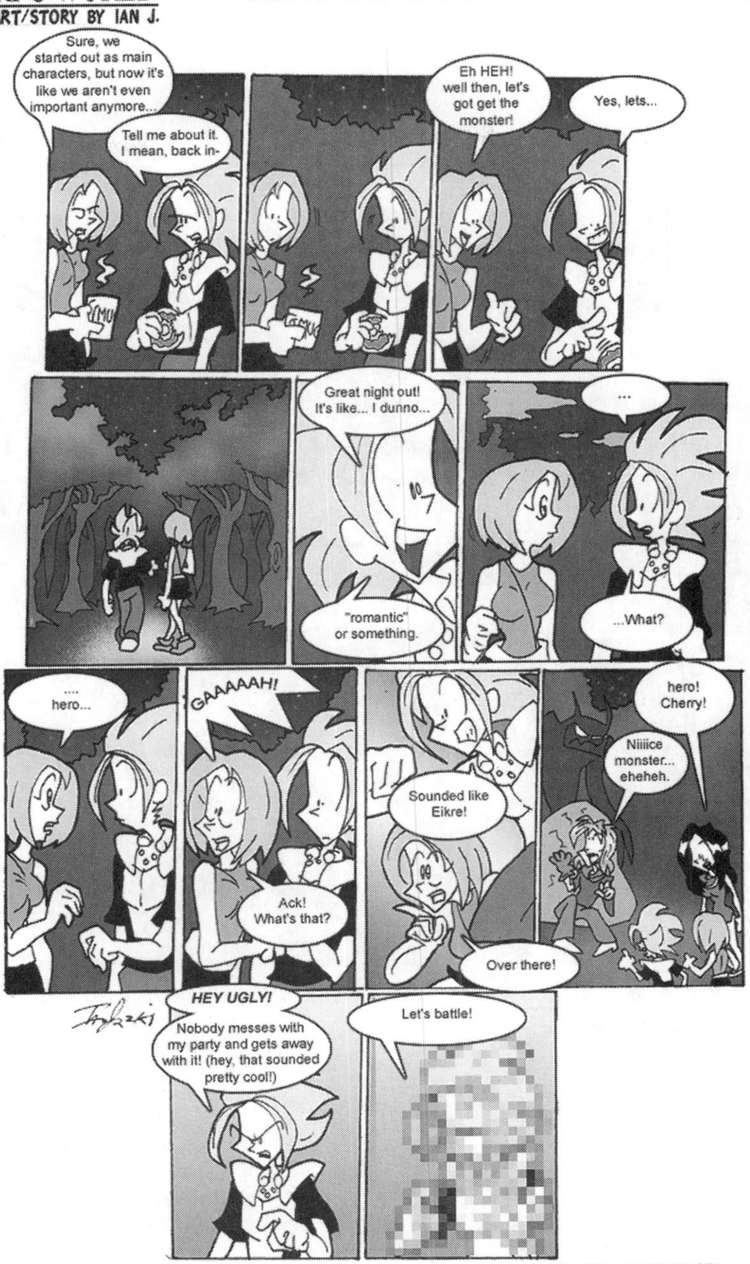

Sure, we started out as main characters, but now it's like we aren't even important anymore...
Tell me about it. I mean, back in-
Eh HEH! well then, let's got get the monster!
Yes, lets...
Great night out! It's like... I dunno...
"romantic" or something.
...
...What?
.... hero...
GAAAAAH!
Ack! What's that?
Sounded like Eikre!
Over there!
hero! Cherry!
Niiiice monster... eheheh.
HEY UGLY!
Nobody messes with my party and gets away with it! (hey, that sounded pretty cool!)
Let's battle!

TO BE CONTINUED!

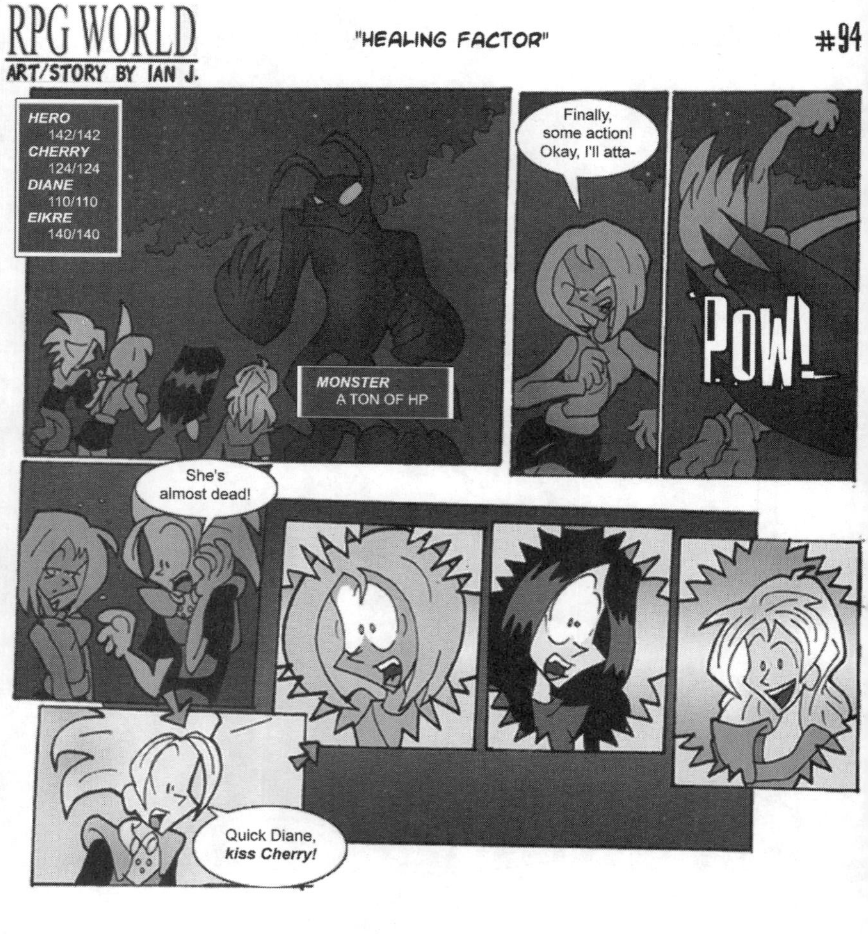
RPG WORLD
ART/STORY BY IAN J.
"HEALING FACTOR"
#94
HERO 142/142
CHERRY 124/124
DIANE 110/110
EIKRE 140/140
MONSTER A TON OF HP
Finally, some action! Okay, I'll atta-
POW!
She's almost dead!
Quick Diane, kiss Cherry!

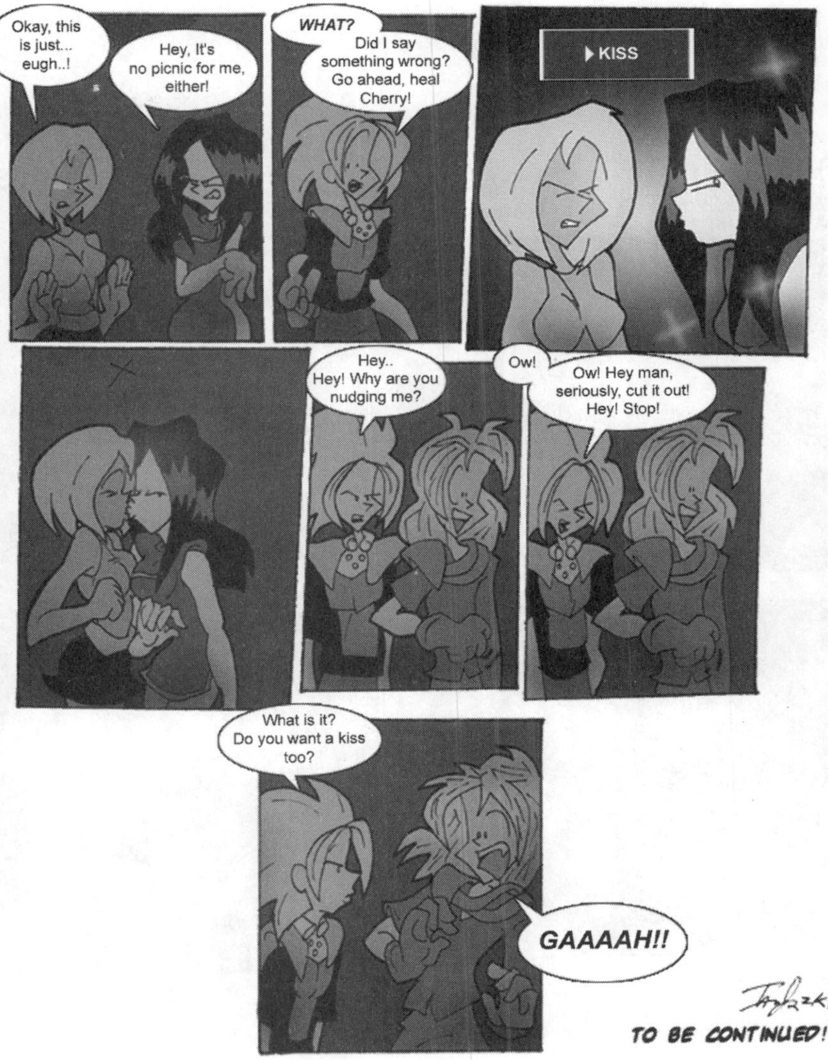
Okay, this is just... eugh..!
Hey, It's no picnic for me, either!
WHAT?
Did I say something wrong? Go ahead, heal Cherry!
KISS
Hey..
Hey! Why are you nudging me?
Ow!
Ow! Hey man, seriously, cut it out! Hey! Stop!
What is it? Do you want a kiss too?
GAAAAH!!
TO BE CONTINUED!

RPG WORLD

ART/STORY BY IAN J.

"MONSTER ATTACK!"

#95

GWRAAAH!
FLICK!
!!! Oh my! Now he's almost dead!
Okay, This is pathertic.

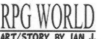

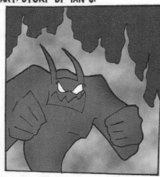

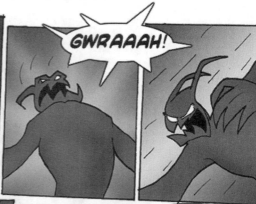

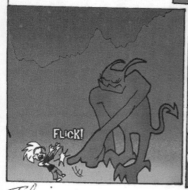

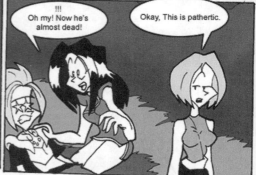

TO BE CONTINUED!

RPG WORLD

"WHAT YOUR WEAKER CHARACTERS ACTUALY THINK" #96

ART/STORY BY IAN J.

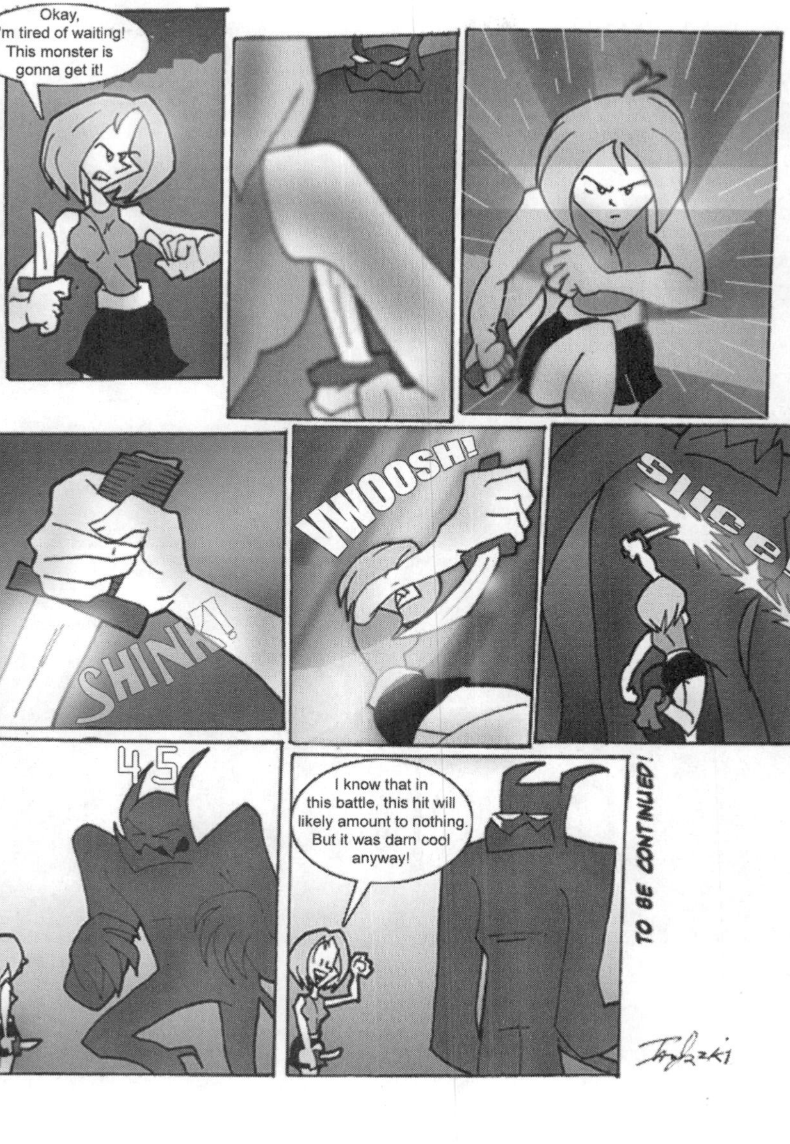

Okay, I'm tired of waiting! This monster is gonna get it!
SHINK!
VWOOSH!
Slice!
45
I know that in this battle, this hit will likely amount to nothing. But it was darn cool anyway!
TO BE CONTINUED!

RPG WORLD

"FOR EVALUATION PURPOSES ONLY"

#97

ART/STORY BY IAN J.

Okay, If we're gonna beat this monster, we need to evaluate the situation and come up with a strategy.
Okay- Pro: The monster appears to have a low defense.
POW!
Alright then, Con: We are all going to die.

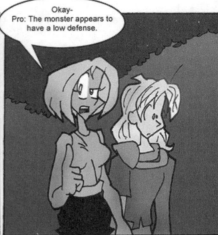

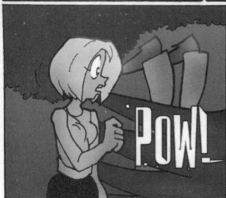

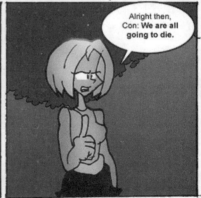

TO BE CONTINUED!

RPG WORLD

ART/STORY BY IAN J.

"STAFF WANTED"

#98

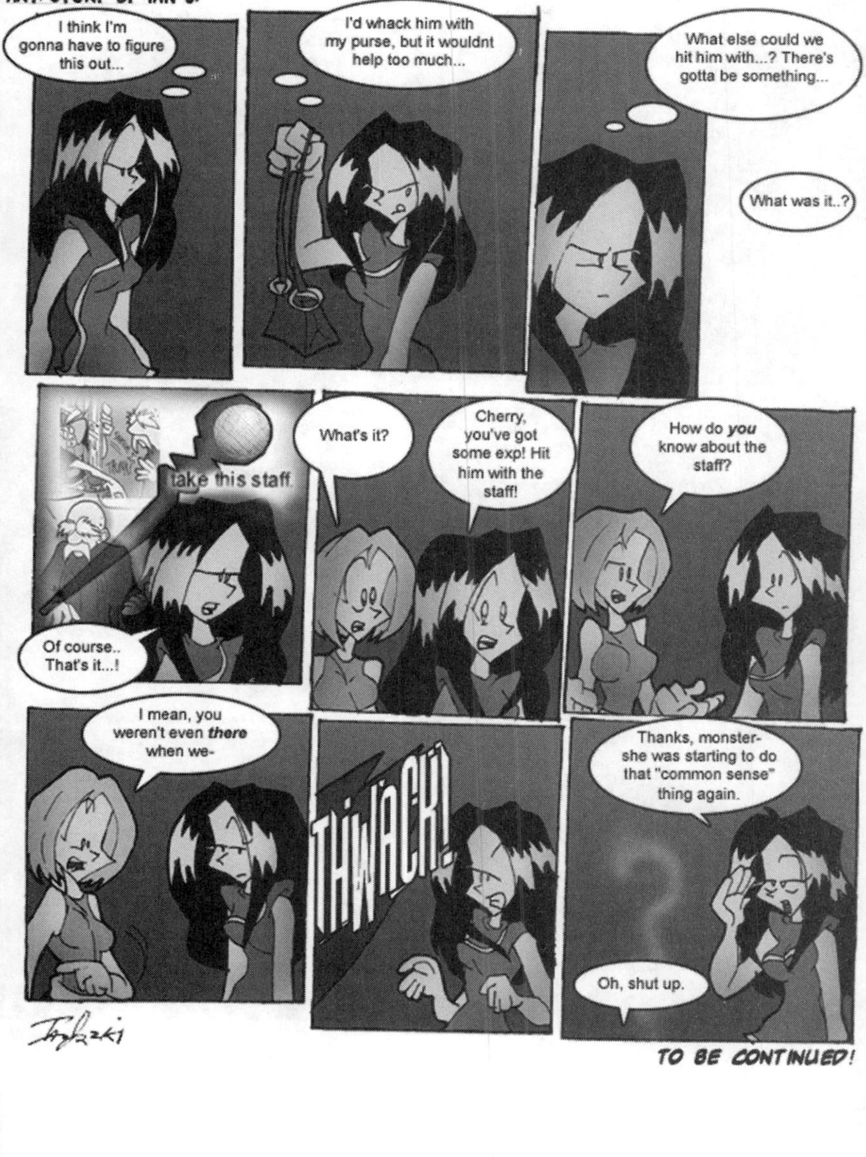
I think I'm gonna have to figure this out...
I'd whack him with my purse, but it wouldnt help too much...
What else could we hit him with...? There's gotta be something...
What was it..?
take this staff
Of course.. That's it...!
What's it?
Cherry, you've got some exp! Hit him with the staff!
How do *you* know about the staff?
I mean, you weren't even *there* when we-
THWACK!
Thanks, monster- she was starting to do that "common sense" thing again.
Oh, shut up.

TO BE CONTINUED!

RPG WORLD

ART/STORY BY IAN J.

"INVENTORY CHECK"

#99

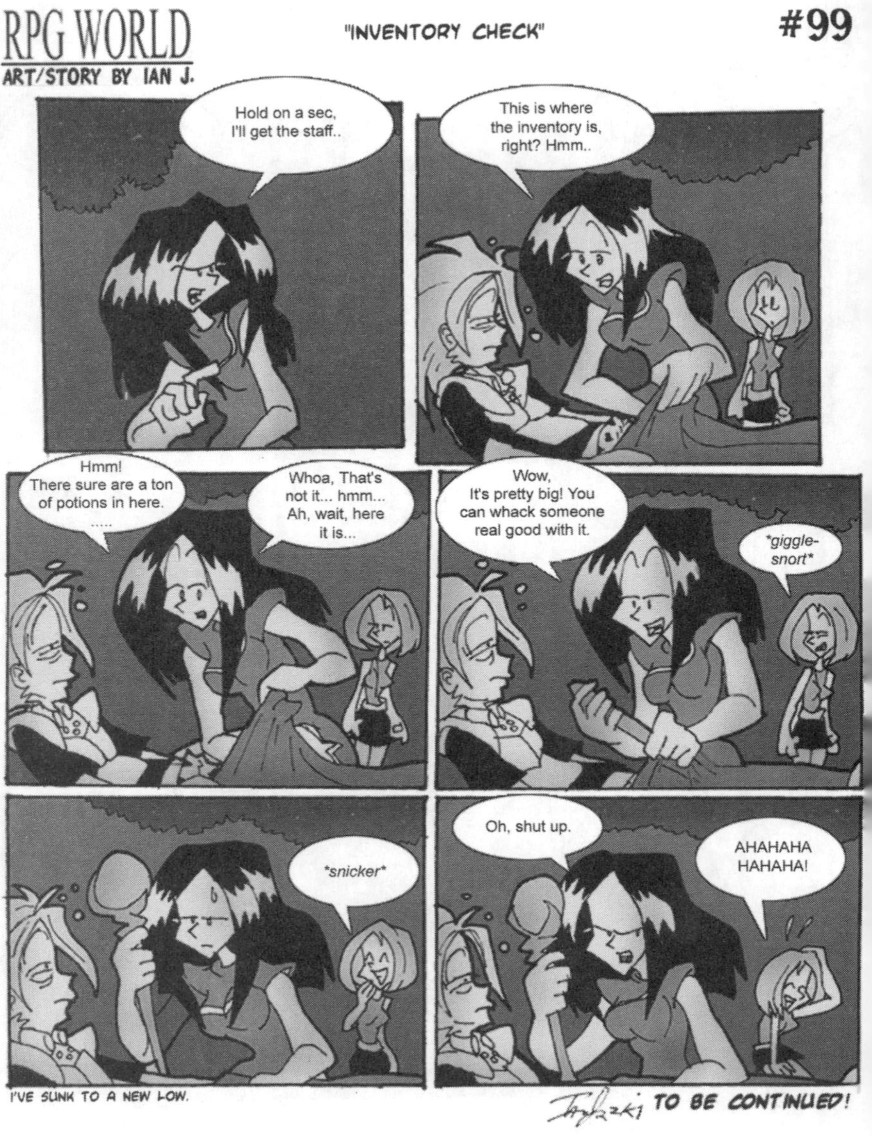
Hold on a sec,
I'll get the staff..
This is where
the inventory is,
right? Hmm..
Hmm!
There sure are a ton
of potions in here.
.....
Whoa, That's
not it... hmm...
Ah, wait, here
it is...
Wow,
It's pretty big! You
can whack someone
real good with it.
*giggle-
snort*
snicker
Oh, shut up.
AHAHAHA
HAHAHA!

I'VE SUNK TO A NEW LOW.

TO BE CONTINUED!

RPG WORLD

ART/STORY BY IAN J.

RPG WORLD #100 SUPER SPECIAL:
"A MONSTROUS BATTLE"

#100

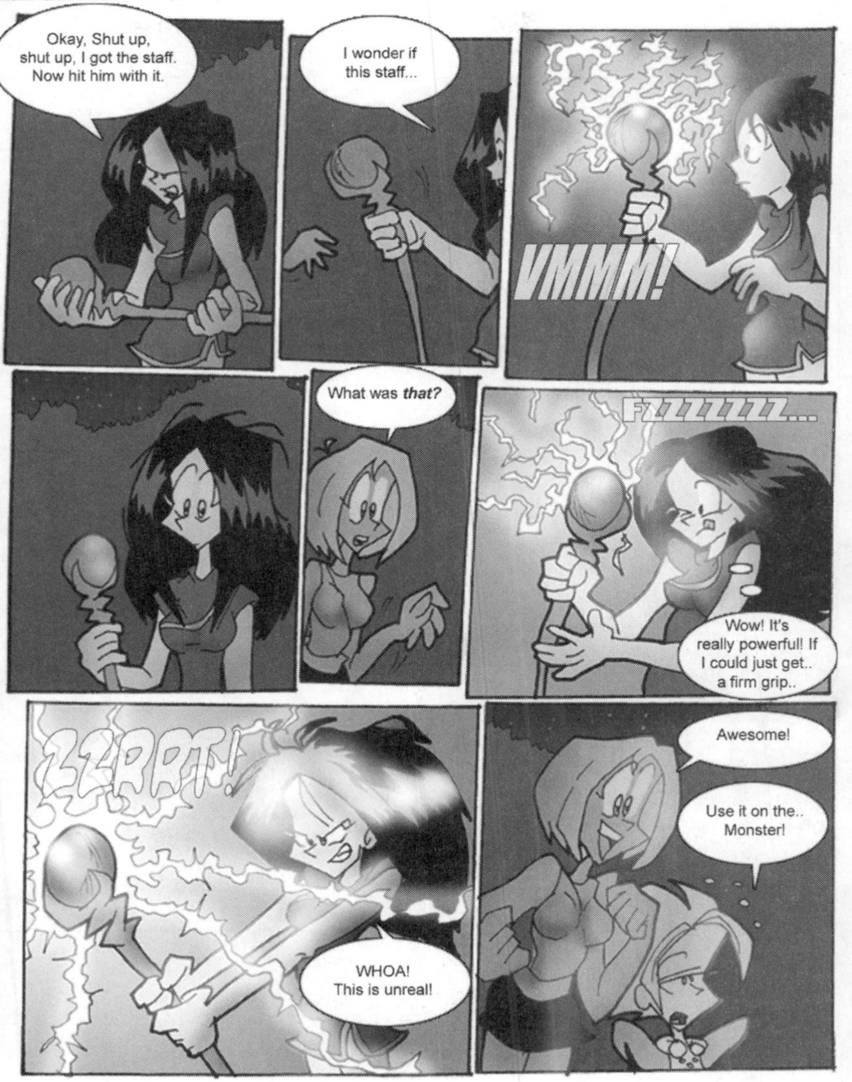

Okay, Shut up, shut up, I got the staff. Now hit him with it.
I wonder if this staff...
VMMM!
What was *that?*
FZZZZZZZ...
Wow! It's really powerful! If I could just get.. a firm grip..
ZZRRRT!
WHOA! This is unreal!
Awesome!
Use it on the.. Monster!

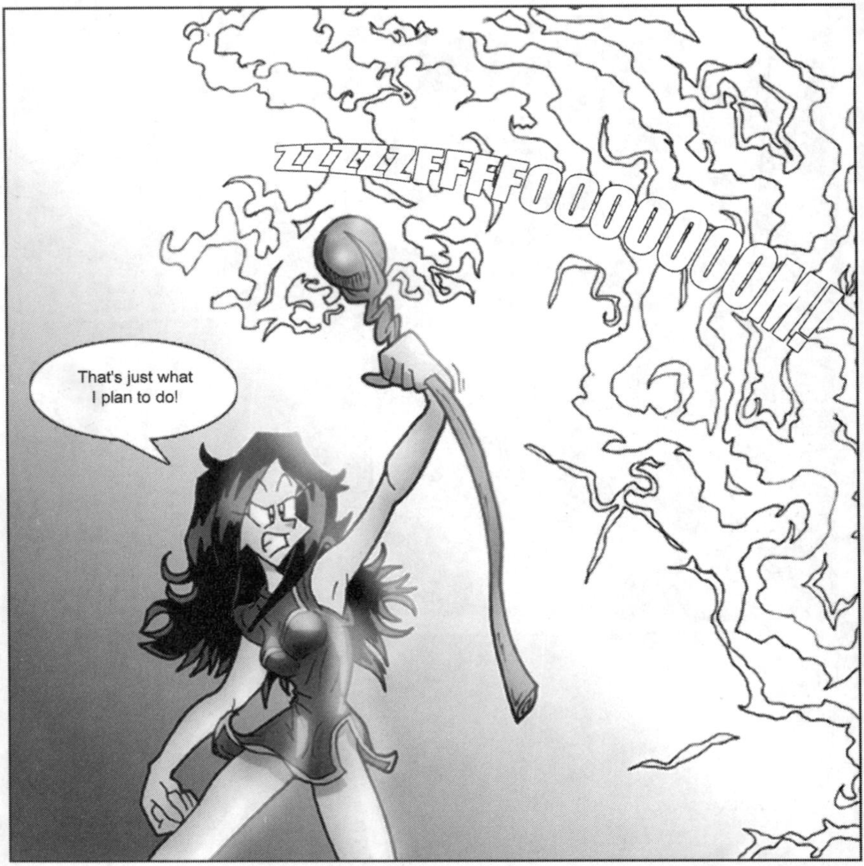
ZZZZZZFFFFOOOOOOOOOM!!
That's just what I plan to do!

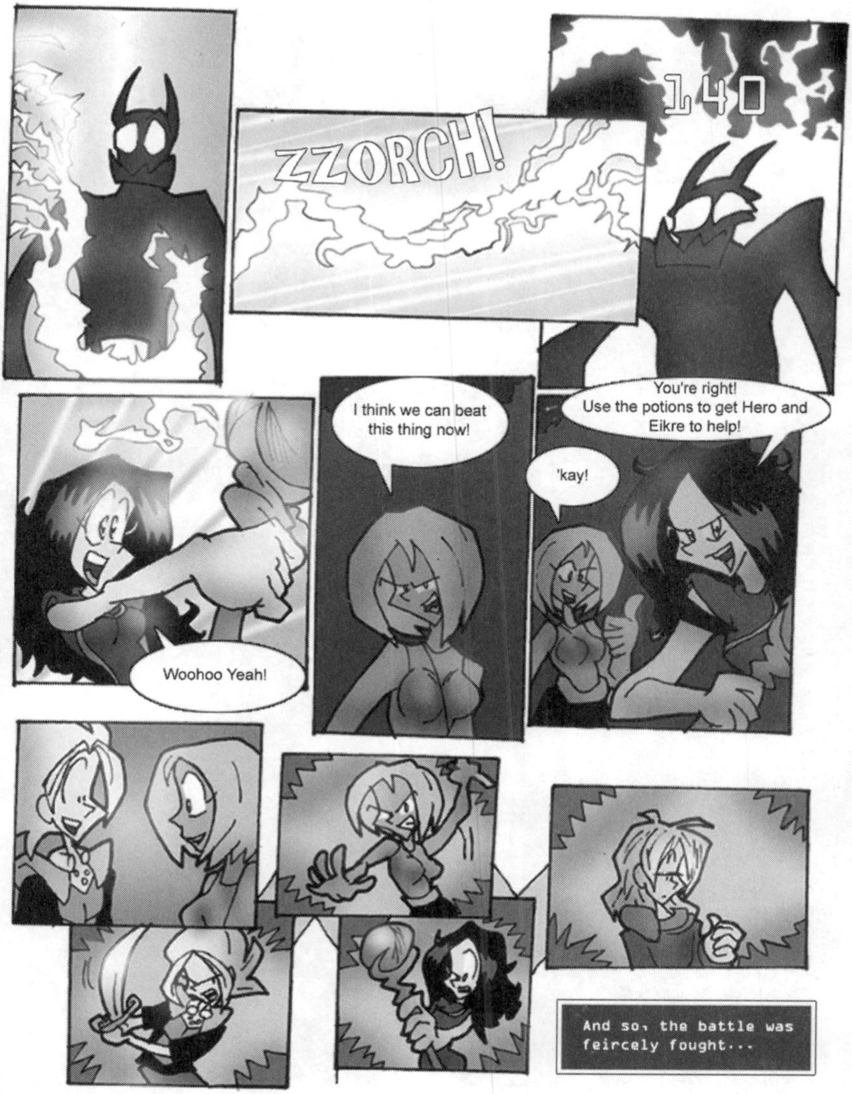
ZZORCH!
140
Woohoo Yeah!
I think we can beat this thing now!
You're right! Use the potions to get Hero and Eikre to help!
'kay!
And so, the battle was feircely fought...

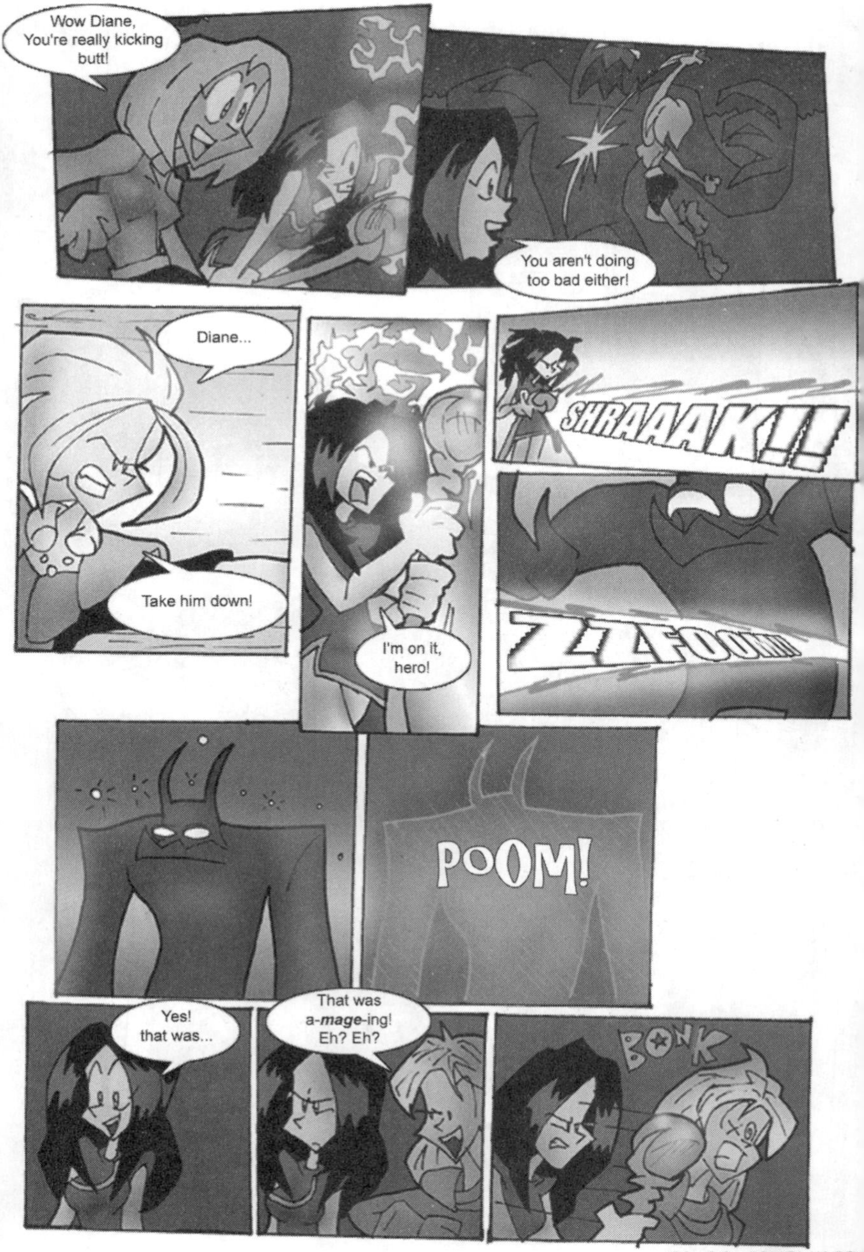

Wow Diane, You're really kicking butt!
You aren't doing too bad either!
Diane...
Take him down!
I'm on it, hero!
SHRAAAK!!!
POOM!
Yes! that was...
That was a-***mage***-ing! Eh? Eh?
BONK

TO BE CONTINUED!

RPG WORLD

ART/STORY BY IAN J

"WRAP-UP"

#101

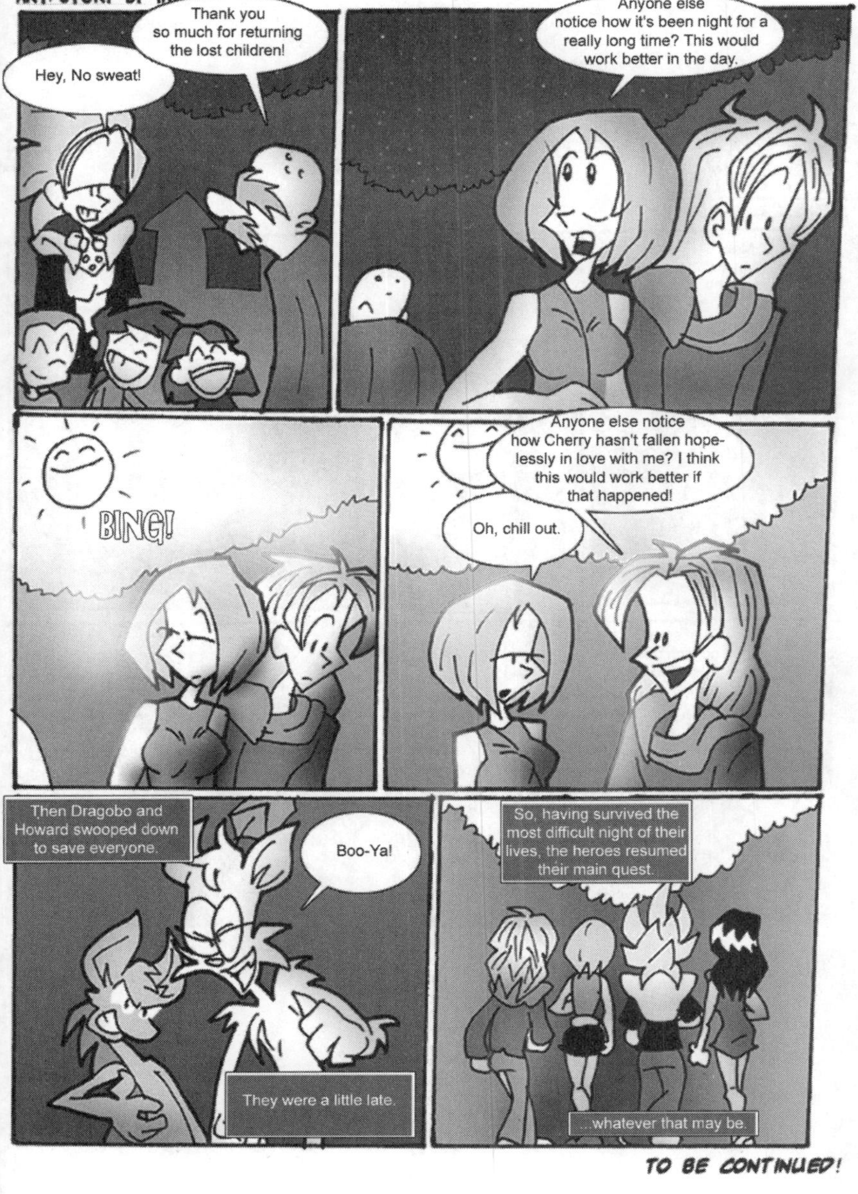

Thank you so much for returning the lost children!
Hey, No sweat!
Anyone else notice how it's been night for a really long time? This would work better in the day.
BING!
Anyone else notice how Cherry hasn't fallen hope-lessly in love with me? I think this would work better if that happened!
Oh, chill out.
Then Dragobo and Howard swooped down to save everyone.
Boo-Ya!
They were a little late.
So, having survived the most difficult night of their lives, the heroes resumed their main quest.
...whatever that may be.

TO BE CONTINUED!

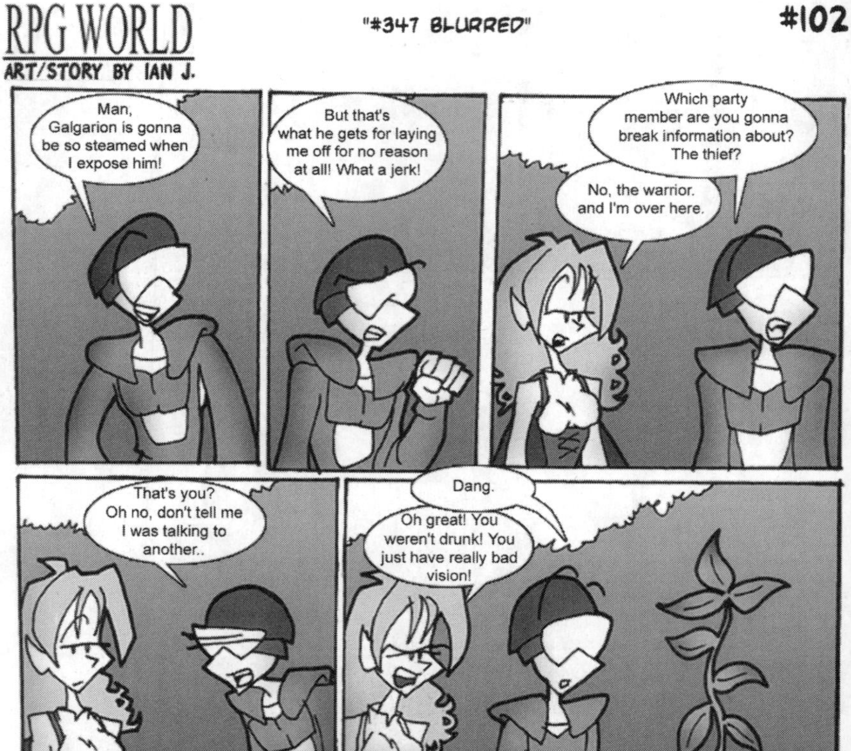
RPG WORLD
ART/STORY BY IAN J.
"#347 BLURRED"
#102
Man, Galgarion is gonna be so steamed when I expose him!
But that's what he gets for laying me off for no reason at all! What a jerk!
Which party member are you gonna break information about? The thief?
No, the warrior. and I'm over here.
That's you? Oh no, don't tell me I was talking to another..
Dang.
Oh great! You weren't drunk! You just have really bad vision!
TO BE CONTINUED!

RPG WORLD

ART/STORY BY IAN J.

"BOSS LADY"

#103

So Boss, what are we gonna do. Boss, what's our next plan?
Stop calling me "BOSS"!
But... You *are* our boss.... ....Um..... When can Larry and I buy new clothes?
Okay, there's only one thing we can do...
Go to my Ex-boyfriend **Galgarion**'s hideout and see if he'll give us some money!
Oh... okay... sounds like a plan... um...
...boss.
GARRRR!

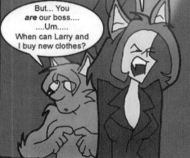

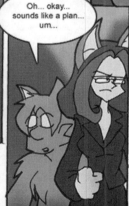

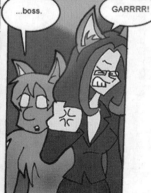

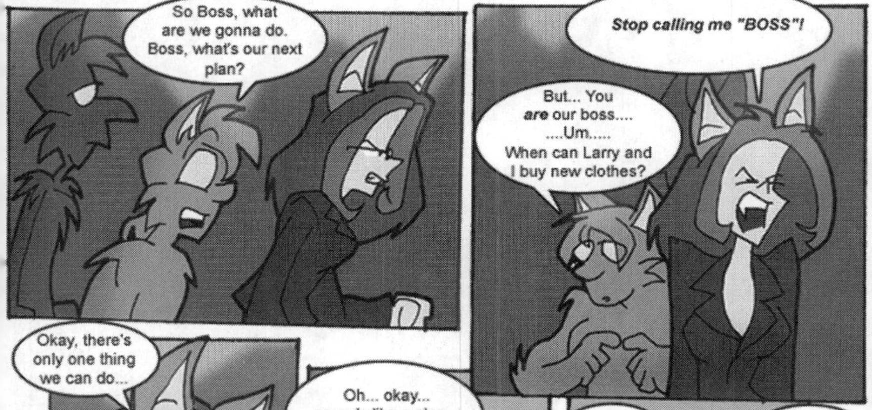

TO BE CONTINUED!

RPG WORLD

ART/STORY BY IAN J.

"PARTING PATHS"

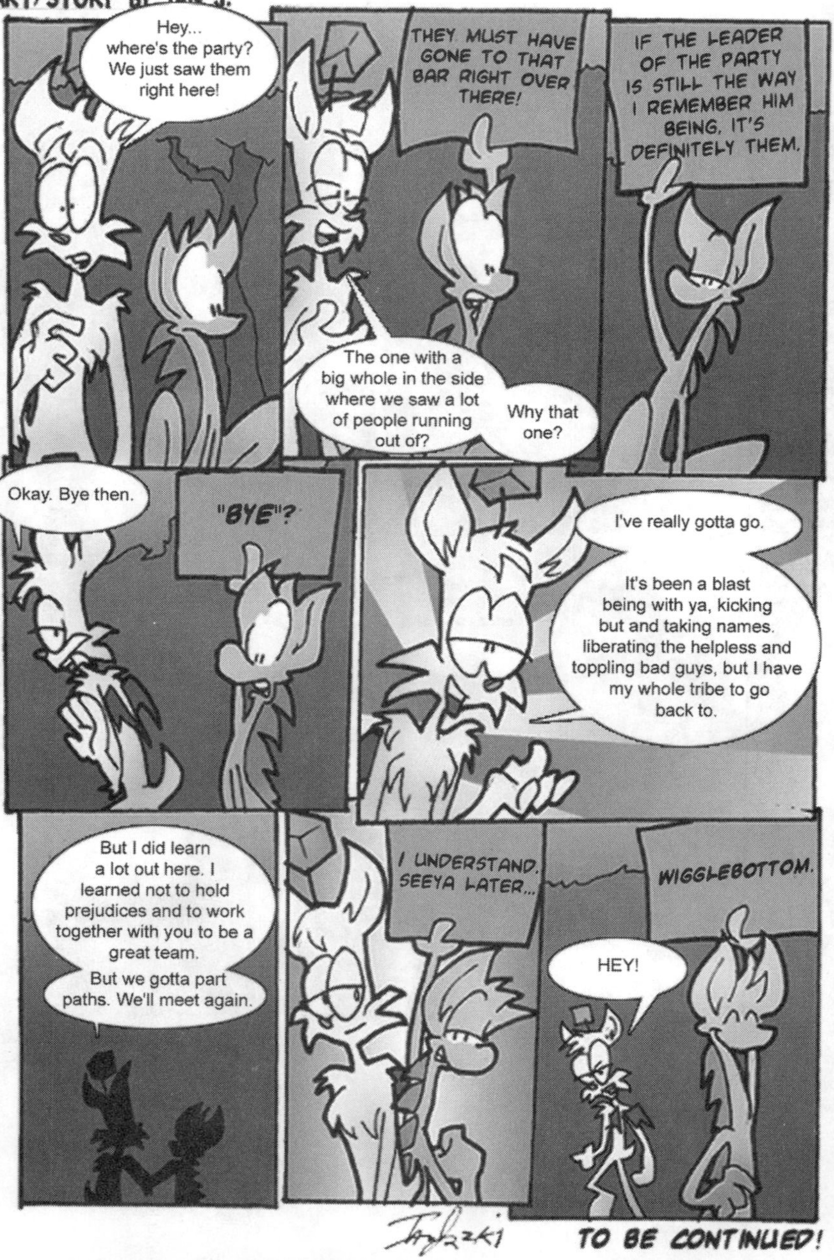
Hey... where's the party? We just saw them right here!
THEY MUST HAVE GONE TO THAT BAR RIGHT OVER THERE!
The one with a big whole in the side where we saw a lot of people running out of?
Why that one?
IF THE LEADER OF THE PARTY IS STILL THE WAY I REMEMBER HIM BEING, IT'S DEFINITELY THEM.
Okay. Bye then.
"BYE"?
I've really gotta go.
It's been a blast being with ya, kicking but and taking names. liberating the helpless and toppling bad guys, but I have my whole tribe to go back to.
But I did learn a lot out here. I learned not to hold prejudices and to work together with you to be a great team.
But we gotta part paths. We'll meet again.
I UNDERSTAND, SEEYA LATER...
WIGGLEBOTTOM.
HEY!

TO BE CONTINUED!

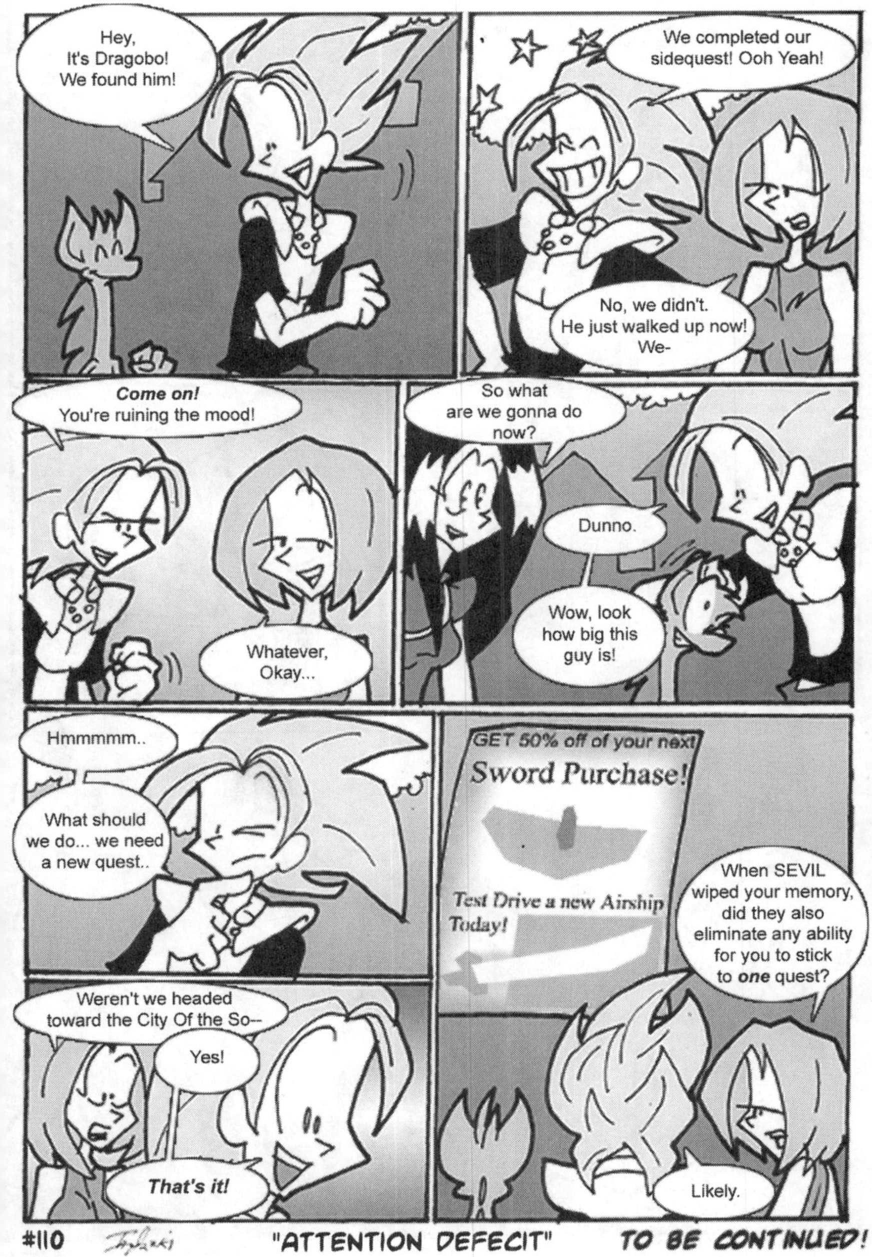

Hey, It's Dragobo! We found him!
We completed our sidequest! Ooh Yeah!
No, we didn't. He just walked up now! We-
Come on! You're ruining the mood!
Whatever, Okay...
So what are we gonna do now?
Dunno.
Wow, look how big this guy is!
Hmmmmm..
What should we do... we need a new quest..
Weren't we headed toward the City Of the So--
Yes!
That's it!
GET 50% off of your next
Sword Purchase!
Test Drive a new Airship Today!
When SEVIL wiped your memory, did they also eliminate any ability for you to stick to *one* quest?
Likely.

#110 "ATTENTION DEFECIT" TO BE CONTINUED!

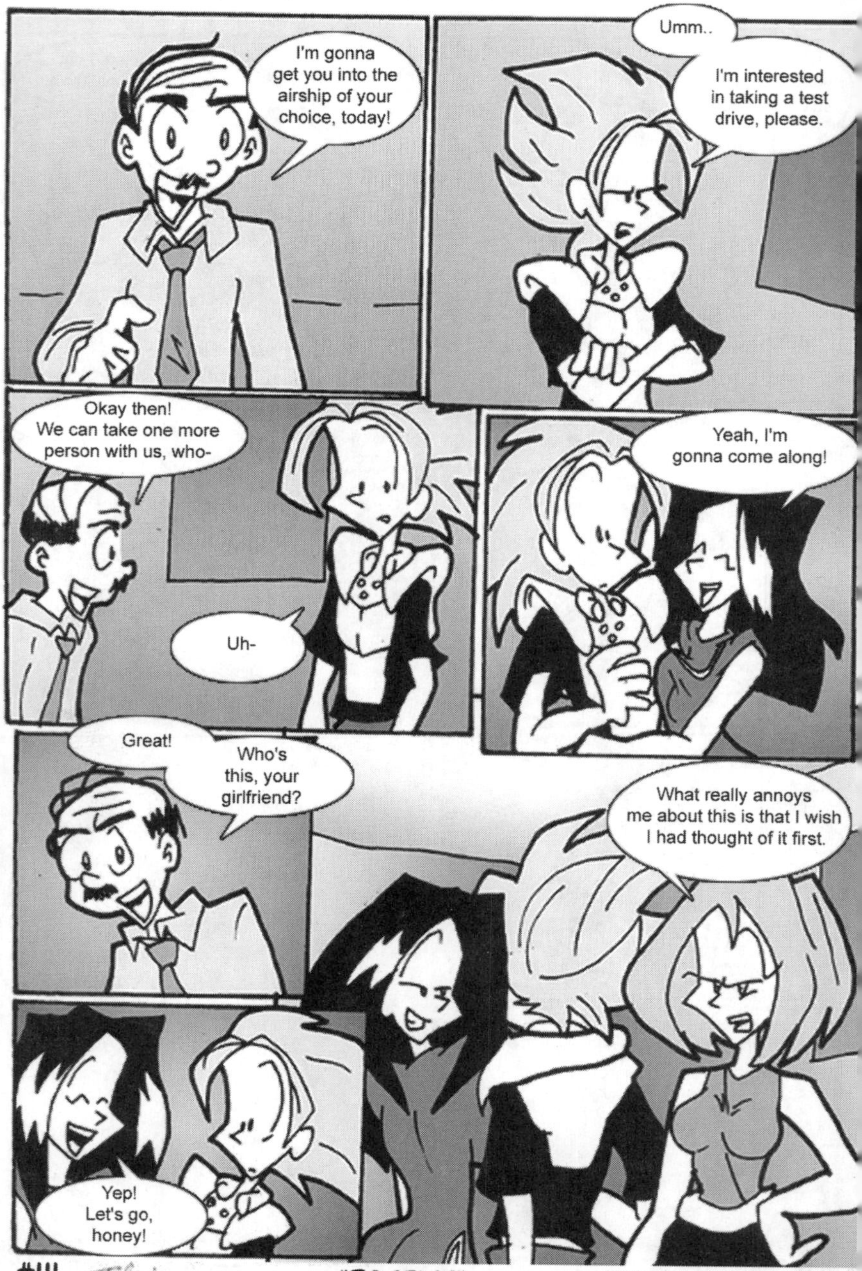
I'm gonna get you into the airship of your choice, today!
Umm..
I'm interested in taking a test drive, please.
Okay then! We can take one more person with us, who-
Uh-
Yeah, I'm gonna come along!
Great!
Who's this, your girlfriend?
Yep! Let's go, honey!
What really annoys me about this is that I wish I had thought of it first.

#111 "TACTICS" TO BE CONTINUED!

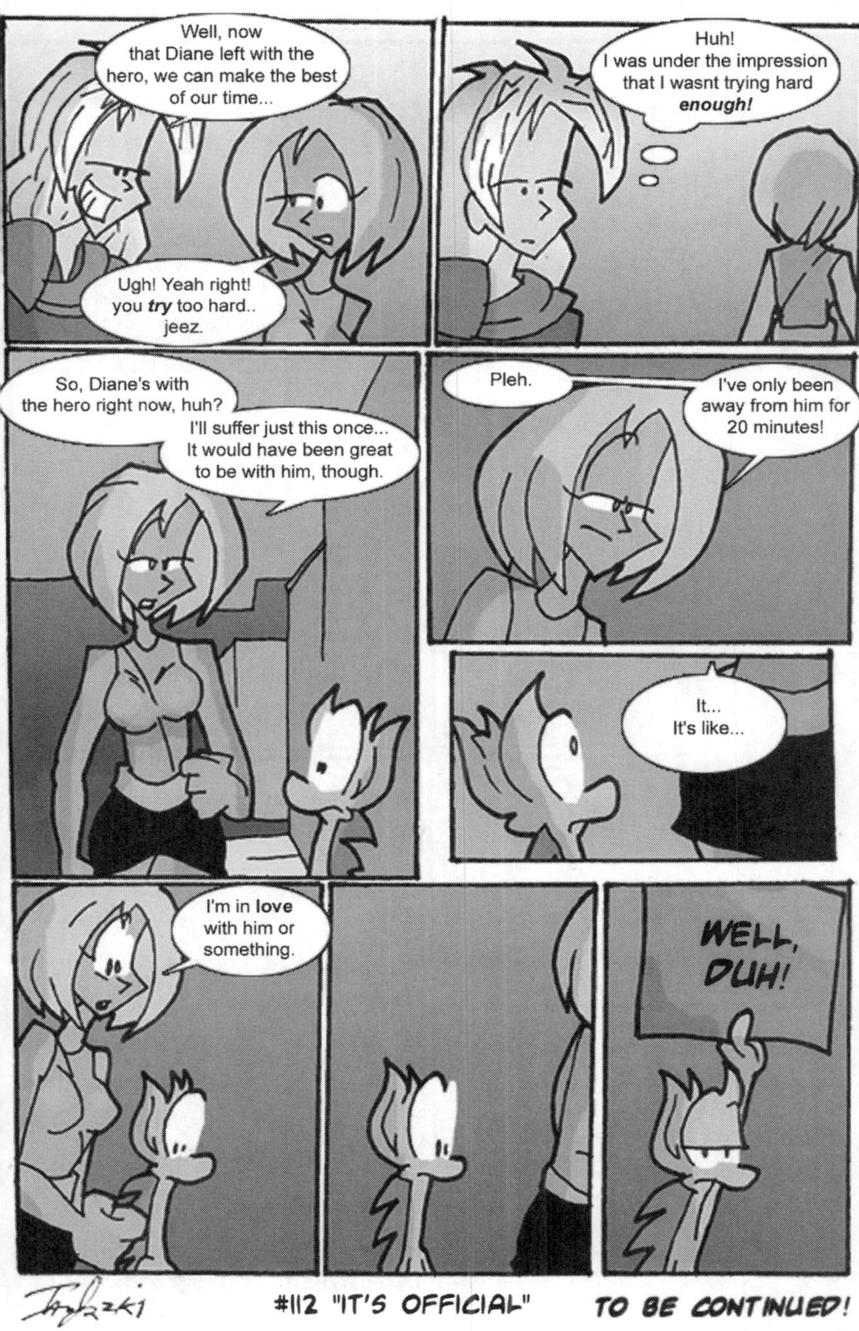
Well, now that Diane left with the hero, we can make the best of our time...
Ugh! Yeah right! you *try* too hard.. jeez.
Huh! I was under the impression that I wasnt trying hard ***enough!***
So, Diane's with the hero right now, huh?
I'll suffer just this once... It would have been great to be with him, though.
Pleh.
I've only been away from him for 20 minutes!
It... It's like...
I'm in **love** with him or something.
WELL, DUH!

Jay Lazki #112 "IT'S OFFICIAL" TO BE CONTINUED!

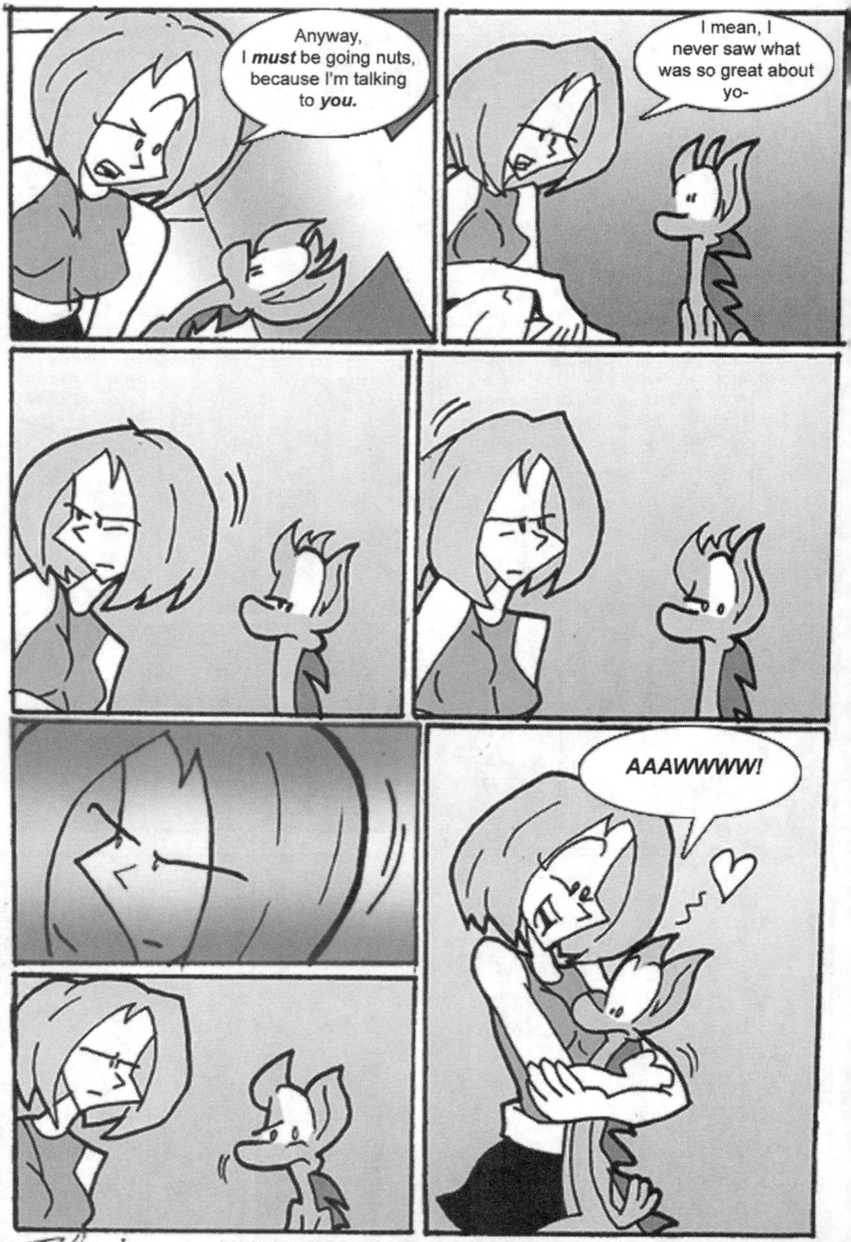
Anyway, I *must* be going nuts, because I'm talking to *you.*
I mean, I never saw what was so great about yo-
AAAWWWW!

Jay 2K1

#113 "LOVE THE DRAGOBO" TO BE CONTINUED!

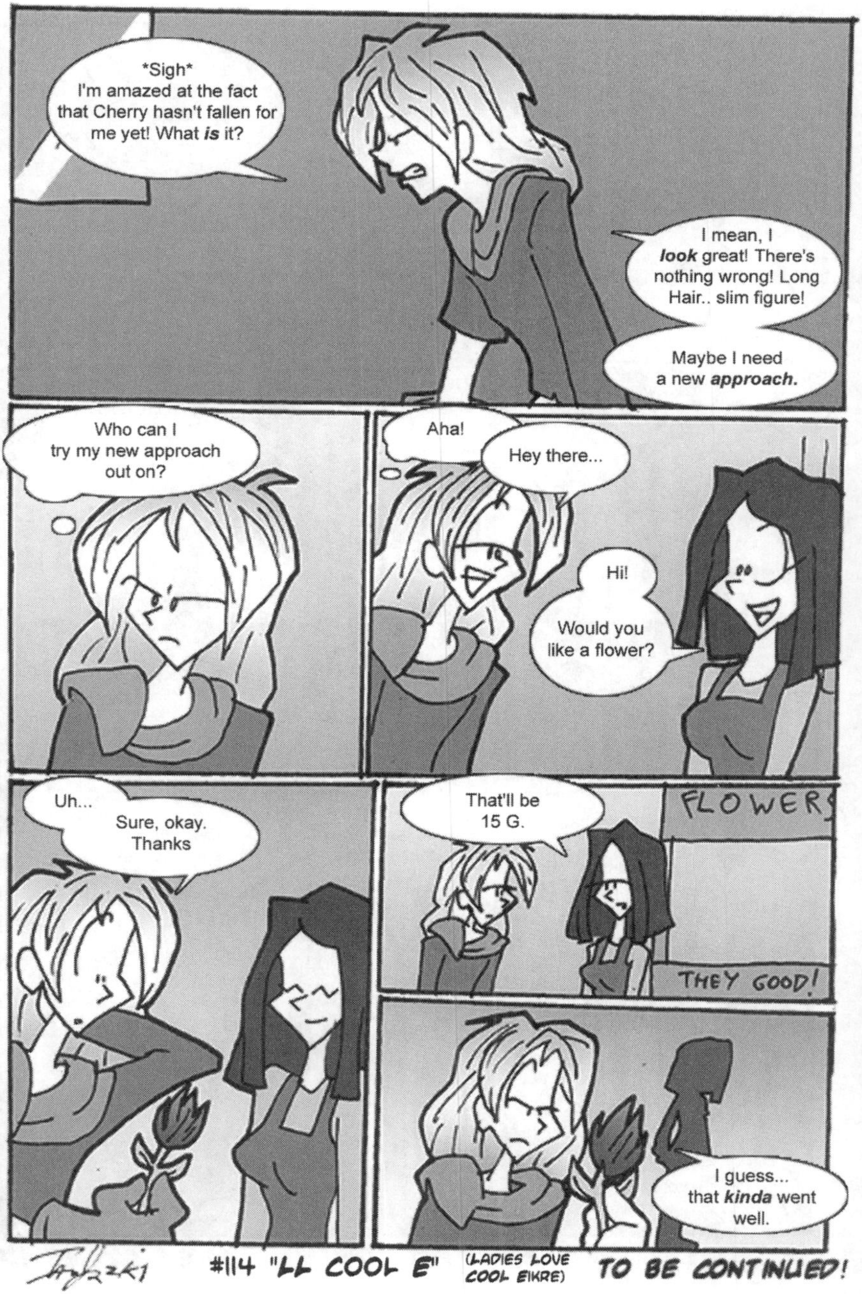
Sigh
I'm amazed at the fact that Cherry hasn't fallen for me yet! What *is* it?
I mean, I *look* great! There's nothing wrong! Long Hair.. slim figure!
Maybe I need a new ***approach.***
Who can I try my new approach out on?
Aha!
Hey there...
Hi!
Would you like a flower?
Uh...
Sure, okay. Thanks
That'll be 15 G.
FLOWERS
THEY GOOD!
I guess... that *kinda* went well.
#114 "LL COOL E" (LADIES LOVE COOL EIKRE)
TO BE CONTINUED!

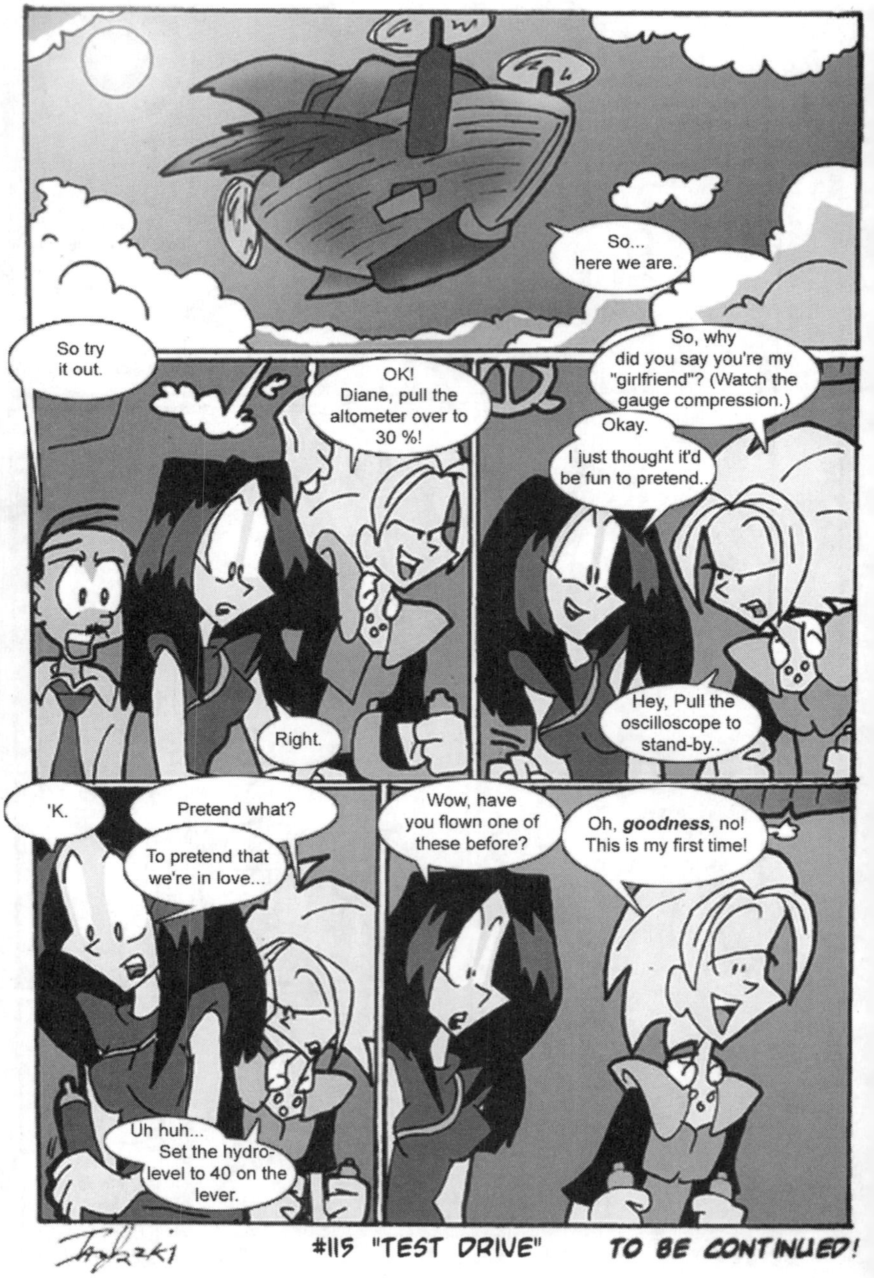

So...
here we are.
So try it out.
OK! Diane, pull the altometer over to 30 %!
Right.
So, why did you say you're my "girlfriend"? (Watch the gauge compression.)
Okay. I just thought it'd be fun to pretend..
Hey, Pull the oscilloscope to stand-by..
'K.
Pretend what?
To pretend that we're in love...
Uh huh... Set the hydro-level to 40 on the lever.
Wow, have you flown one of these before?
Oh, ***goodness,*** no! This is my first time!

#115 "TEST DRIVE" TO BE CONTINUED!

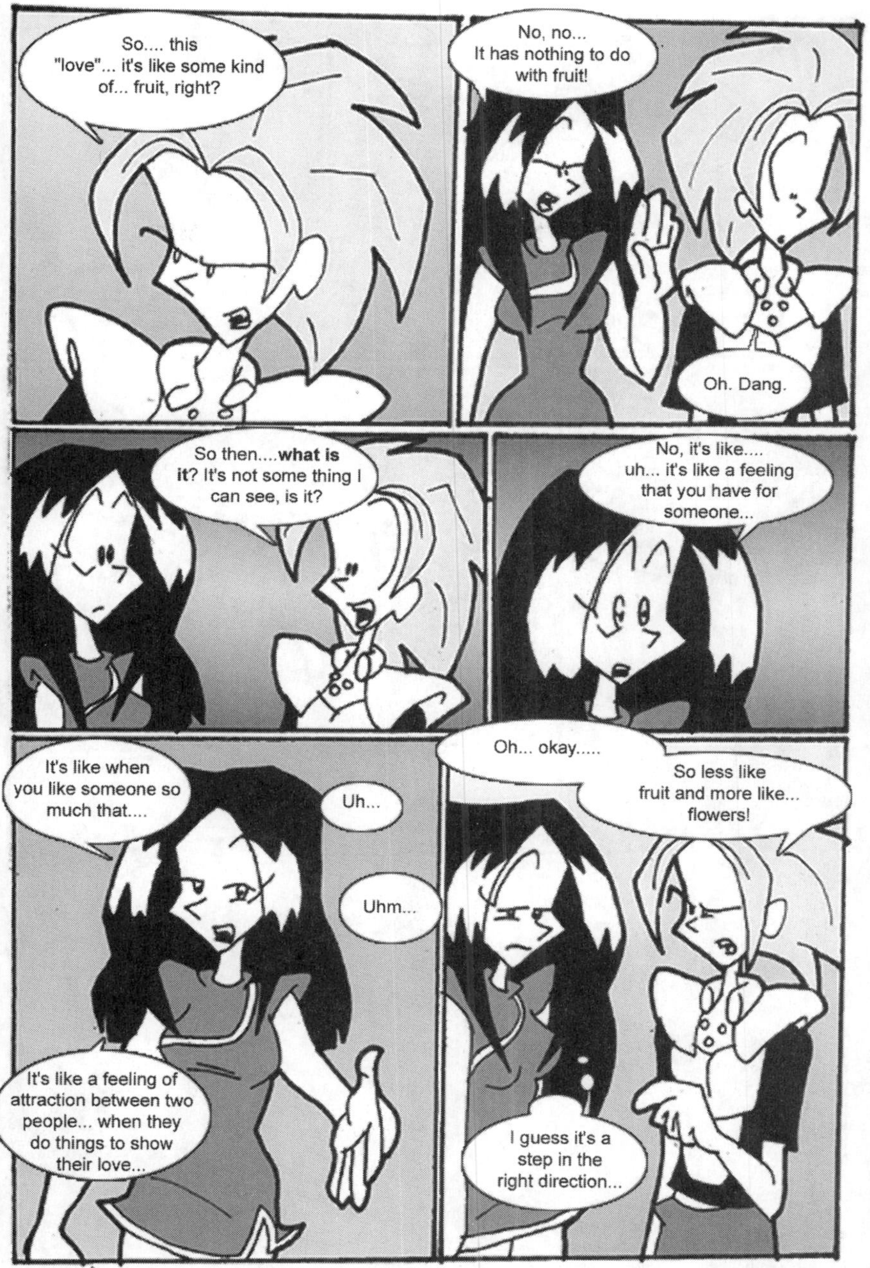

So.... this "love"... it's like some kind of... fruit, right?
No, no... It has nothing to do with fruit!
Oh. Dang.
So then....**what is it**? It's not some thing I can see, is it?
No, it's like.... uh... it's like a feeling that you have for someone...
It's like when you like someone so much that....
Uh...
Uhm...
It's like a feeling of attraction between two people... when they do things to show their love...
Oh... okay.....
So less like fruit and more like... flowers!
I guess it's a step in the right direction...

Jaydazki

#116 "DEFINITION"

TO BE CONTINUED!

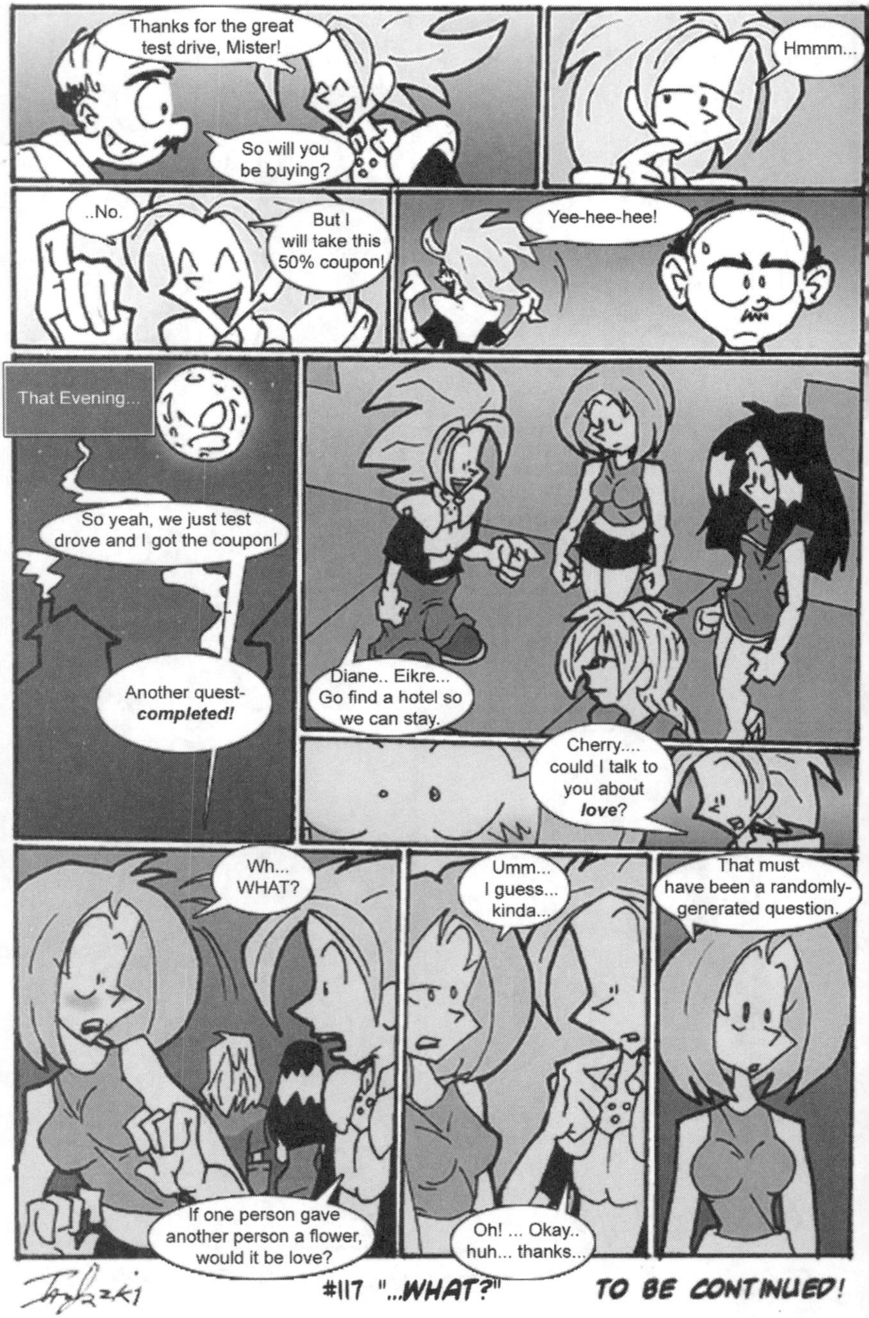
Thanks for the great test drive, Mister!
So will you be buying?
Hmmm...
..No.
But I will take this 50% coupon!
Yee-hee-hee!
That Evening...
So yeah, we just test drove and I got the coupon!
Another quest- *completed!*
Diane.. Eikre... Go find a hotel so we can stay.
Cherry.... could I talk to you about *love*?
Wh... WHAT?
If one person gave another person a flower, would it be love?
Umm... I guess... kinda...
Oh! ... Okay.. huh... thanks...
That must have been a randomly-generated question.
Inyozaki
#117 "...WHAT?"
TO BE CONTINUED!

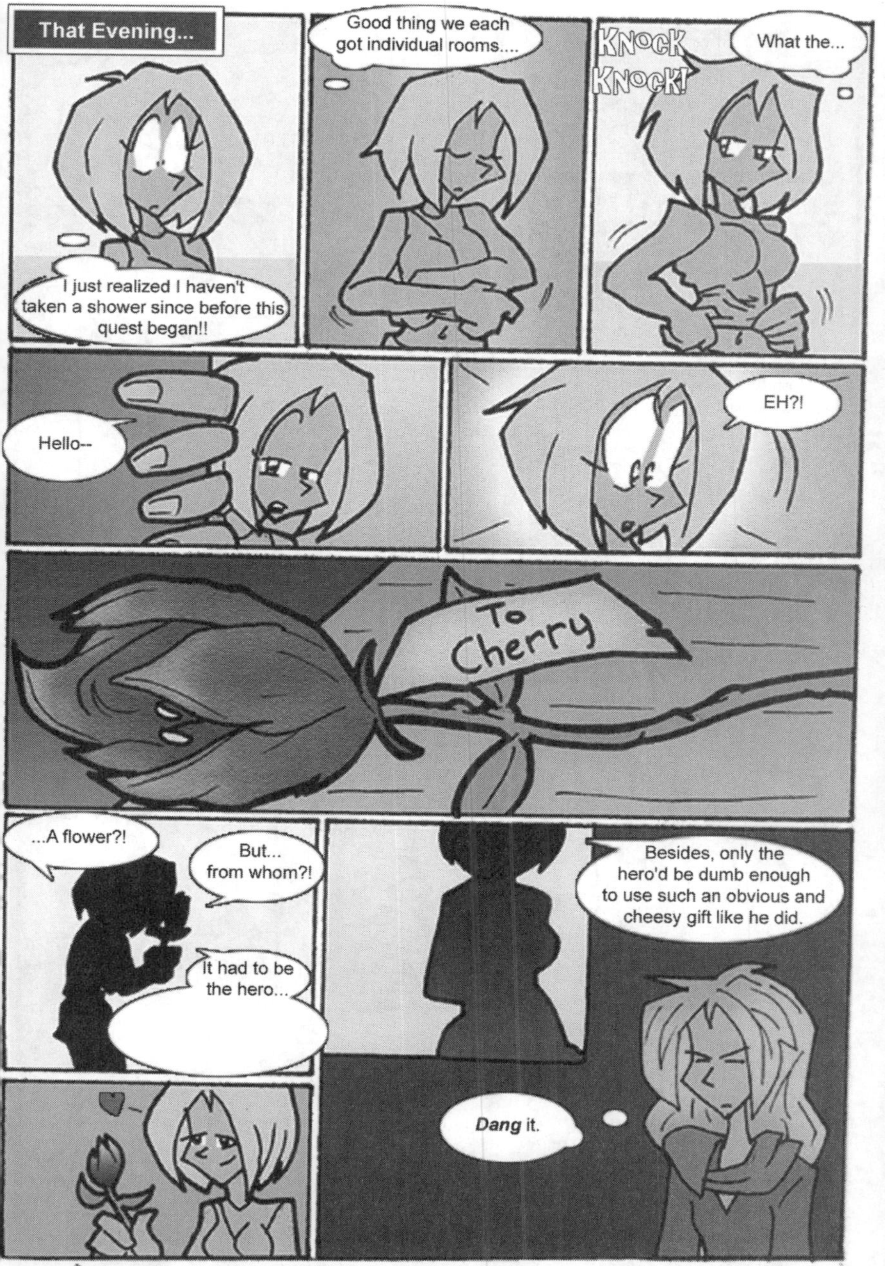
That Evening...
I just realized I haven't taken a shower since before this quest began!!
Good thing we each got individual rooms....
KNOCK KNOCK!
What the...
Hello--
EH?!
To Cherry
...A flower?!
But... from whom?!
It had to be the hero...
Besides, only the hero'd be dumb enough to use such an obvious and cheesy gift like he did.
Dang it.

#118 "DELIVERY"

TO BE CONTINUED!

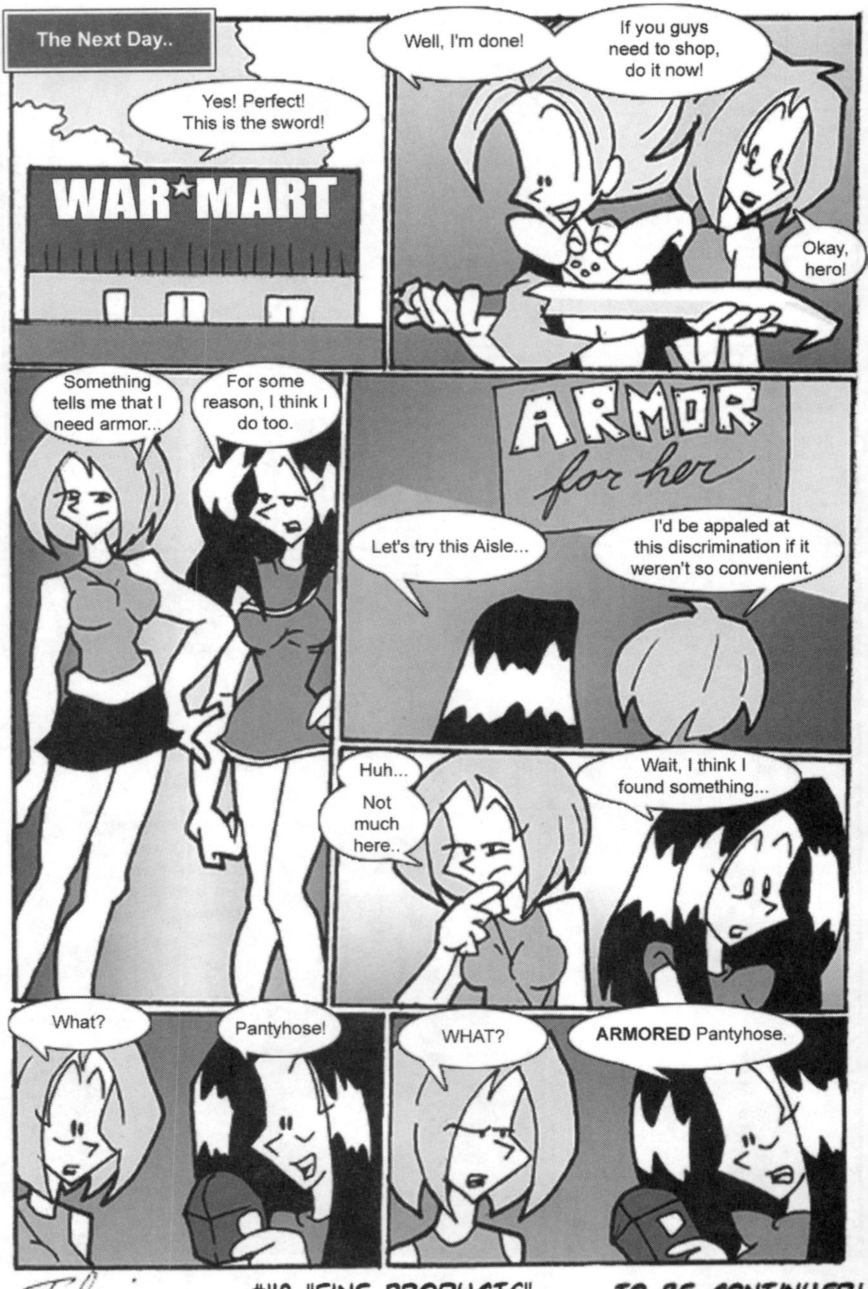
The Next Day..
Yes! Perfect! This is the sword!
WAR★MART
Well, I'm done!
If you guys need to shop, do it now!
Okay, hero!
Something tells me that I need armor...
For some reason, I think I do too.
ARMOR for her
Let's try this Aisle...
I'd be appaled at this discrimination if it weren't so convenient.
Huh...
Not much here..
Wait, I think I found something...
What?
Pantyhose!
WHAT?
ARMORED Pantyhose.

#119 "FINE PRODUCTS"

TO BE CONTINUED!

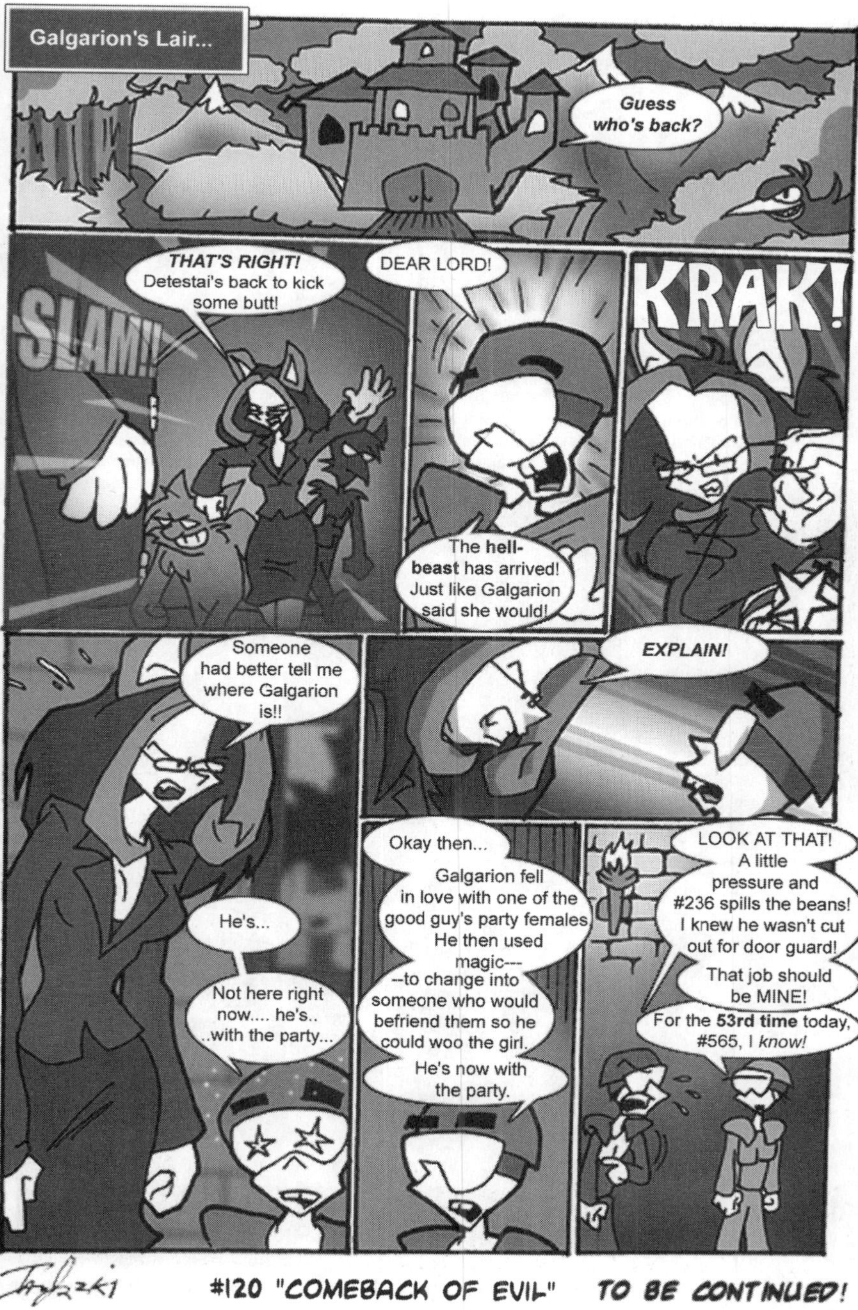
Galgarion's Lair...
Guess who's back?
THAT'S RIGHT! Detestai's back to kick some butt!
SLAM!!
DEAR LORD!
The hell-beast has arrived! Just like Galgarion said she would!
KRAK!
Someone had better tell me where Galgarion is!!
EXPLAIN!
He's...
Not here right now.... he's.. ..with the party...
Okay then...
Galgarion fell in love with one of the good guy's party females He then used magic---
--to change into someone who would befriend them so he could woo the girl.
He's now with the party.
LOOK AT THAT! A little pressure and #236 spills the beans! I knew he wasn't cut out for door guard!
That job should be MINE!
For the 53rd time today, #565, I know!
#120 "COMEBACK OF EVIL"
TO BE CONTINUED!

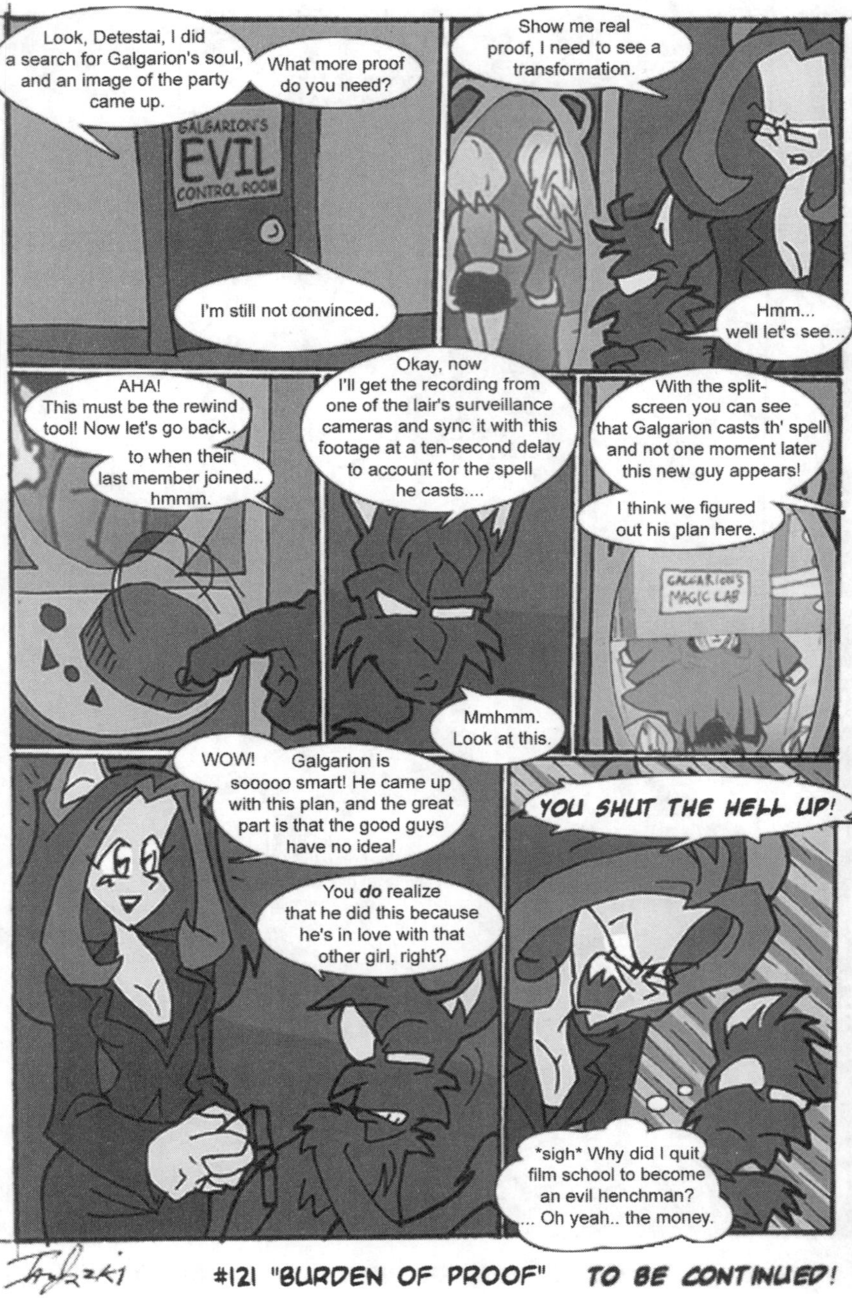
Look, Detestai, I did a search for Galgarion's soul, and an image of the party came up.
What more proof do you need?
GALGARION'S EVIL CONTROL ROOM
I'm still not convinced.
Show me real proof, I need to see a transformation.
Hmm... well let's see...
AHA! This must be the rewind tool! Now let's go back..
to when their last member joined.. hmmm.
Okay, now I'll get the recording from one of the lair's surveillance cameras and sync it with this footage at a ten-second delay to account for the spell he casts....
Mmhmm. Look at this.
With the split-screen you can see that Galgarion casts th' spell and not one moment later this new guy appears!
I think we figured out his plan here.
GALGARION'S MAGIC LAB
WOW! Galgarion is sooooo smart! He came up with this plan, and the great part is that the good guys have no idea!
You *do* realize that he did this because he's in love with that other girl, right?
YOU SHUT THE HELL UP!
sigh Why did I quit film school to become an evil henchman? ... Oh yeah.. the money.

#121 "BURDEN OF PROOF" TO BE CONTINUED!

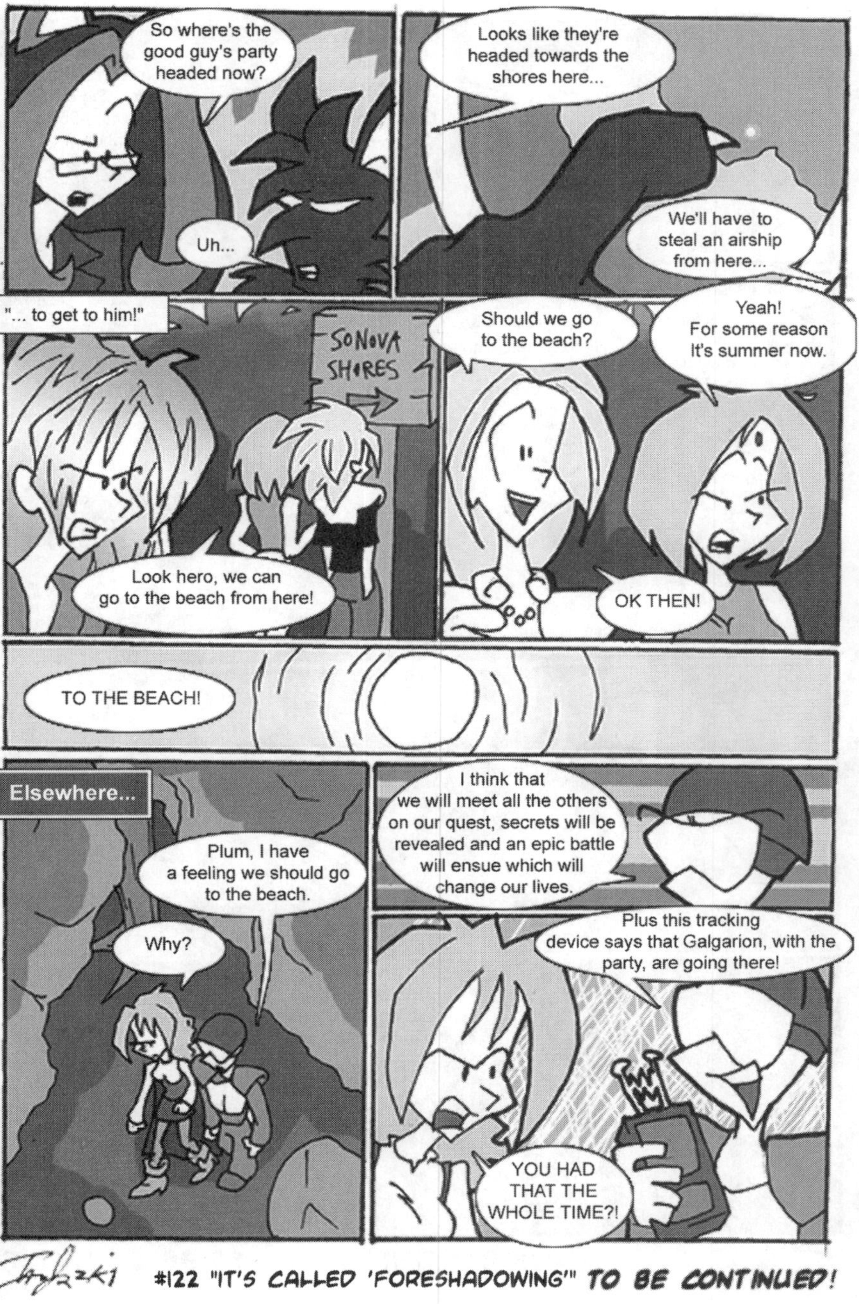
So where's the good guy's party headed now?
Uh...
Looks like they're headed towards the shores here...
We'll have to steal an airship from here...
"... to get to him!"
SONOVA SHORES
Look hero, we can go to the beach from here!
Should we go to the beach?
Yeah! For some reason It's summer now.
OK THEN!
TO THE BEACH!
Elsewhere...
Plum, I have a feeling we should go to the beach.
Why?
I think that we will meet all the others on our quest, secrets will be revealed and an epic battle will ensue which will change our lives.
Plus this tracking device says that Galgarion, with the party, are going there!
YOU HAD THAT THE WHOLE TIME?!

#122 "IT'S CALLED 'FORESHADOWING'" TO BE CONTINUED!

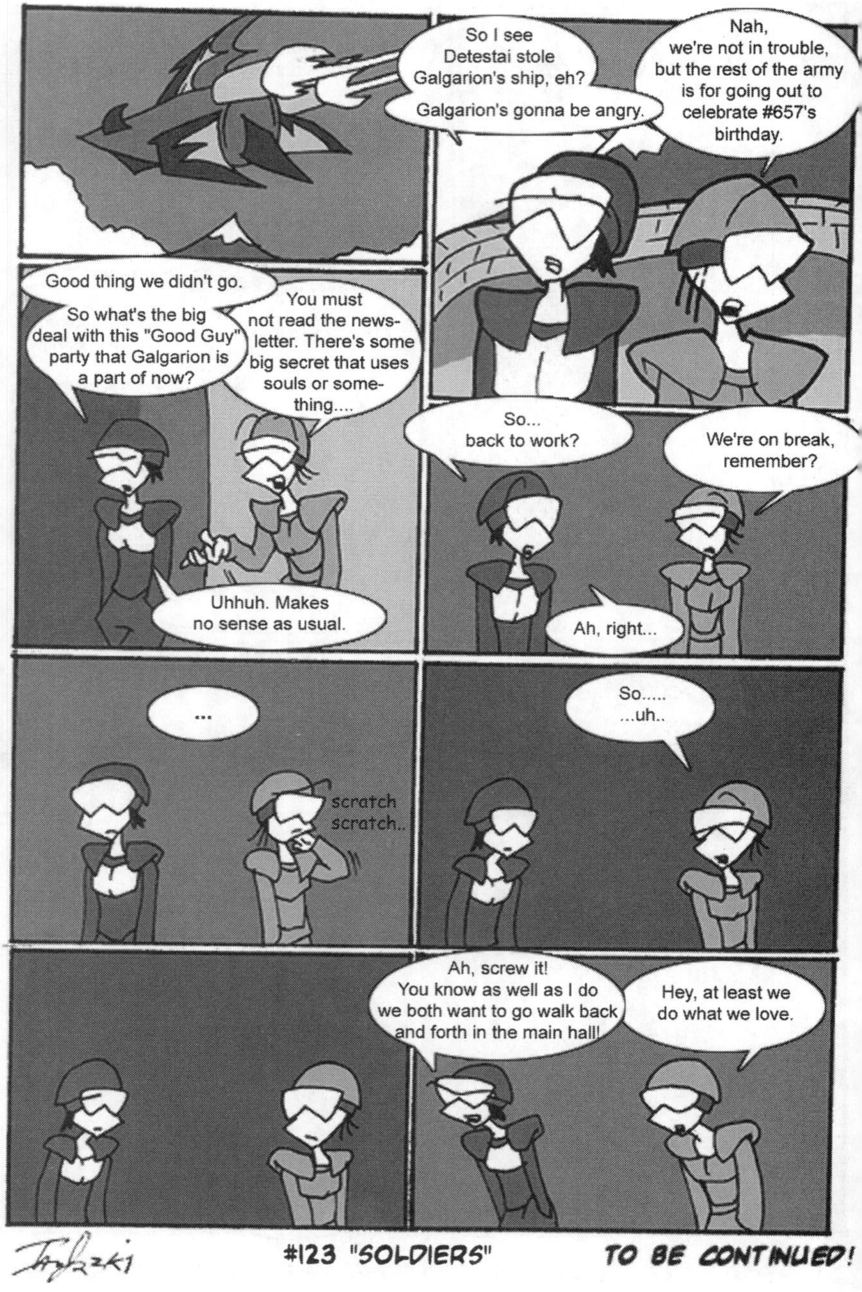
So I see Detestai stole Galgarion's ship, eh?
Galgarion's gonna be angry.
Nah, we're not in trouble, but the rest of the army is for going out to celebrate #657's birthday.
Good thing we didn't go.
So what's the big deal with this "Good Guy" party that Galgarion is a part of now?
You must not read the news-letter. There's some big secret that uses souls or some-thing....
Uhhuh. Makes no sense as usual.
So... back to work?
We're on break, remember?
Ah, right...
...
scratch scratch..
So..... ...uh..
Ah, screw it! You know as well as I do we both want to go walk back and forth in the main hall!
Hey, at least we do what we love.
#123 "SOLDIERS"
TO BE CONTINUED!

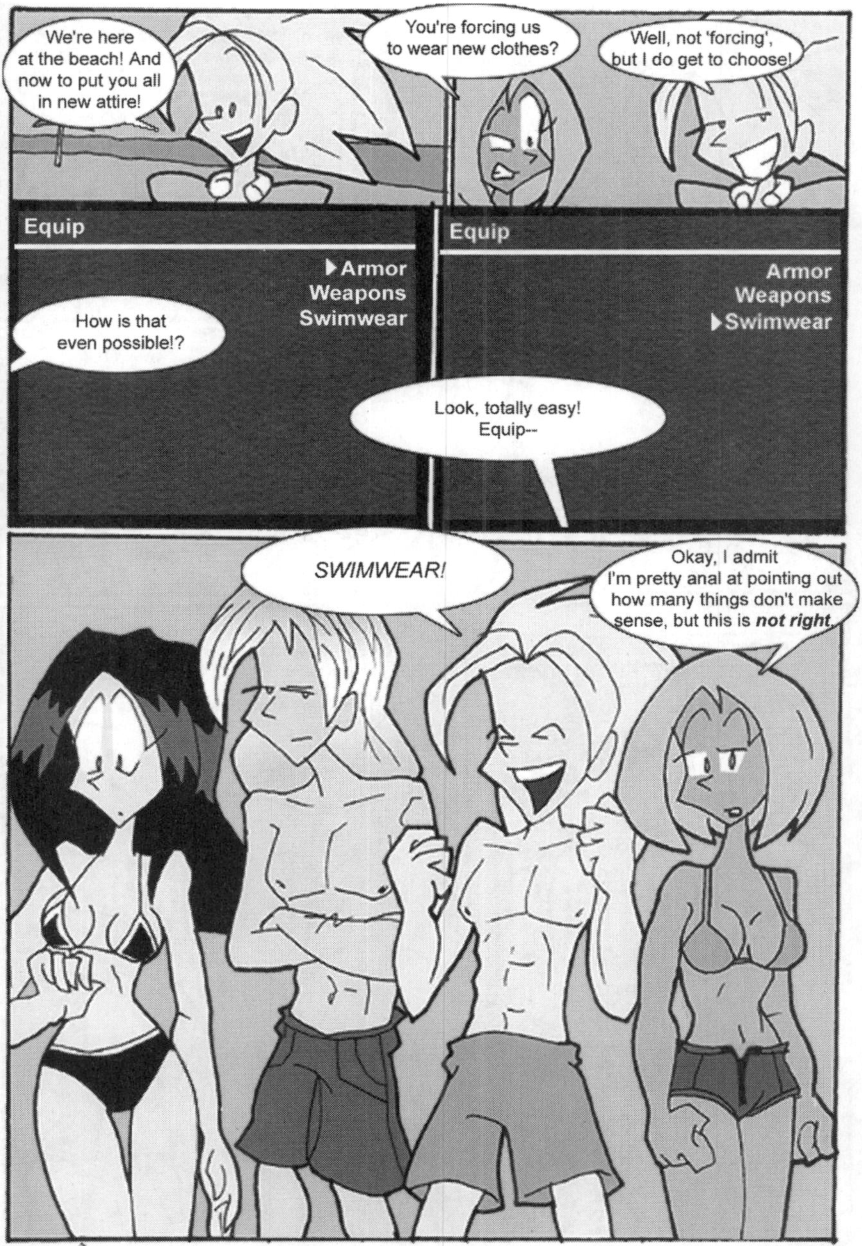
We're here at the beach! And now to put you all in new attire!
You're forcing us to wear new clothes?
Well, not 'forcing', but I do get to choose!
Equip
Armor
Weapons
Swimwear
How is that even possible!?
Equip
Armor
Weapons
Swimwear
Look, totally easy! Equip--
SWIMWEAR!
Okay, I admit I'm pretty anal at pointing out how many things don't make sense, but this is *not right*.

Inyozaki #124 "EQUIP SWIMWEAR" TO BE CONTINUED!

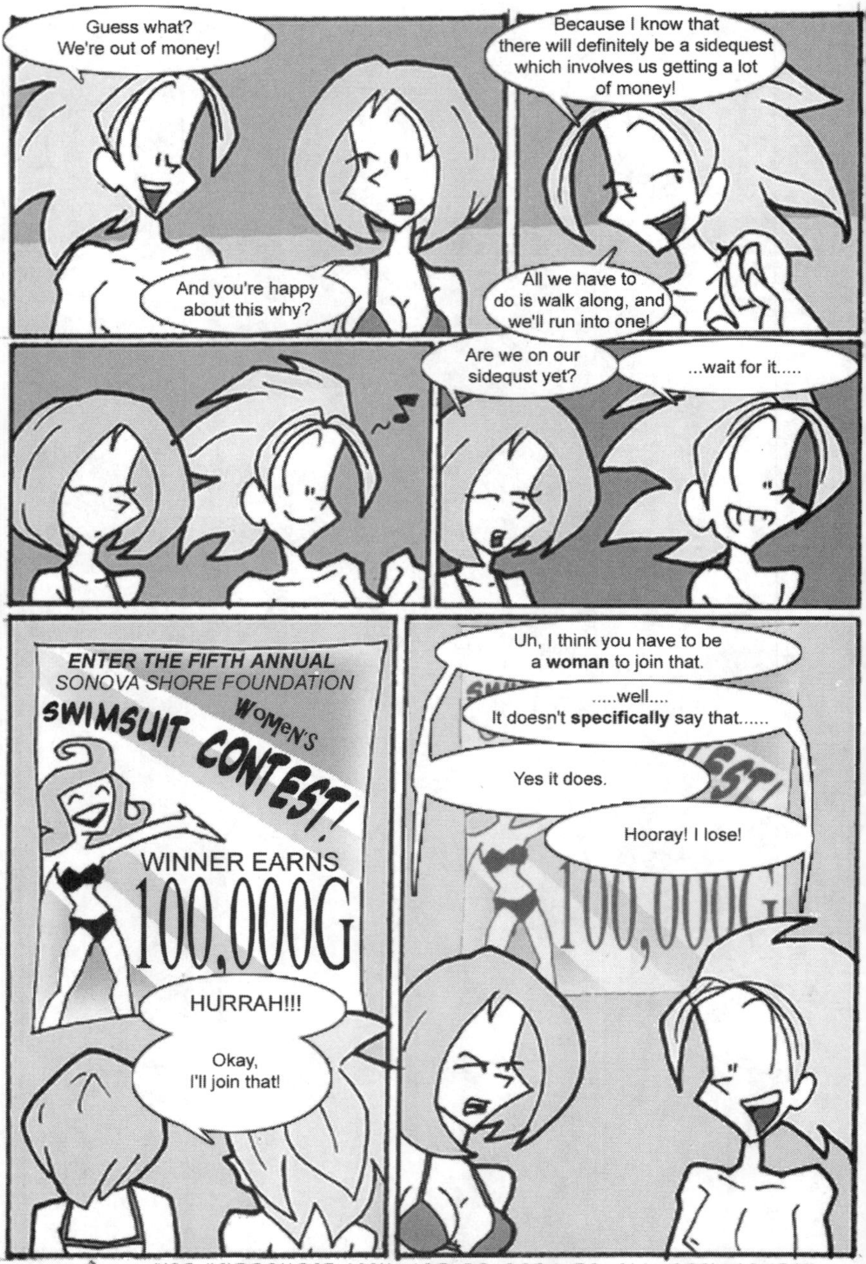

Guess what? We're out of money!
And you're happy about this why?
Because I know that there will definitely be a sidequest which involves us getting a lot of money!
All we have to do is walk along, and we'll run into one!
Are we on our sidequst yet?
...wait for it.....
ENTER THE FIFTH ANNUAL
SONOVA SHORE FOUNDATION
WOMEN'S
SWIMSUIT CONTEST!
WINNER EARNS
100,000G
HURRAH!!!
Okay, I'll join that!
Uh, I think you have to be a **woman** to join that.
.....well.... It doesn't **specifically** say that......
Yes it does.
Hooray! I lose!

#125 "SIDEQUEST MAY NOT BE OPEN TO ALL APPLICANTS"

TO BE CONTINUED!

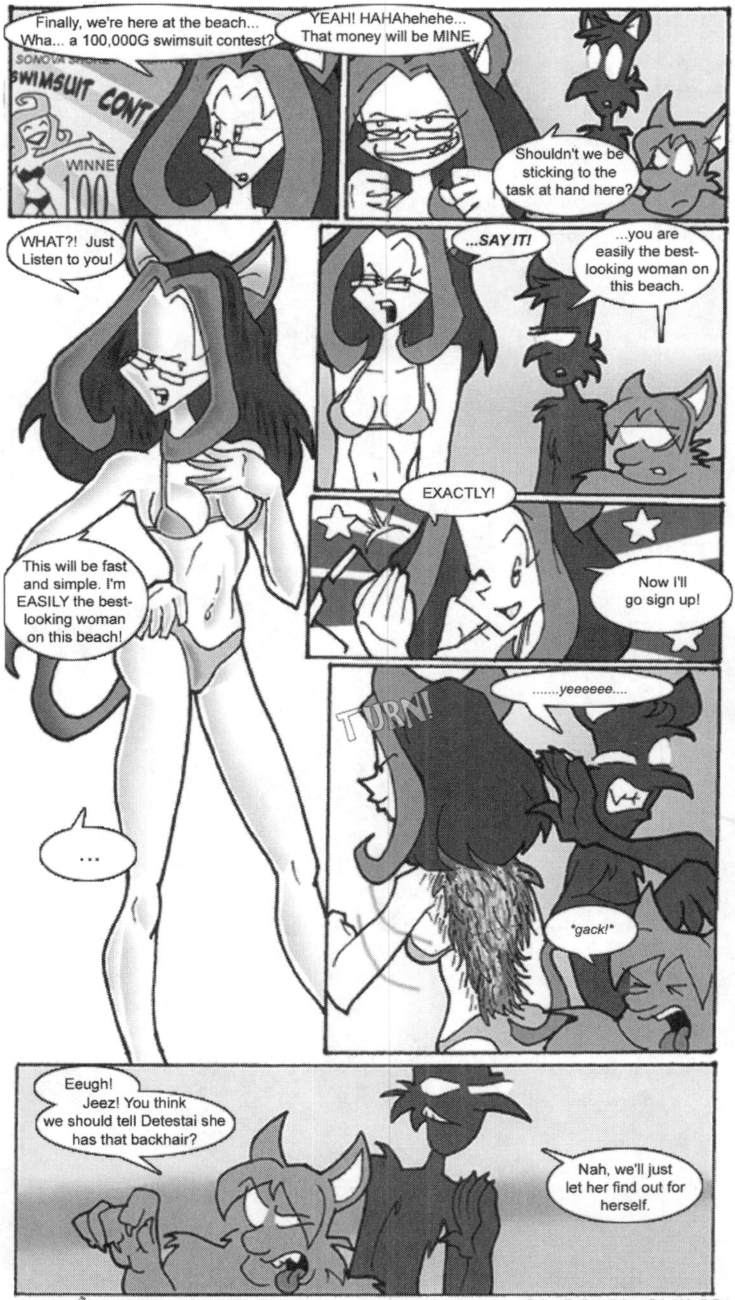

Finally, we're here at the beach... Wha... a 100,000G swimsuit contest?
SWIMSUIT CONT
WINNER
100
YEAH! HAHAhehehe... That money will be MINE.
Shouldn't we be sticking to the task at hand here?
WHAT?! Just Listen to you!
This will be fast and simple. I'm EASILY the best-looking woman on this beach!
...
...SAY IT!
...you are easily the best-looking woman on this beach.
EXACTLY!
Now I'll go sign up!
TURN!
.......yeeeeee....
gack!
Eeugh! Jeez! You think we should tell Detestai she has that backhair?
Nah, we'll just let her find out for herself.

#126 "WHY CAT-HUMANS ARE GROSS" TO BE CONTINUED!

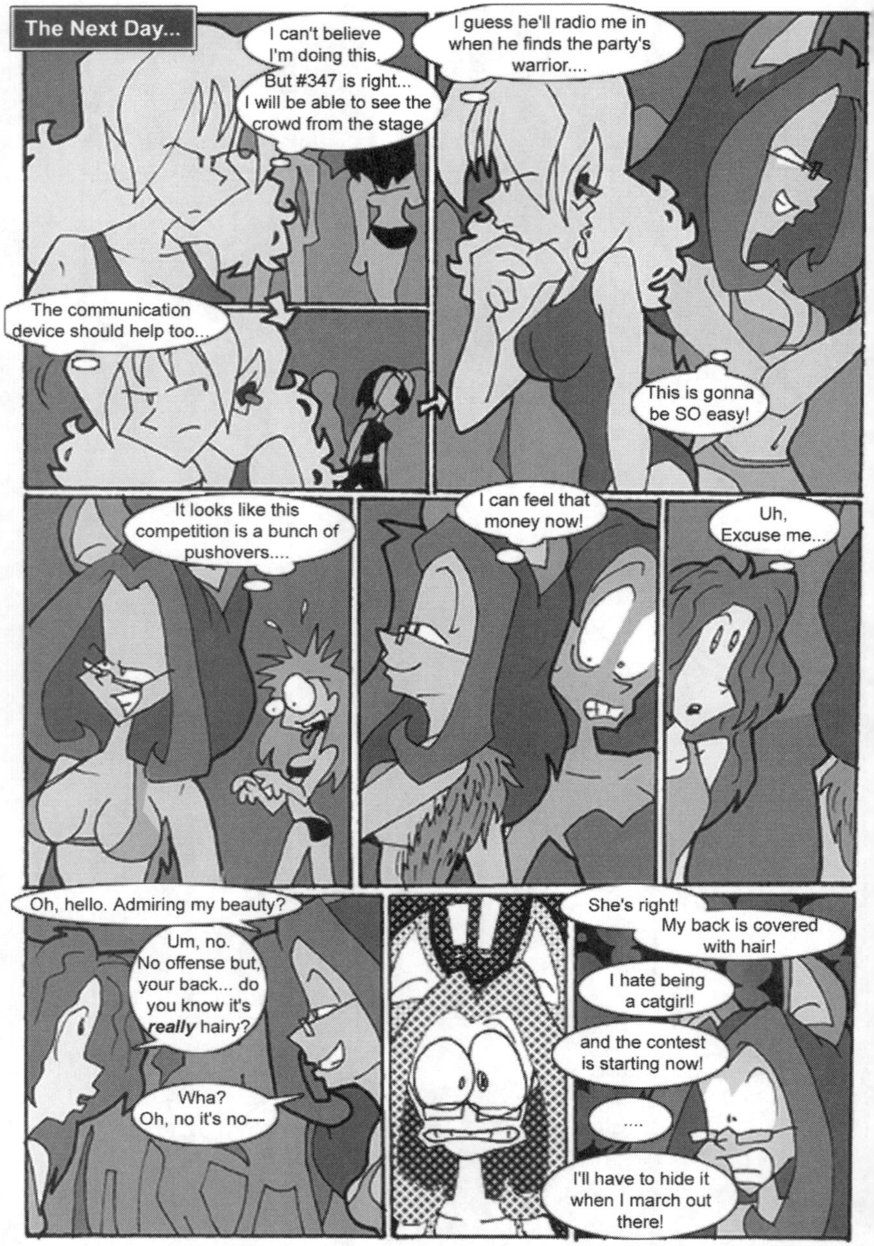
The Next Day...
I can't believe I'm doing this.
But #347 is right... I will be able to see the crowd from the stage
The communication device should help too...
I guess he'll radio me in when he finds the party's warrior....
This is gonna be SO easy!
It looks like this competition is a bunch of pushovers....
I can feel that money now!
Uh, Excuse me...
Oh, hello. Admiring my beauty?
Um, no. No offense but, your back... do you know it's *really* hairy?
Wha? Oh, no it's no---
She's right!
My back is covered with hair!
I hate being a catgirl!
and the contest is starting now!
....
I'll have to hide it when I march out there!

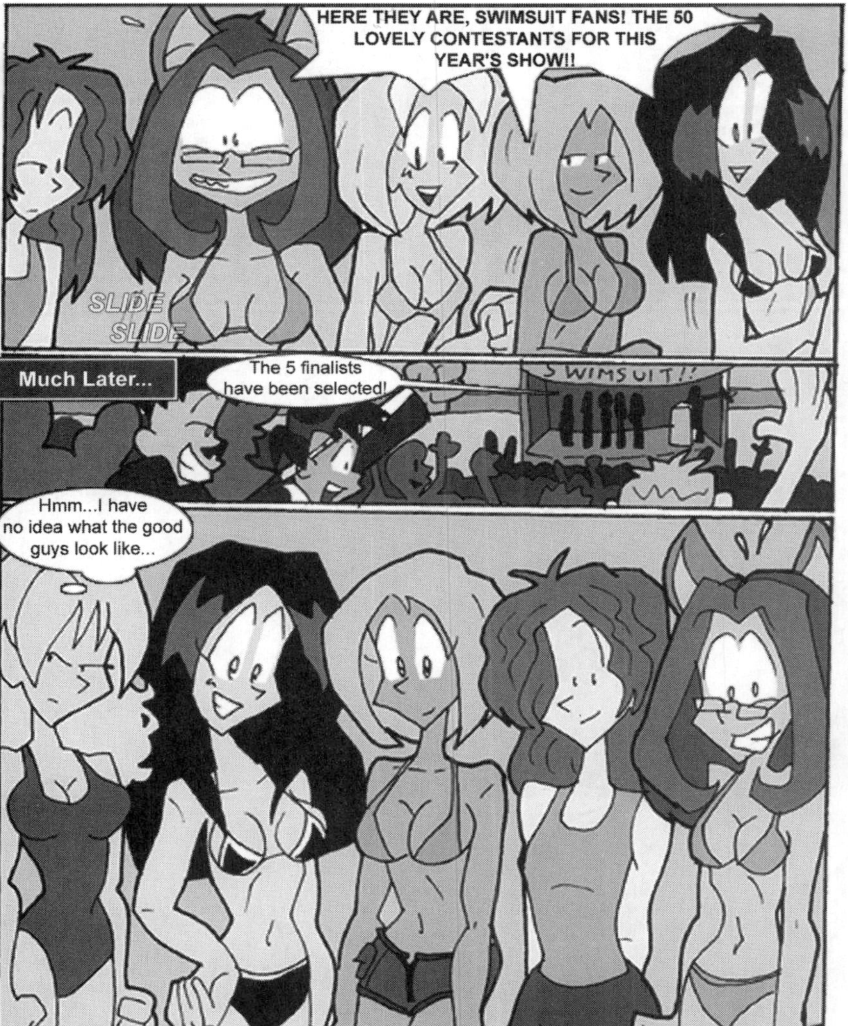
HERE THEY ARE, SWIMSUIT FANS! THE 50 LOVELY CONTESTANTS FOR THIS YEAR'S SHOW!!
SLIDE
SLIDE
Much Later...
The 5 finalists have been selected!
SWIMSUIT!!
Hmm...I have no idea what the good guys look like...
How did I make it this far?
Someone please shoot me!

WOW! ALL 4 CHARACTERS MADE IT TO THE FINAL ROUND! HOW CONVENIENT.

#127 "FANSERVICE" TO BE CONTINUED!

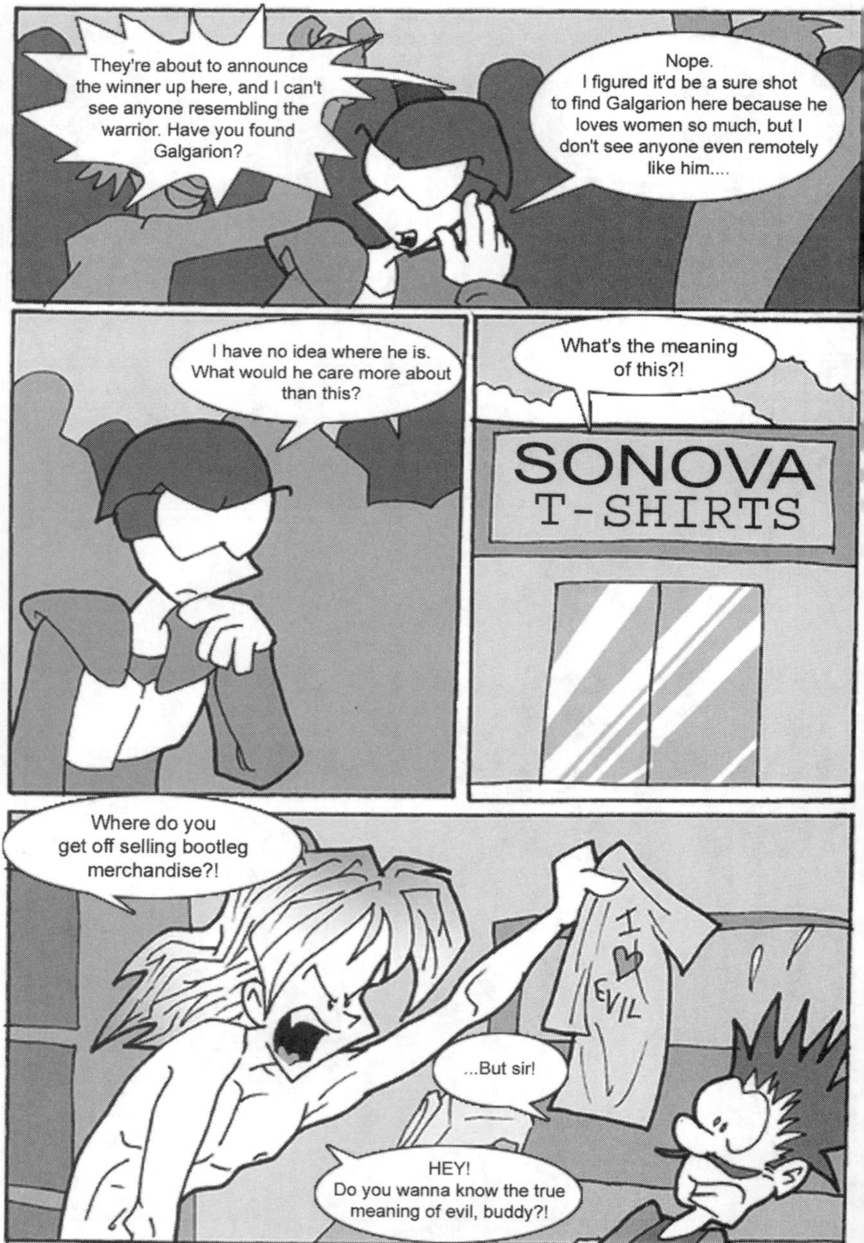
They're about to announce the winner up here, and I can't see anyone resembling the warrior. Have you found Galgarion?
Nope. I figured it'd be a sure shot to find Galgarion here because he loves women so much, but I don't see anyone even remotely like him....
I have no idea where he is. What would he care more about than this?
What's the meaning of this?!
SONOVA T-SHIRTS
Where do you get off selling bootleg merchandise?!
I ♥ EVIL
...But sir!
HEY! Do you wanna know the true meaning of evil, buddy?!

Inazaki #128 "THERE'S A LESSON IN THIS" TO BE CONTINUED!

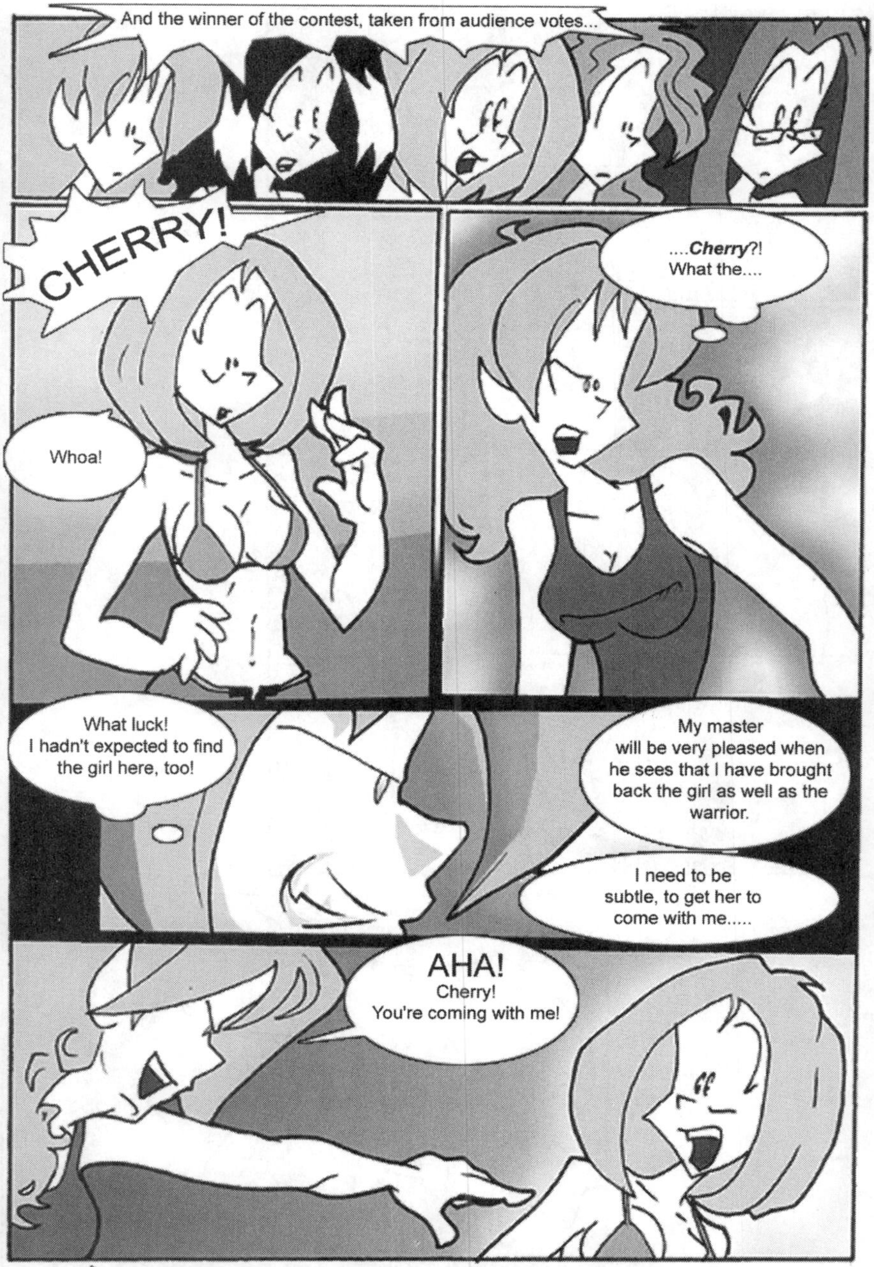
And the winner of the contest, taken from audience votes...
CHERRY!
Whoa!
....Cherry?!
What the....
What luck!
I hadn't expected to find the girl here, too!
My master will be very pleased when he sees that I have brought back the girl as well as the warrior.
I need to be subtle, to get her to come with me.....
AHA!
Cherry!
You're coming with me!

#129 "ABOUT AS SUBTLE AS AN 18-WHEELER"

TO BE CONTINUED!

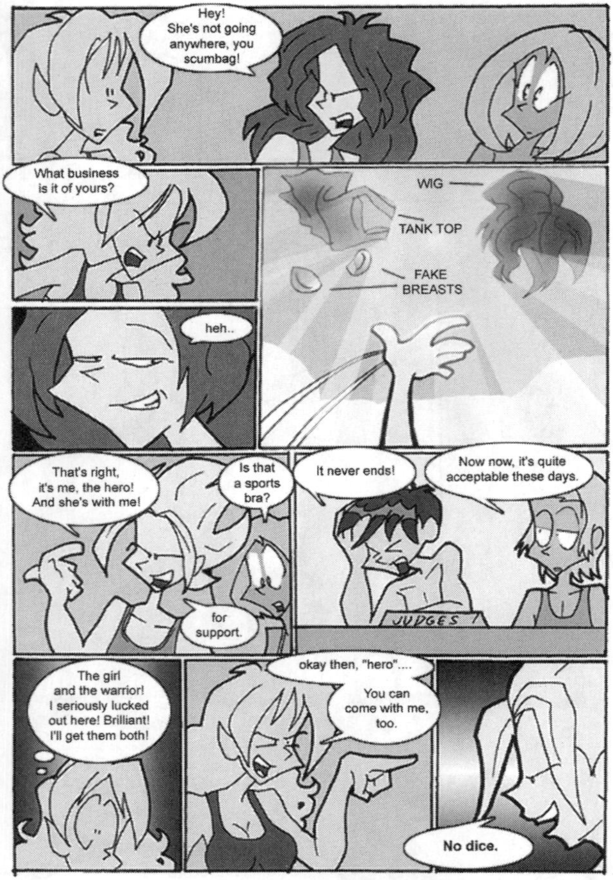

Hey! She's not going anywhere, you scumbag!
What business is it of yours?
WIG
TANK TOP
FAKE BREASTS
heh..
That's right, it's me, the hero! And she's with me!
Is that a sports bra?
for support.
It never ends!
Now now, it's quite acceptable these days.
JUDGES
The girl and the warrior! I seriously lucked out here! Brilliant! I'll get them both!
okay then, "hero"....
You can come with me, too.
No dice.

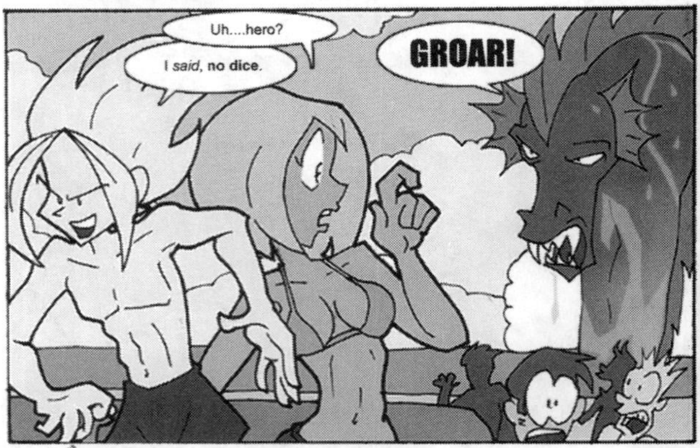

Uh....hero?
I *said*, no dice.
GROAR!

#130 "STILL GLAD YOU VOTED FOR 'HER'?"

EDITORIAL ASSISTANCE PROVIDED BY JOSH MIRMAN.

TO BE CONTINUED!

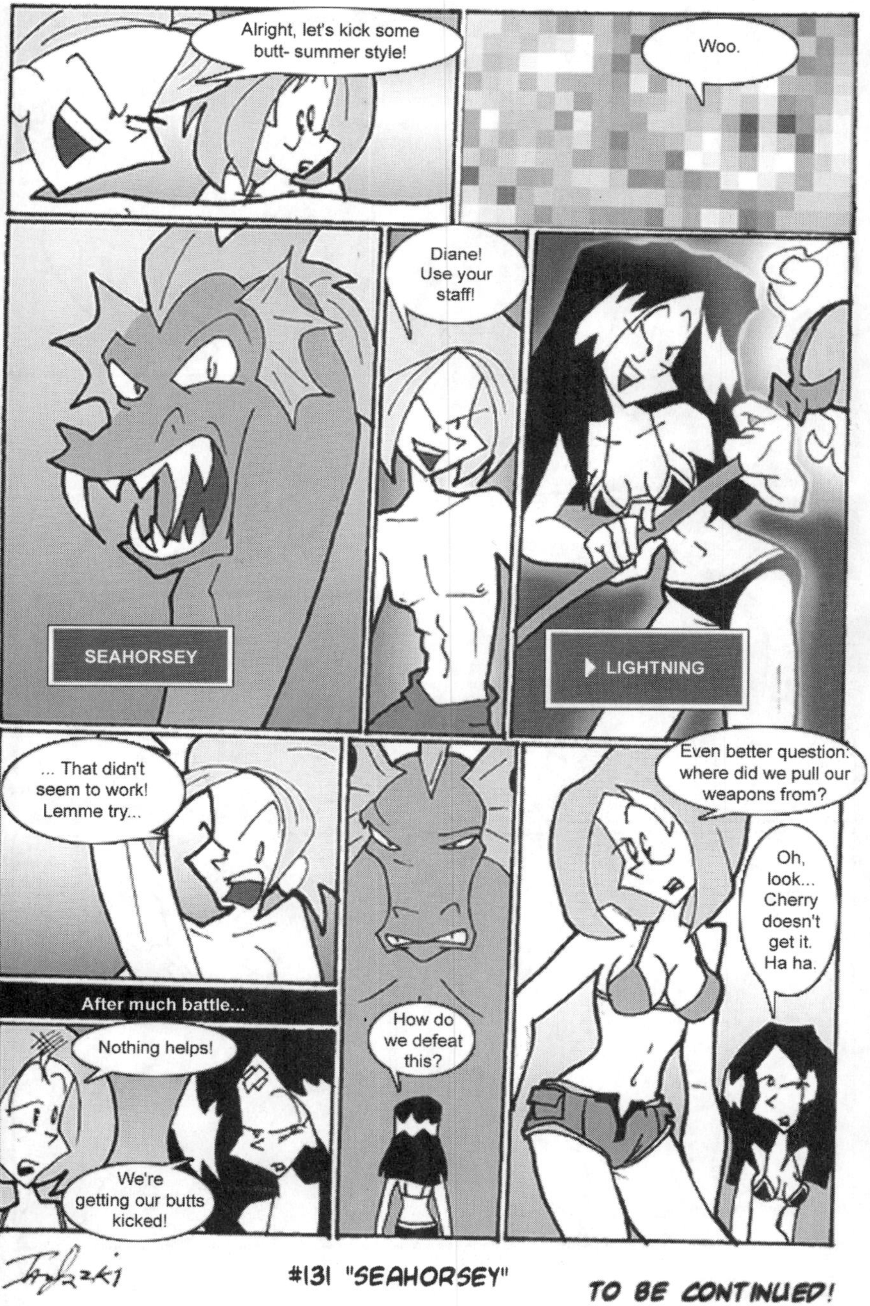
Alright, let's kick some butt- summer style!
Woo.
SEAHORSEY
Diane! Use your staff!
LIGHTNING
... That didn't seem to work! Lemme try...
After much battle...
Nothing helps!
We're getting our butts kicked!
How do we defeat this?
Even better question: where did we pull our weapons from?
Oh, look... Cherry doesn't get it. Ha ha.

#131 "SEAHORSEY"

TO BE CONTINUED!

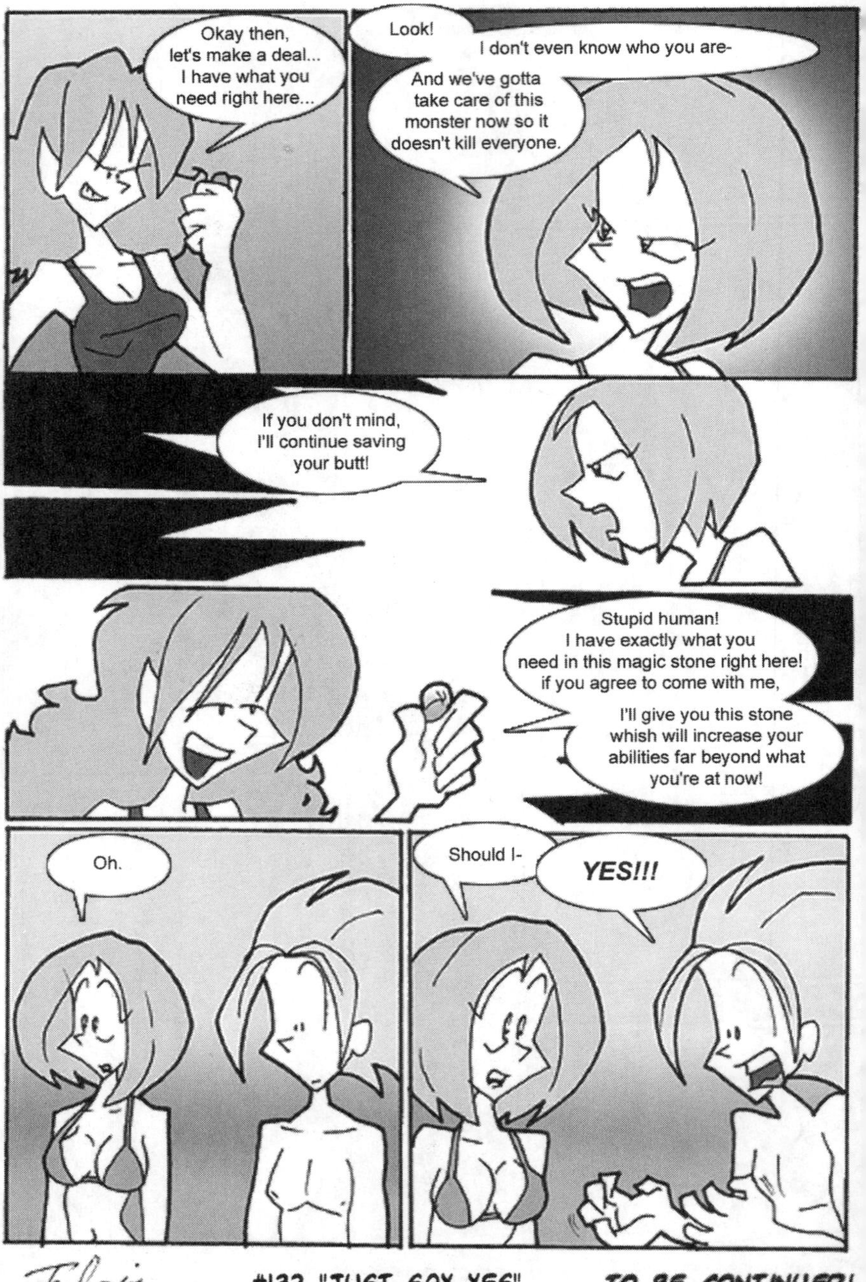
Okay then, let's make a deal... I have what you need right here...
Look!
I don't even know who you are-
And we've gotta take care of this monster now so it doesn't kill everyone.
If you don't mind, I'll continue saving your butt!
Stupid human! I have exactly what you need in this magic stone right here! if you agree to come with me,
I'll give you this stone whish will increase your abilities far beyond what you're at now!
Oh.
Should I-
YES!!!

#132 "JUST SAY YES"

TO BE CONTINUED!

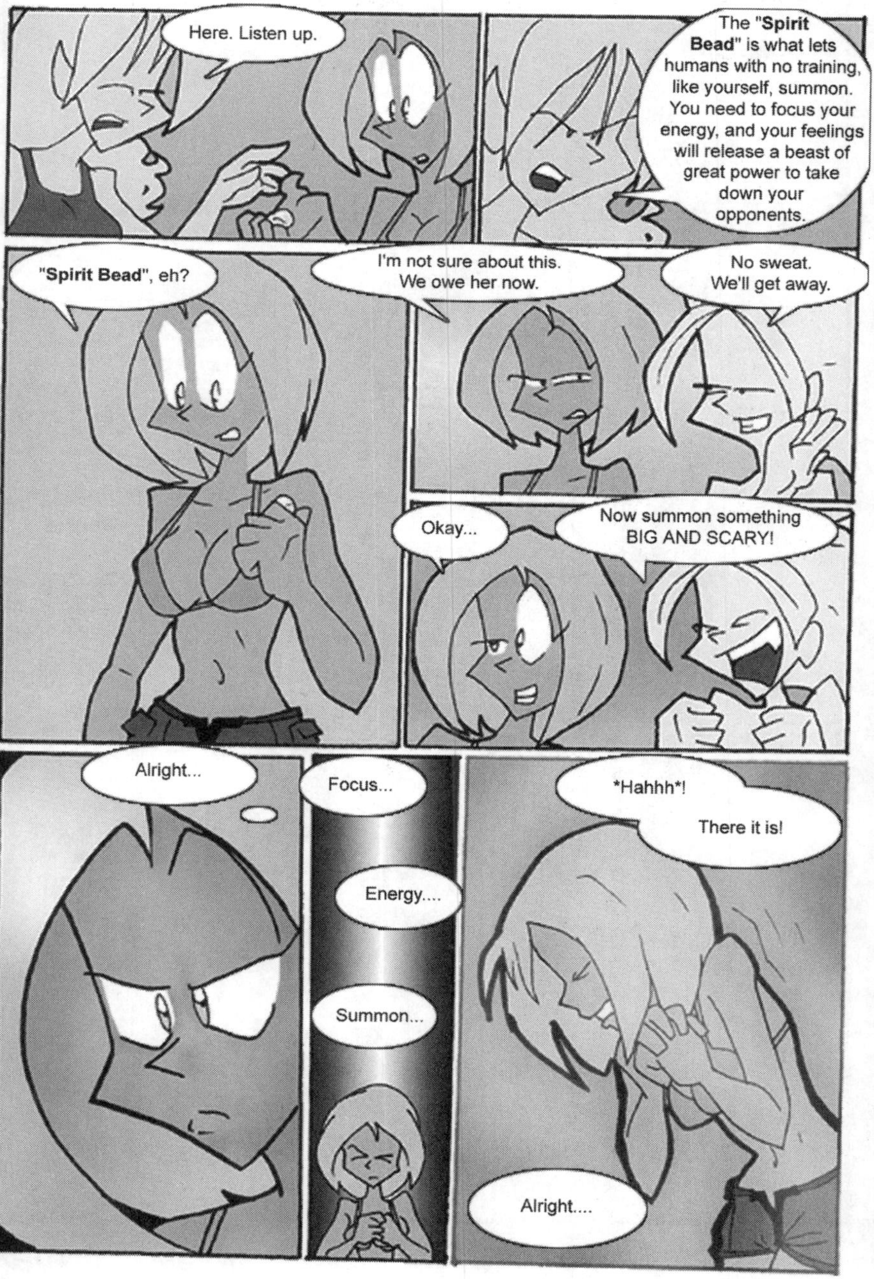

Here. Listen up.
The "**Spirit Bead**" is what lets humans with no training, like yourself, summon. You need to focus your energy, and your feelings will release a beast of great power to take down your opponents.
"**Spirit Bead**", eh?
I'm not sure about this. We owe her now.
No sweat. We'll get away.
Okay...
Now summon something BIG AND SCARY!
Alright...
Focus...
Energy....
Summon...
Hahhh!
There it is!
Alright....

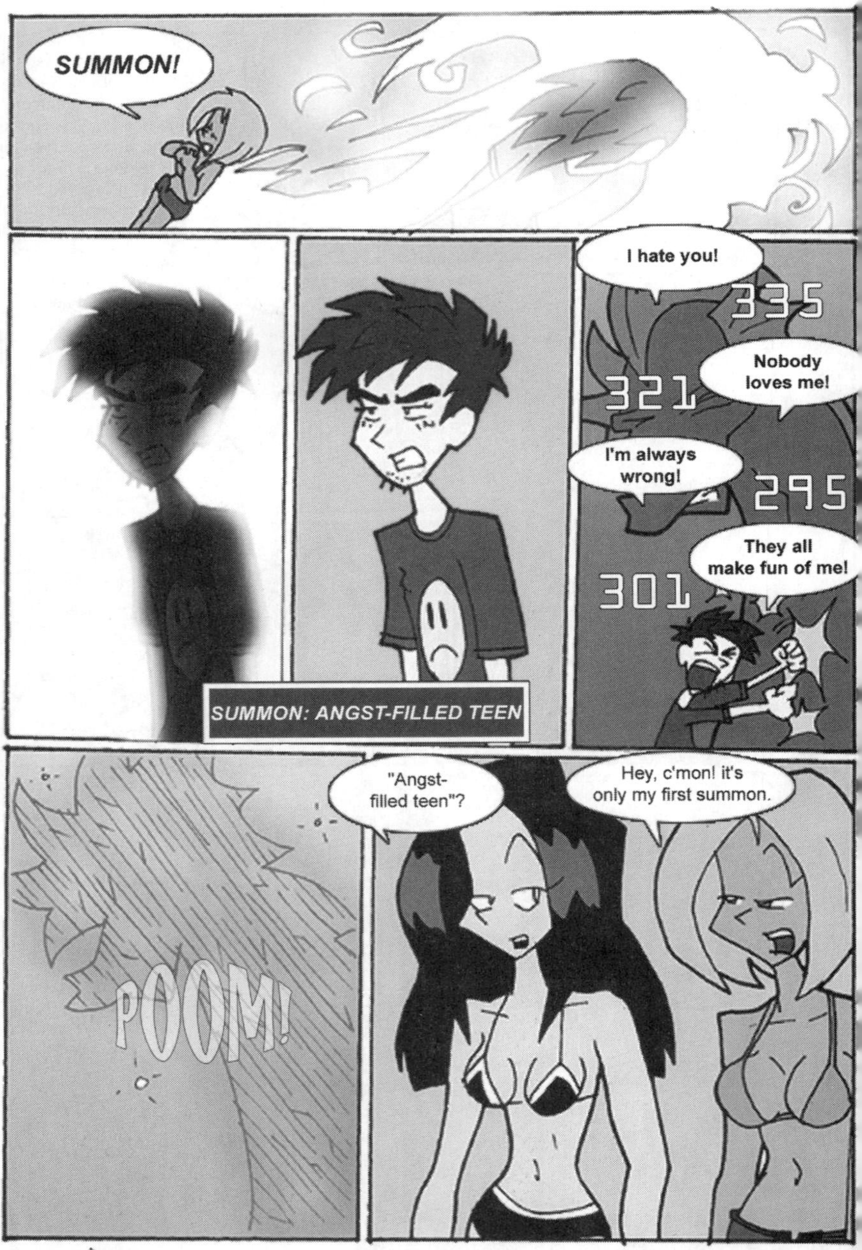
SUMMON!
I hate you!
335
Nobody loves me!
321
I'm always wrong!
295
They all make fun of me!
301
SUMMON: ANGST-FILLED TEEN
POOM!
"Angst-filled teen"?
Hey, c'mon! it's only my first summon.

#133 "SUMMON UP SOME TROUBLE"

TO BE CONTINUED

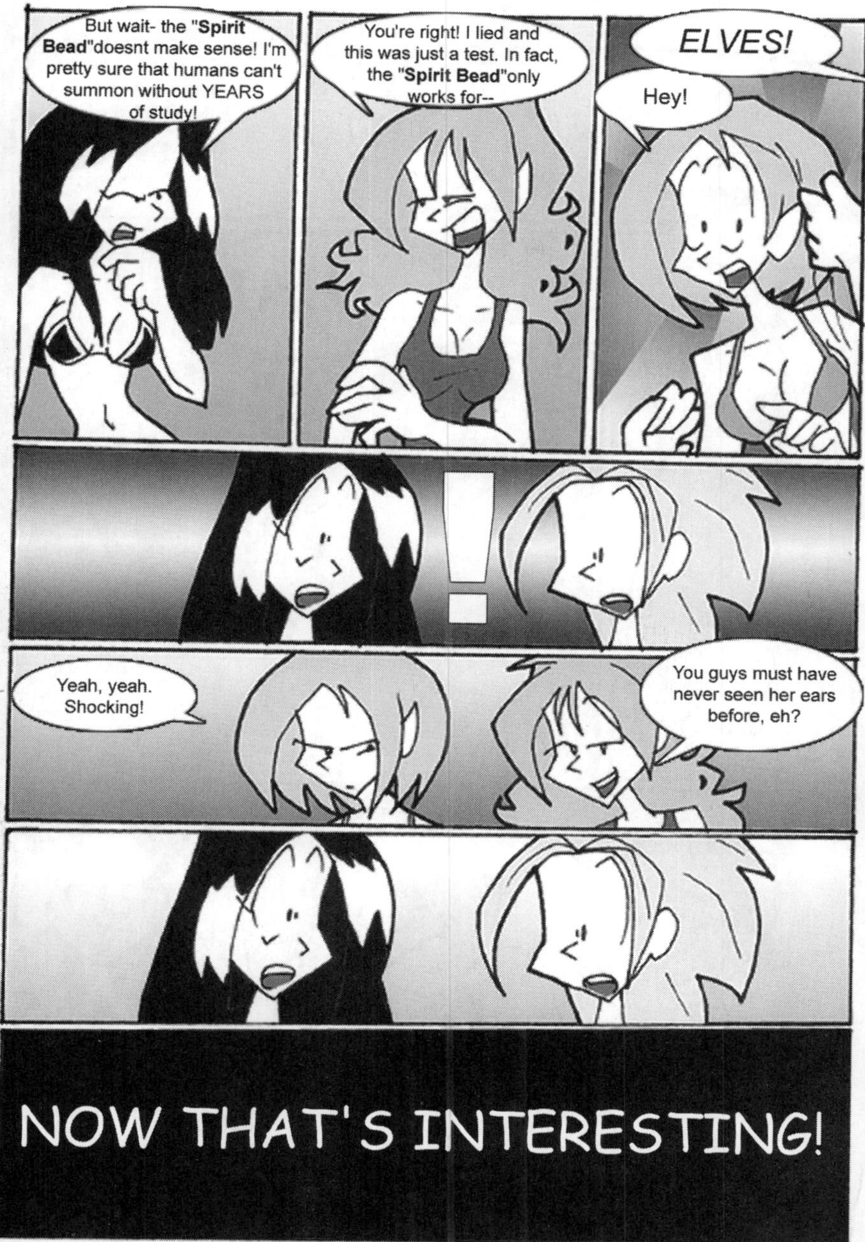
But wait- the "Spirit Bead"doesnt make sense! I'm pretty sure that humans can't summon without YEARS of study!
You're right! I lied and this was just a test. In fact, the "Spirit Bead"only works for--
Hey!
ELVES!
!
Yeah, yeah. Shocking!
You guys must have never seen her ears before, eh?
NOW THAT'S INTERESTING!

(Check Comic #1 to see Cherry's elf ears. Yep, they've been there all along, folks!)

Inazuki

#134 "SHOCKING!"

TO BE CONTINUED!

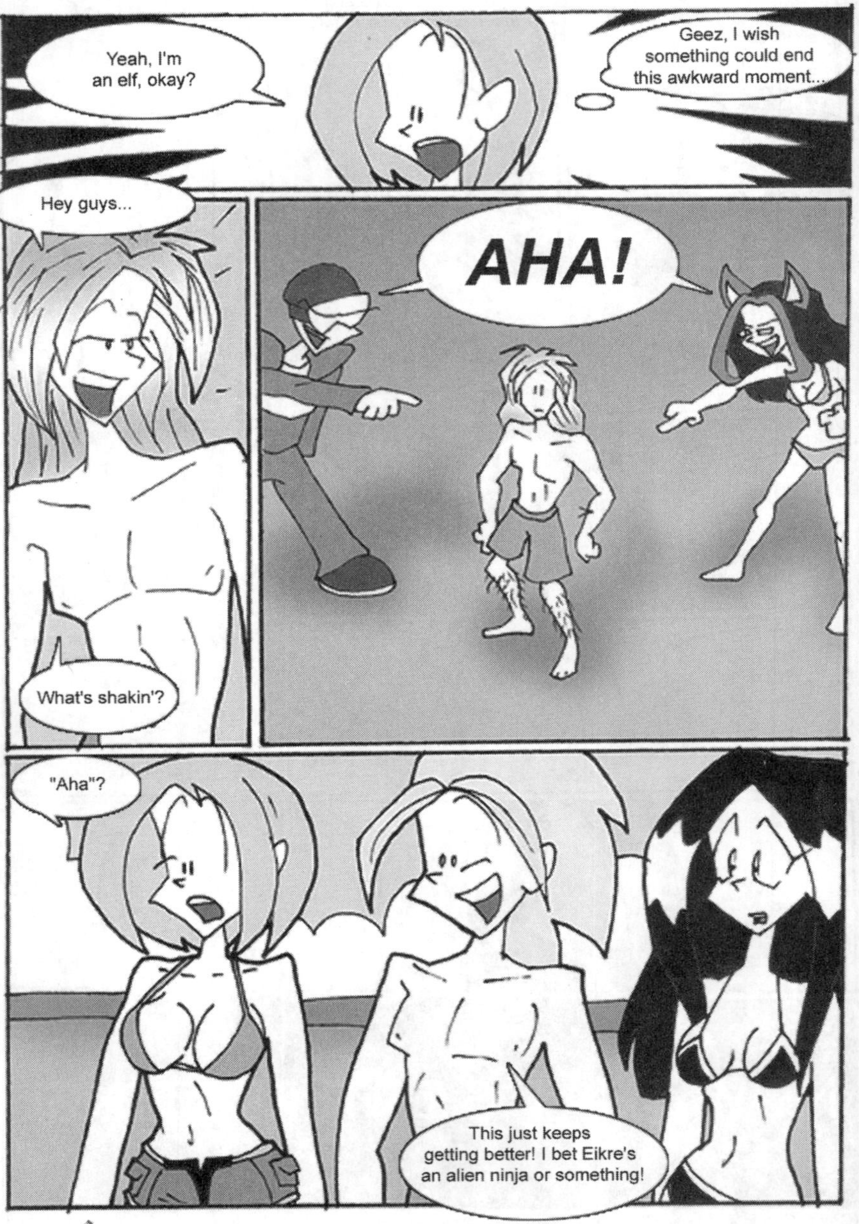

Yeah, I'm an elf, okay?
Geez, I wish something could end this awkward moment...
Hey guys...
What's shakin'?
AHA!
"Aha"?
This just keeps getting better! I bet Eikre's an alien ninja or something!

Jay Lazki #135 "AHA" TO BE CONTINUED!

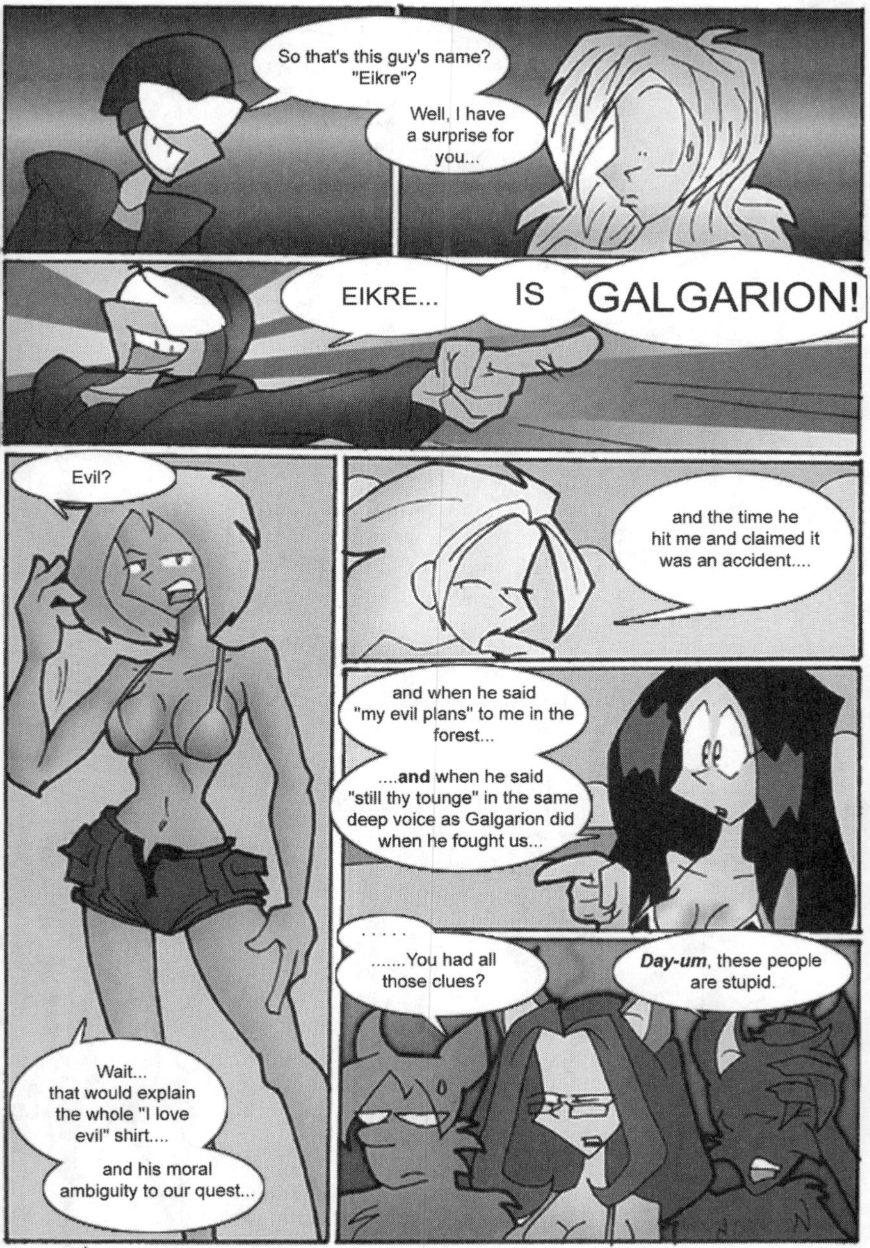

So that's this guy's name? "Eikre"?
Well, I have a surprise for you...
EIKRE...
IS
GALGARION!
Evil?
and the time he hit me and claimed it was an accident....
and when he said "my evil plans" to me in the forest...
....**and** when he said "still thy tounge" in the same deep voice as Galgarion did when he fought us...
Wait... that would explain the whole "I love evil" shirt....
and his moral ambiguity to our quest...
. . . . .
.......You had all those clues?
Day-um, these people are stupid.

#136 "TOTAL OBVIOUSNESS"

TO BE CONTINUED!

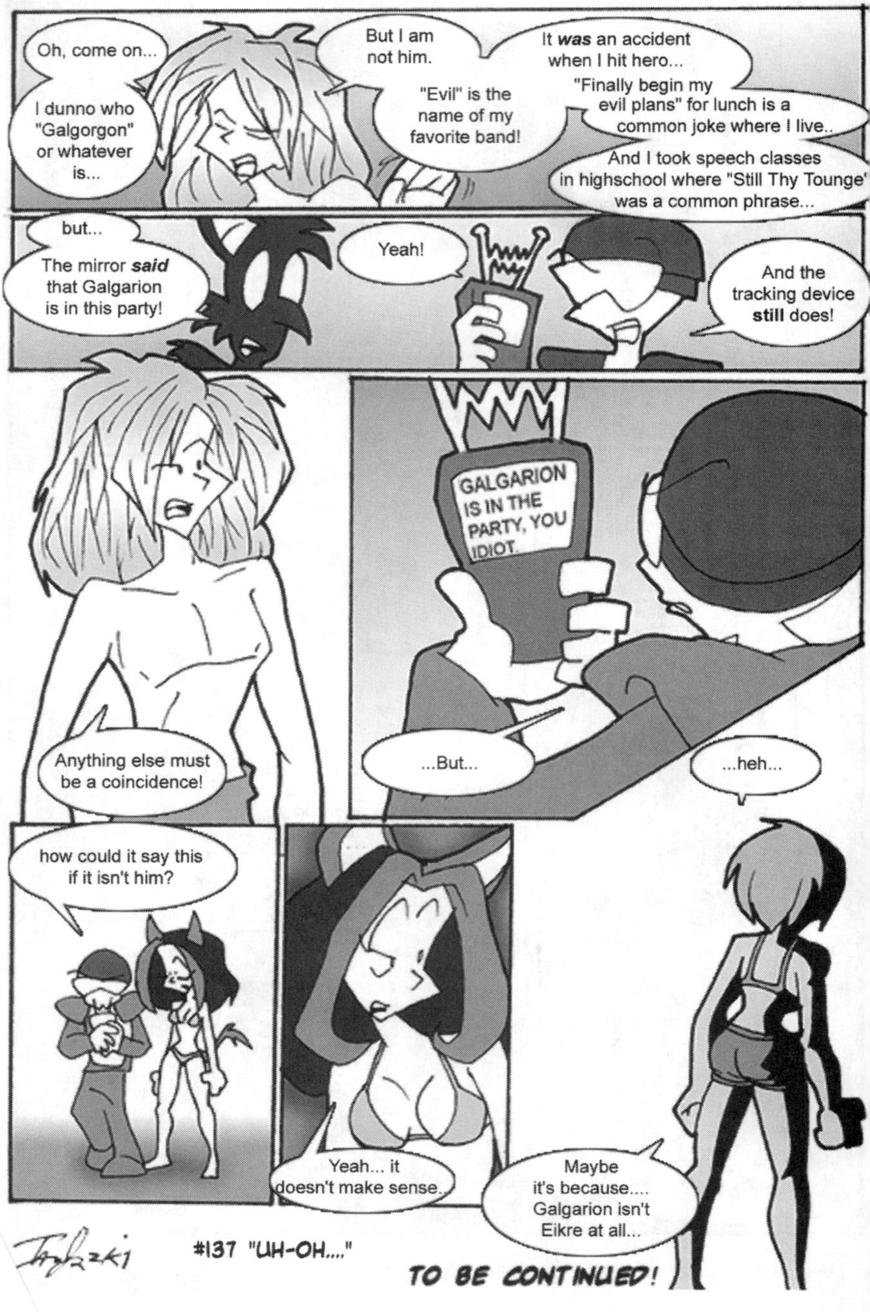
Oh, come on...
I dunno who "Galgorgon" or whatever is...
But I am not him.
"Evil" is the name of my favorite band!
It **was** an accident when I hit hero...
"Finally begin my evil plans" for lunch is a common joke where I live..
And I took speech classes in highschool where "Still Thy Tounge" was a common phrase...
but...
The mirror **said** that Galgarion is in this party!
Yeah!
And the tracking device **still** does!
Anything else must be a coincidence!
GALGARION IS IN THE PARTY, YOU IDIOT.
...But...
...heh...
how could it say this if it isn't him?
Yeah... it doesn't make sense..
Maybe it's because.... Galgarion isn't Eikre at all...
#137 "UH-OH...."
TO BE CONTINUED!

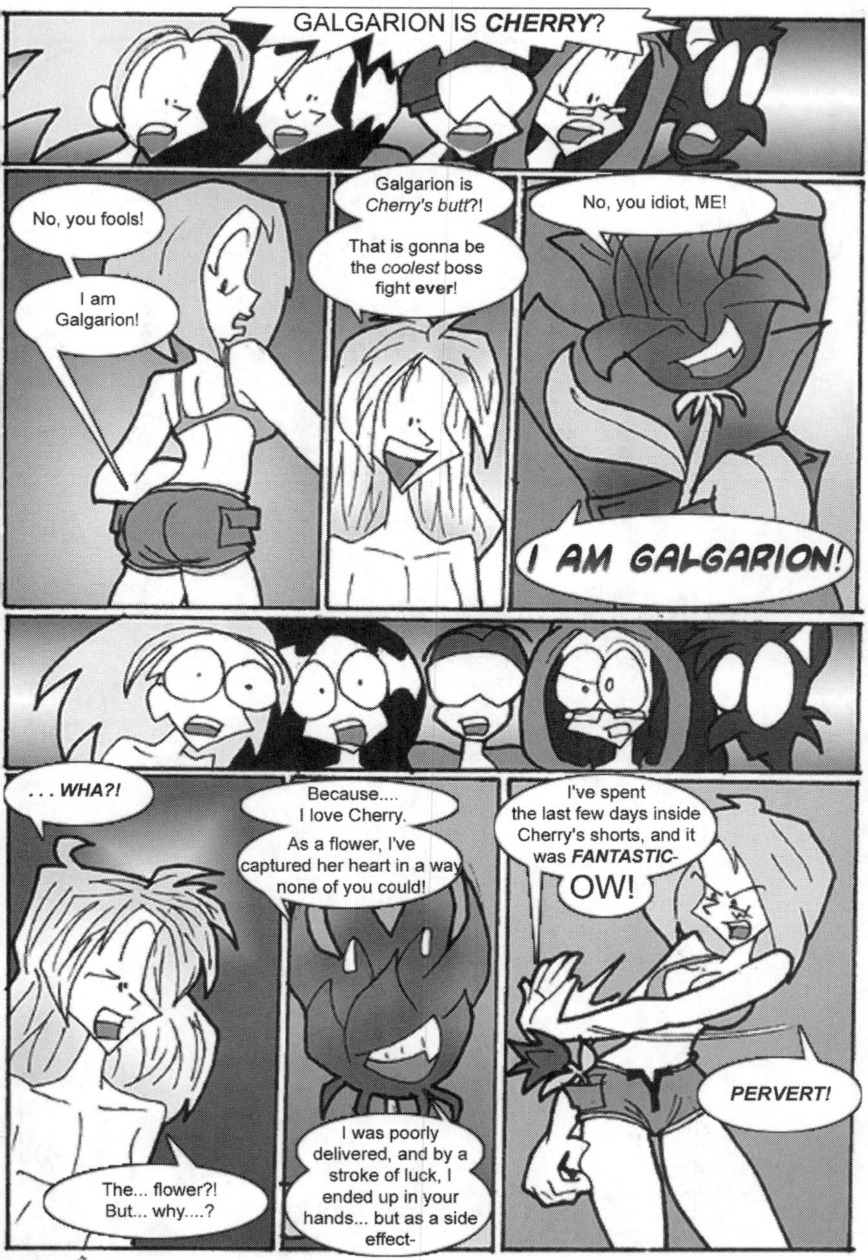

GALGARION IS ***CHERRY***?
No, you fools!
I am Galgarion!
Galgarion is *Cherry's butt*?!
That is gonna be the *coolest* boss fight **ever**!
No, you idiot, ME!
I AM GALGARION!
. . . WHA?!
The... flower?! But... why....?
Because.... I love Cherry.
As a flower, I've captured her heart in a way none of you could!
I was poorly delivered, and by a stroke of luck, I ended up in your hands... but as a side effect-
I've spent the last few days inside Cherry's shorts, and it was ***FANTASTIC***-
OW!
PERVERT!

#138 "EVIL.. UNVEILED!"

TO BE CONTINUED!

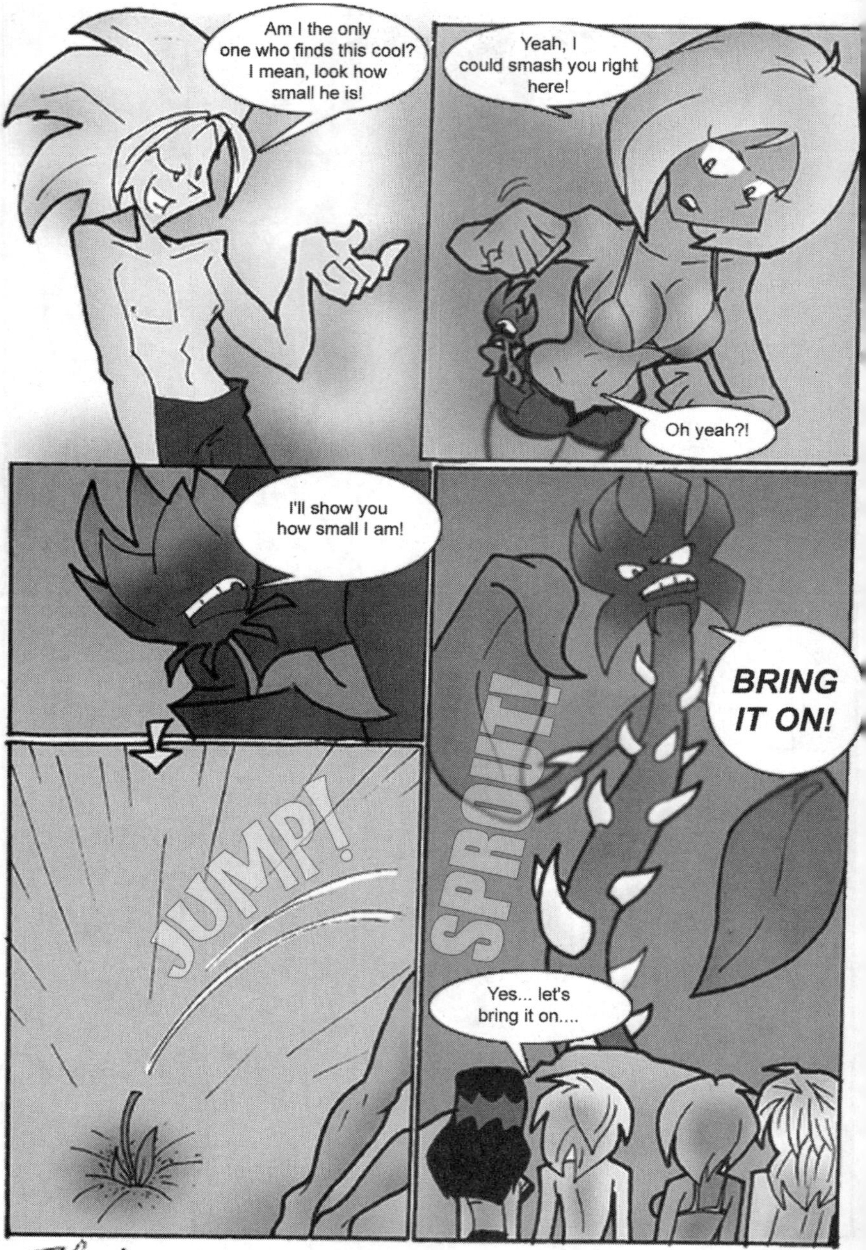
Am I the only one who finds this cool? I mean, look how small he is!
Yeah, I could smash you right here!
Oh yeah?!
I'll show you how small I am!
JUMP!
SPROUT!
BRING IT ON!
Yes... let's bring it on....

#139 "OH YEAH?"

TO BE CONTINUED!

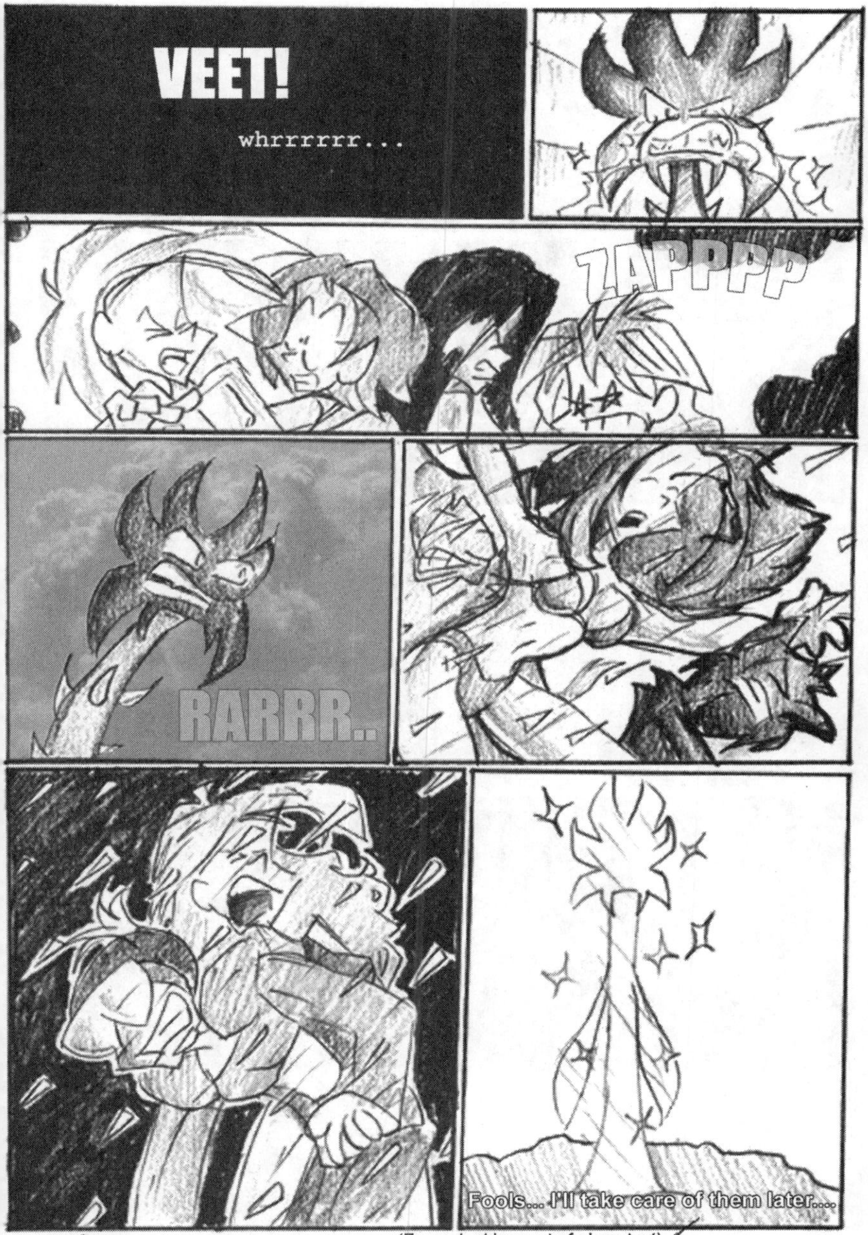
VEET!
whrrrrrr...
ZAPPPP
RARRR..
Fools... I'll take care of them later....
(Funny looking, out of place text)

#140 "FULL MOTION BEATING" TO BE CONTINUED!

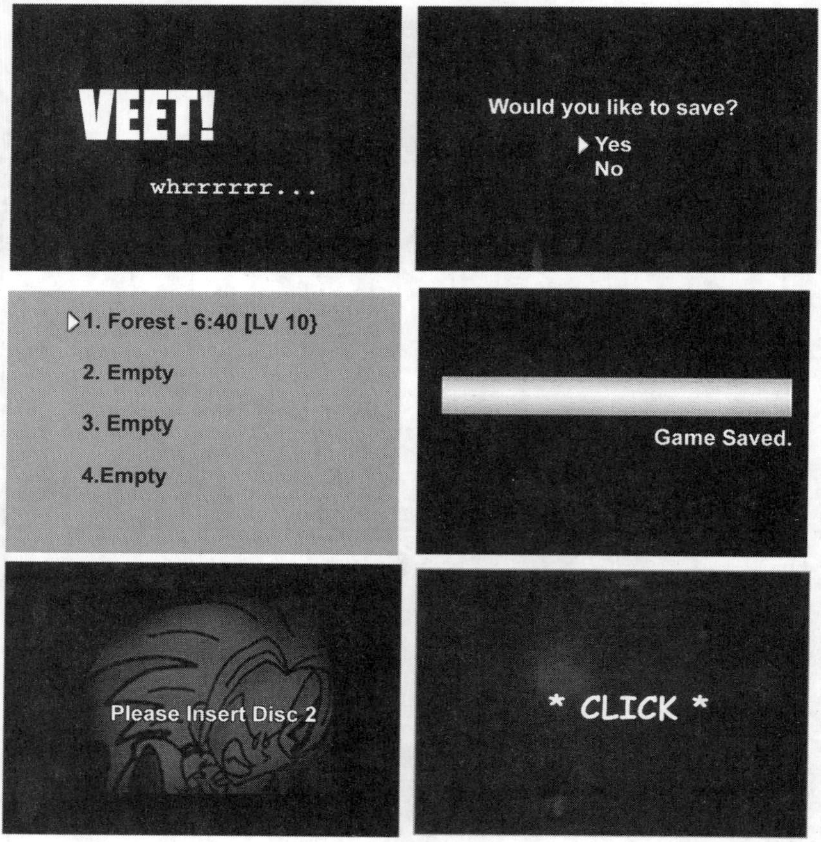
VEET!
whrrrrrr...
Would you like to save?
Yes
No
1. Forest - 6:40 [LV 10}
2. Empty
3. Empty
4.Empty
Game Saved.
Please Insert Disc 2
* CLICK *

SUPPLEMENTAL MATERIALS

WHAT FOLLOWS IS A COLLECTION OF EXTRA MATERIAL PRODUCED
DURING RPG WORLD'S FIRST YEAR ONLINE. WHILE NOT REALLY NEEDED
TO UNDERSTAND THE CONTINUITY OF THE STORY, THEY COMPLETE
THE EXPERIENCE.

INCLUDED:

"JIM, THE GUY WHO PLAYS RPG WORLD"
STARRING DAVID BARNES AND ZAK ELTZROTH

"IT HAD TO HAPPEN"
THE ADVENTURERS!/RPG WORLD CROSSOVER
A COLLABORATION INCLUDING WRITING AND ART BY MARK SHALLOW

ASSORTED PINUPS AND OTHER PROMO GRAPHICS

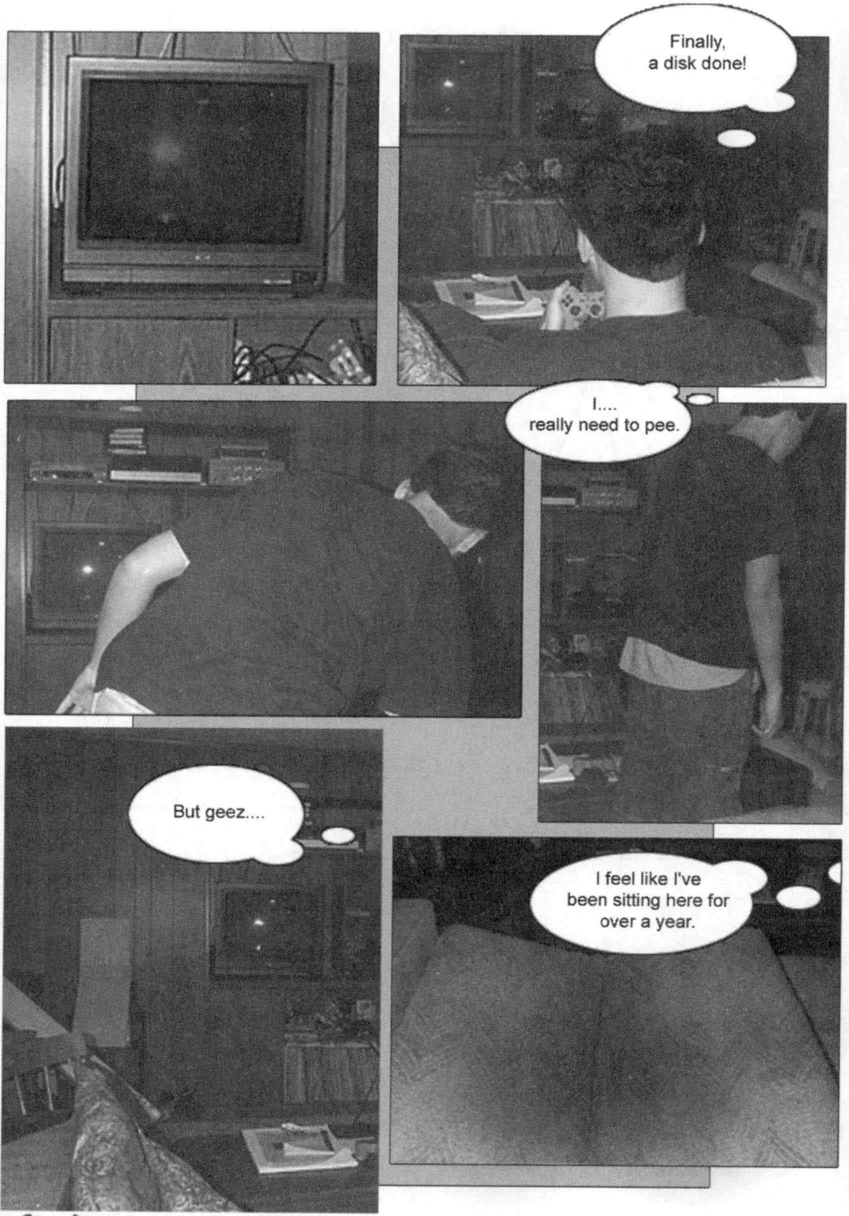
Finally,
a disk done!
I....
really need to pee.
But geez....
I feel like I've
been sitting here for
over a year.

JIM. THE GUY WHO PLAYS RPG WORLD
(By David B, Zak E. and Ian J.)

#1 "Couch Groove"

TO BE CONTINUED!

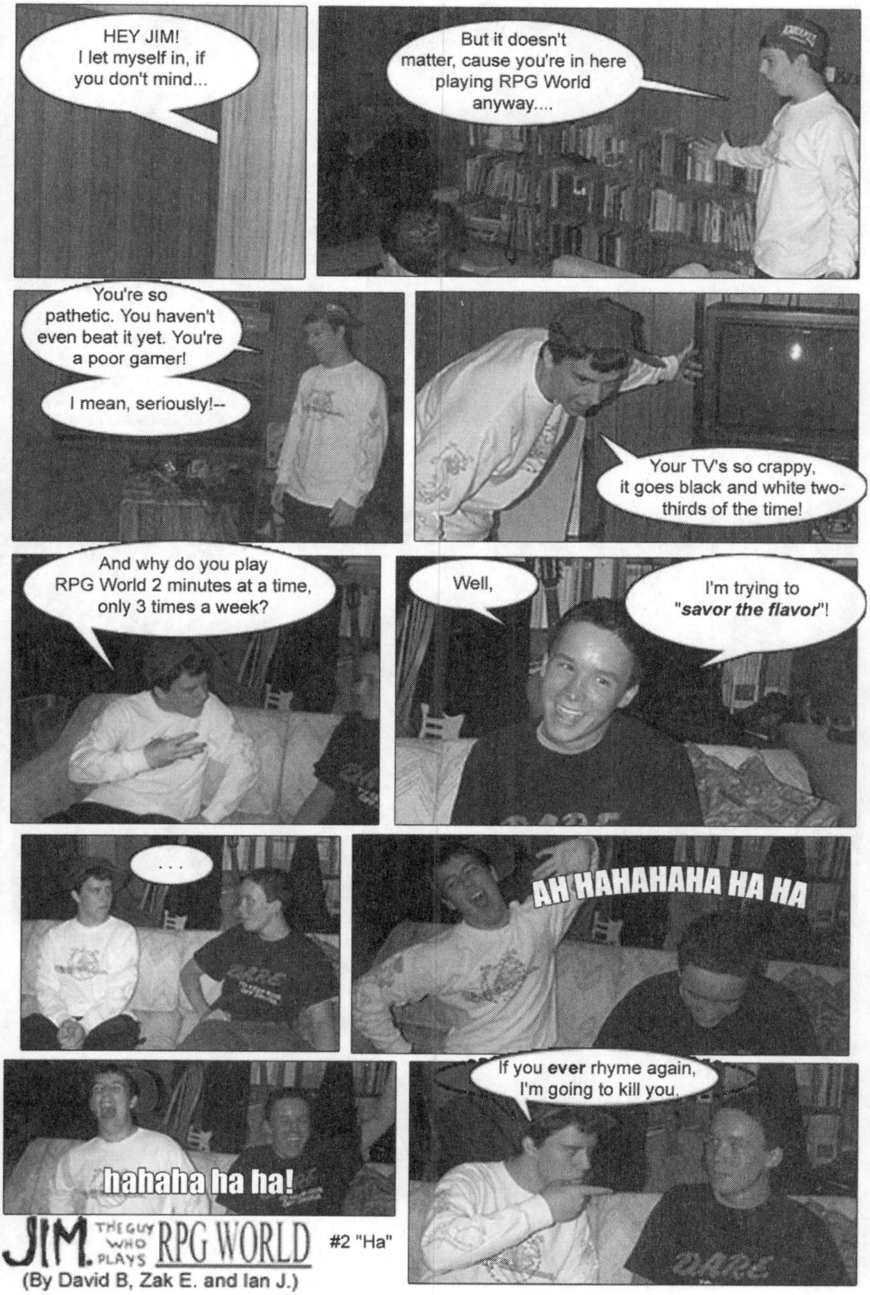
HEY JIM!
I let myself in, if you don't mind...
But it doesn't matter, cause you're in here playing RPG World anyway....
You're so pathetic. You haven't even beat it yet. You're a poor gamer!
I mean, seriously!--
Your TV's so crappy, it goes black and white two-thirds of the time!
And why do you play RPG World 2 minutes at a time, only 3 times a week?
Well,
I'm trying to "*savor the flavor*"!
. . .
AH HAHAHAHA HA HA
hahaha ha ha!
If you **ever** rhyme again, I'm going to kill you.
JIM. THE GUY WHO PLAYS RPG WORLD
#2 "Ha"
(By David B, Zak E. and Ian J.)

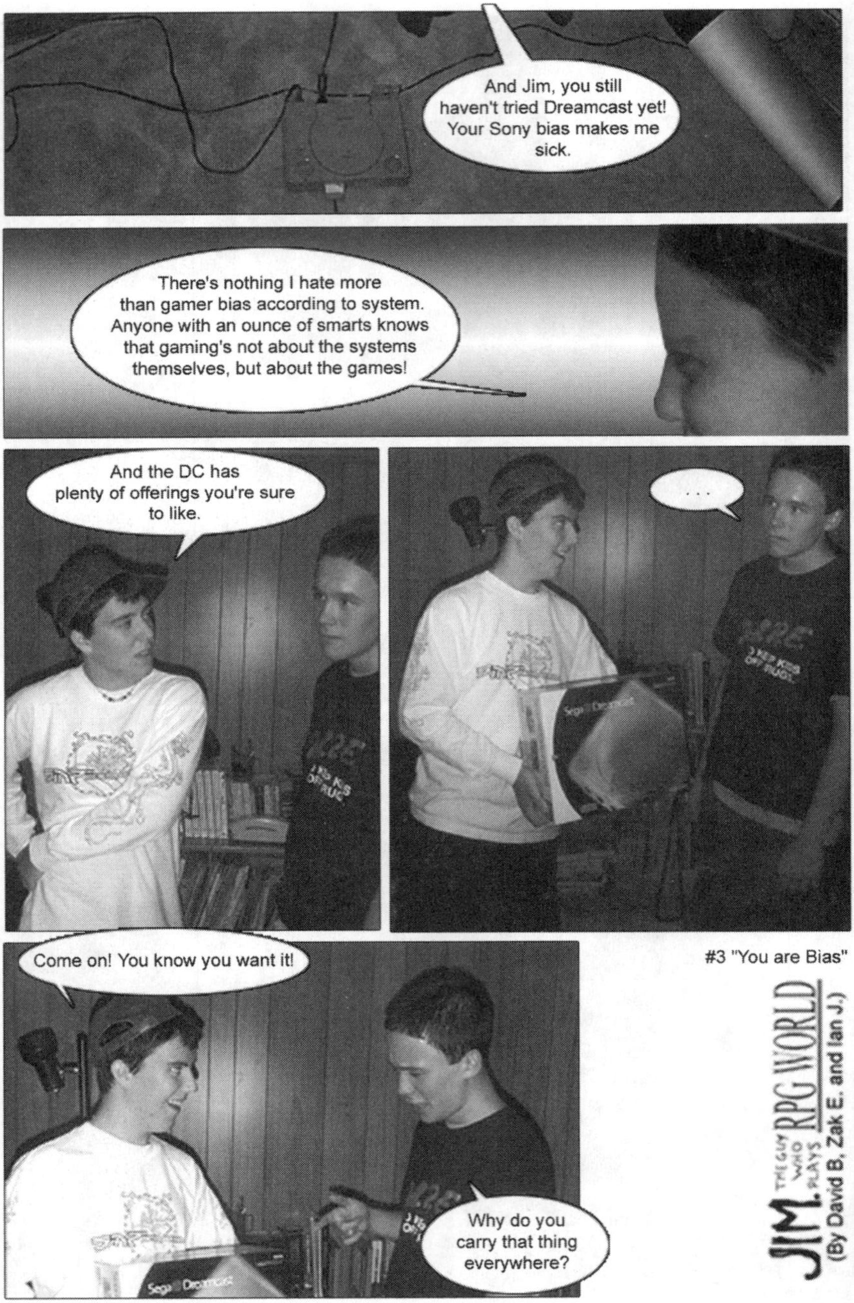
And Jim, you still haven't tried Dreamcast yet! Your Sony bias makes me sick.
There's nothing I hate more than gamer bias according to system. Anyone with an ounce of smarts knows that gaming's not about the systems themselves, but about the games!
And the DC has plenty of offerings you're sure to like.
. . .
Come on! You know you want it!
Why do you carry that thing everywhere?

#3 "You are Bias"

JIM. THE GUY WHO PLAYS RPG WORLD
(By David B, Zak E. and Ian J.)

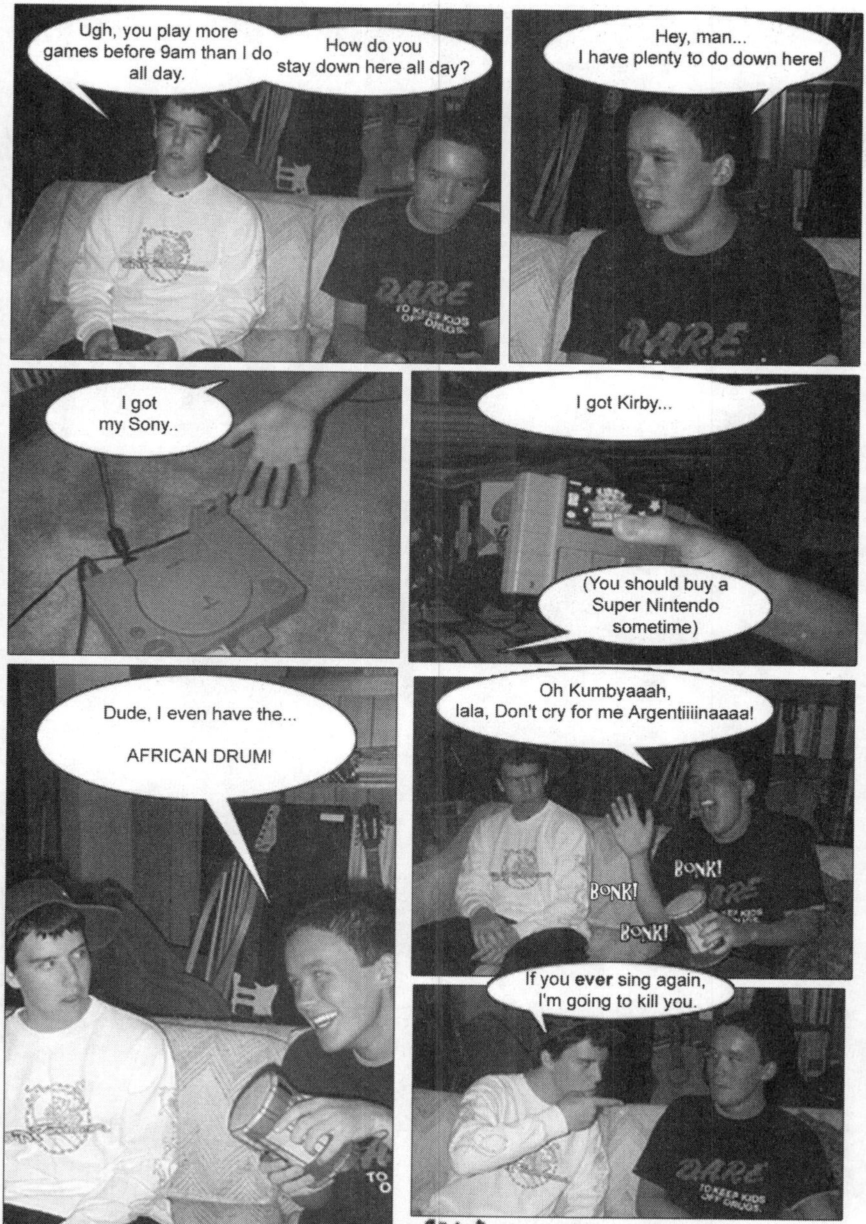
Ugh, you play more games before 9am than I do all day.
How do you stay down here all day?
Hey, man... I have plenty to do down here!
I got my Sony..
I got Kirby...
(You should buy a Super Nintendo sometime)
Dude, I even have the... AFRICAN DRUM!
Oh Kumbyaaah, lala, Don't cry for me Argentiiiinaaaa!
BONK!
BONK!
BONK!
If you **ever** sing again, I'm going to kill you.

JIM. THE GUY WHO PLAYS RPG WORLD #4 "Performance"

(By David B, Zak E. and Ian J.)

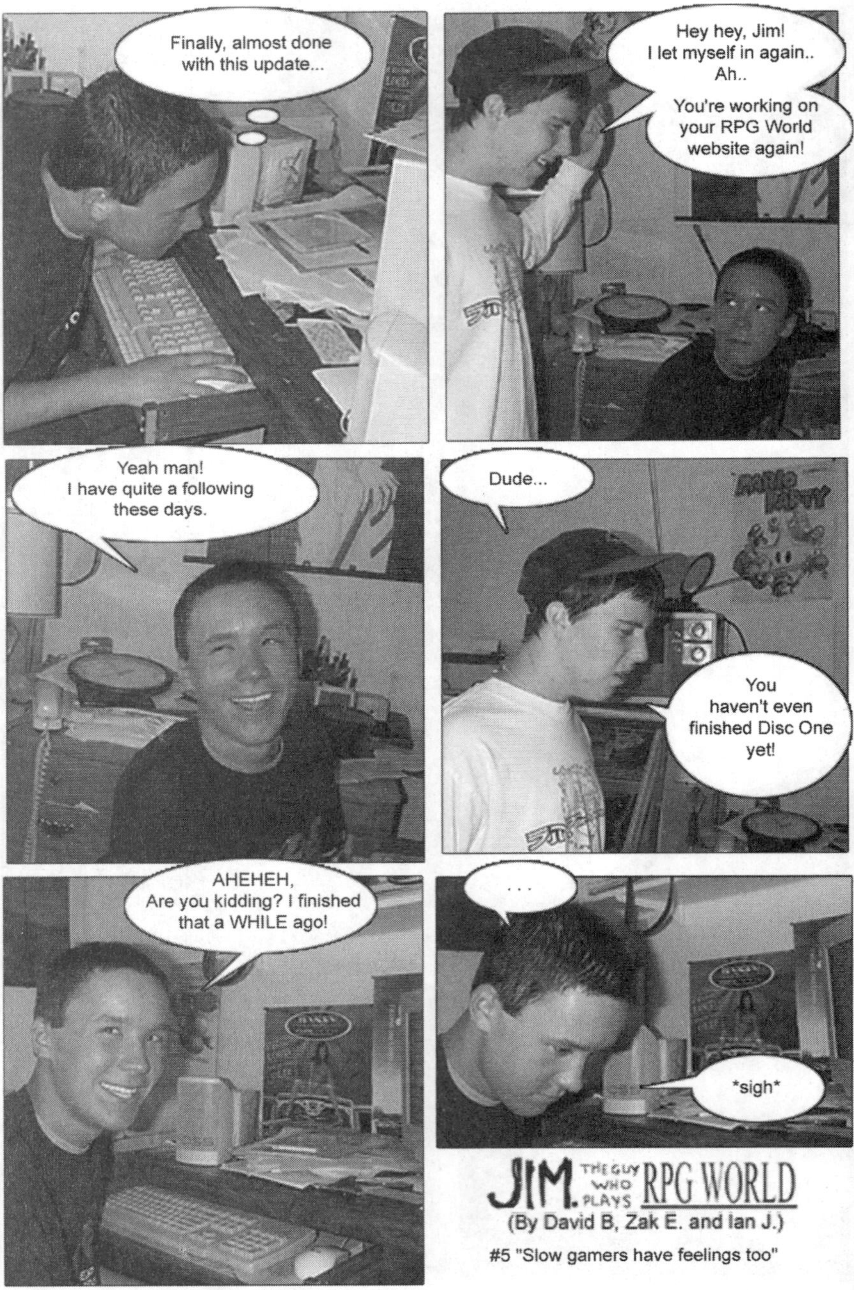

Finally, almost done with this update...
Hey hey, Jim! I let myself in again.. Ah..
You're working on your RPG World website again!
Yeah man! I have quite a following these days.
Dude...
You haven't even finished Disc One yet!
AHEHEH, Are you kidding? I finished that a WHILE ago!
. . .
sigh

JIM. THE GUY WHO PLAYS RPG WORLD

(By David B, Zak E. and Ian J.)

#5 "Slow gamers have feelings too"

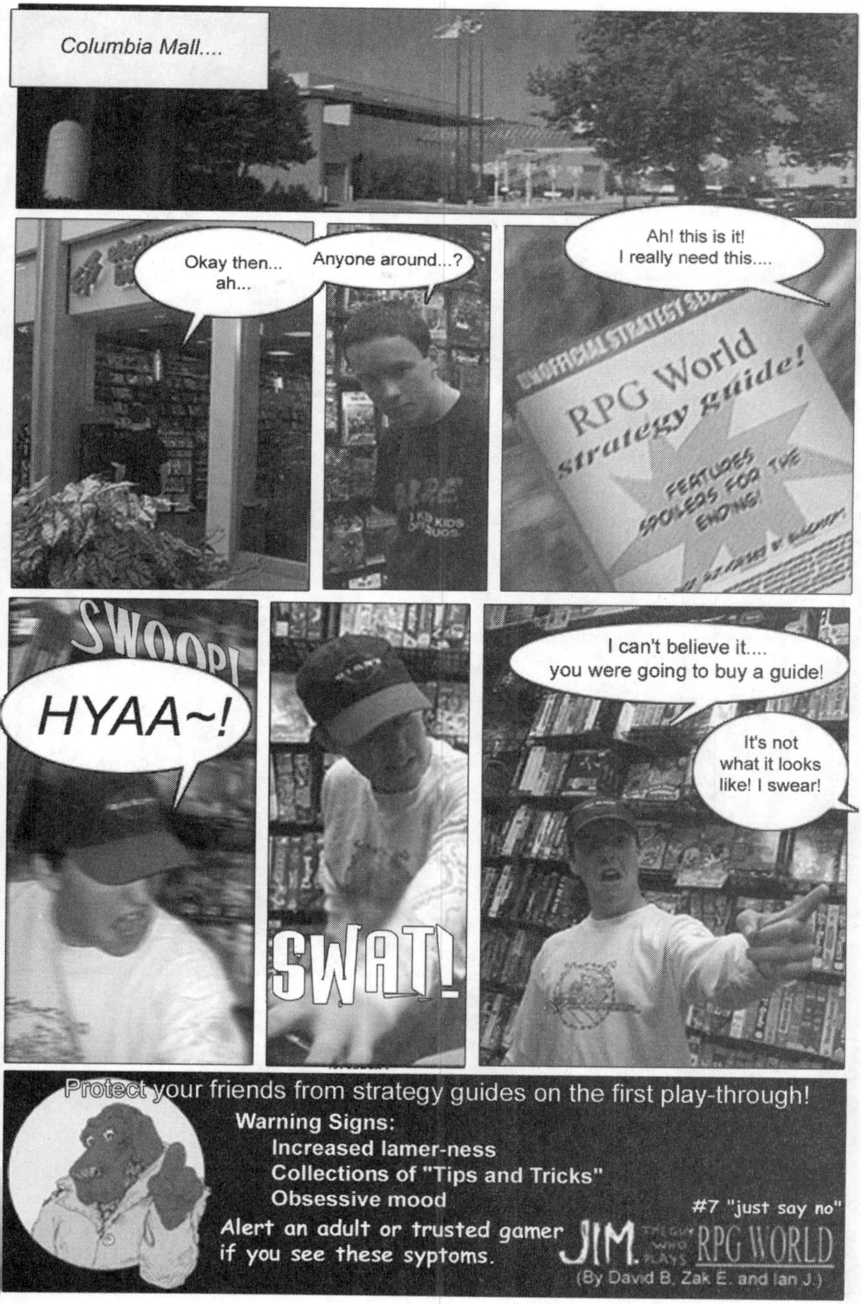
Columbia Mall....
Okay then... ah...
Anyone around...?
Ah! this is it! I really need this....
UNOFFICIAL STRATEGY GUIDE
RPG World strategy guide!
FEATURES SPOILERS FOR THE ENDING!
SWOOP!
HYAA~!
SWAT!
I can't believe it.... you were going to buy a guide!
It's not what it looks like! I swear!
Protect your friends from strategy guides on the first play-through!
Warning Signs:
Increased lamer-ness
Collections of "Tips and Tricks"
Obsessive mood
Alert an adult or trusted gamer if you see these syptoms.
#7 "just say no"
JIM. THE GUY WHO PLAYS RPG WORLD
(By David B, Zak E, and Ian J.)

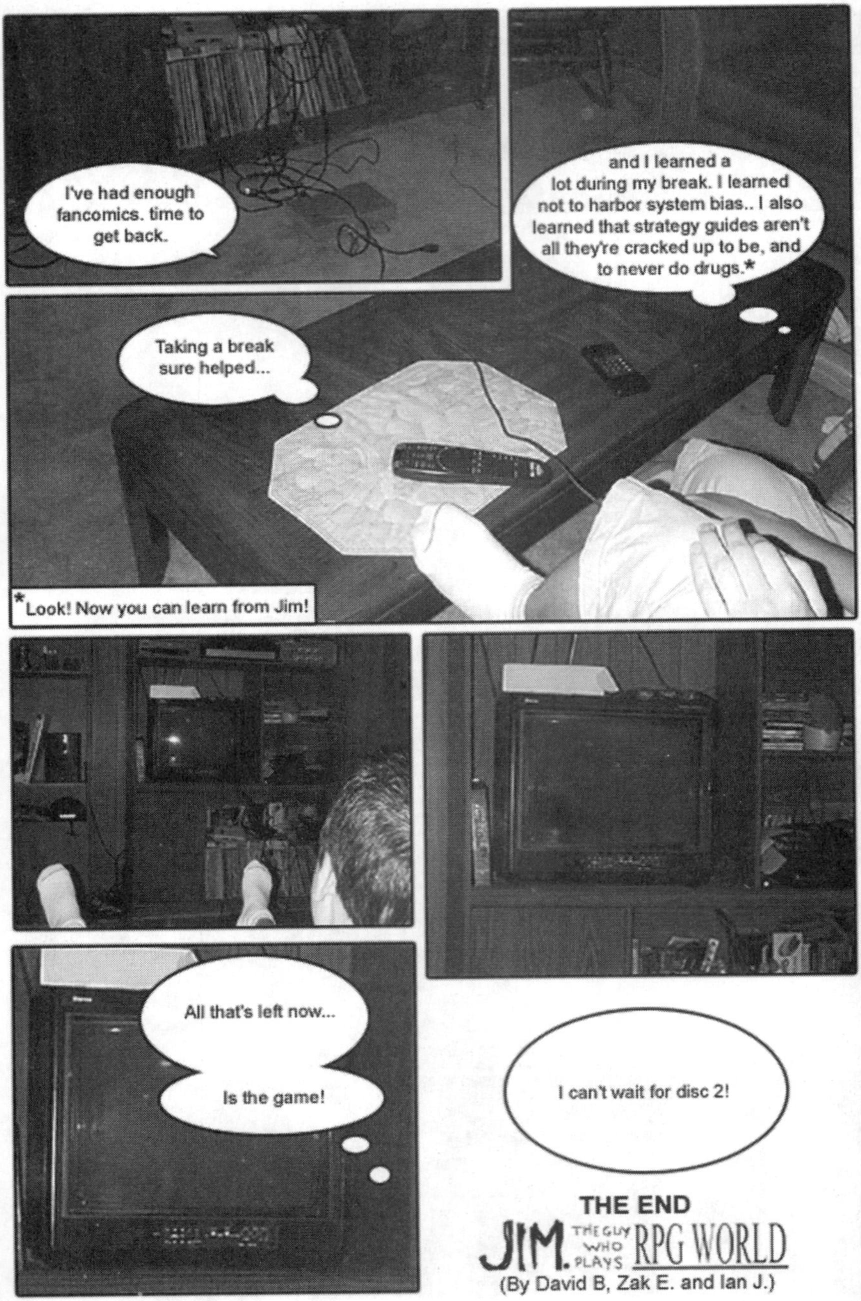
I've had enough fancomics. time to get back.
Taking a break sure helped...
and I learned a lot during my break. I learned not to harbor system bias.. I also learned that strategy guides aren't all they're cracked up to be, and to never do drugs.*
*Look! Now you can learn from Jim!
All that's left now...
Is the game!
I can't wait for disc 2!
THE END
JIM. THE GUY WHO PLAYS RPG WORLD
(By David B, Zak E. and Ian J.)

"IT HAD TO HAPPEN" BY MARK SHALLOW AND IAN JONES-QUARTEY

THIS IS THE INEVITABLE CROSSOVER BETWEEN RPG WORLD AND THE FIRST AND BEST RPG PARODY COMIC ON THE INTERNET, ADVENTURERS! BY MARK SHALLOW. IT CAN BE FOUND AT

WWW.ADVENTURERS-COMIC.COM

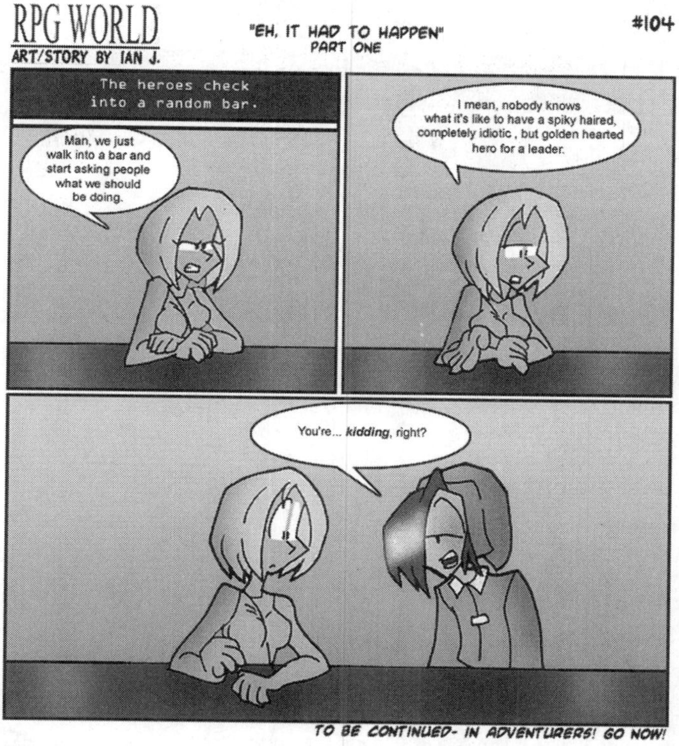

RPG WORLD
ART/STORY BY IAN J.
"EH, IT HAD TO HAPPEN"
PART ONE
#104
The heroes check into a random bar.
Man, we just walk into a bar and start asking people what we should be doing.
I mean, nobody knows what it's like to have a spiky haired, completely idiotic , but golden hearted hero for a leader.
You're... kidding, right?
TO BE CONTINUED- IN ADVENTURERS! GO NOW!

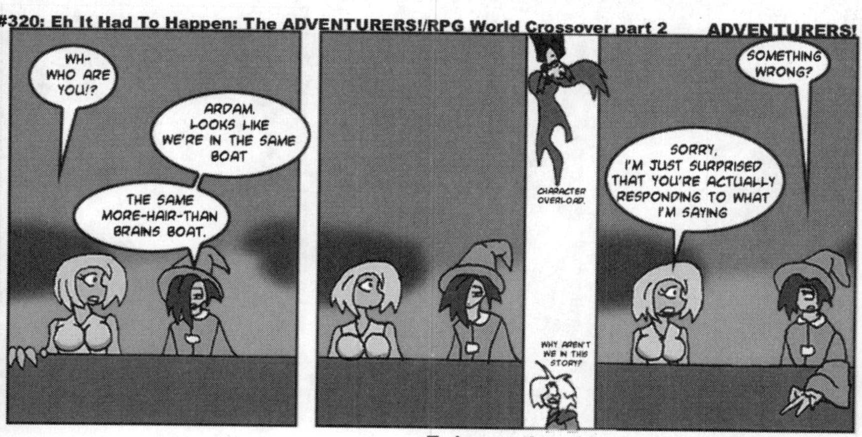

#320: Eh It Had To Happen: The ADVENTURERS!/RPG World Crossover part 2
ADVENTURERS!
WH- WHO ARE YOU!?
ARDAM. LOOKS LIKE WE'RE IN THE SAME BOAT
THE SAME MORE-HAIR-THAN BRAINS BOAT.
CHARACTER OVERLOAD.
WHY AREN'T WE IN THIS STORY?
SOMETHING WRONG?
SORRY, I'M JUST SURPRISED THAT YOU'RE ACTUALLY RESPONDING TO WHAT I'M SAYING

To be continued in tommorow's RPG WORLD

RPG WORLD

ART/STORY BY IAN J.

"EH, IT HAD TO HAPPEN"
THE ADVENTURERS / RPG WORLD CROSSOVER
PART THREE

#105

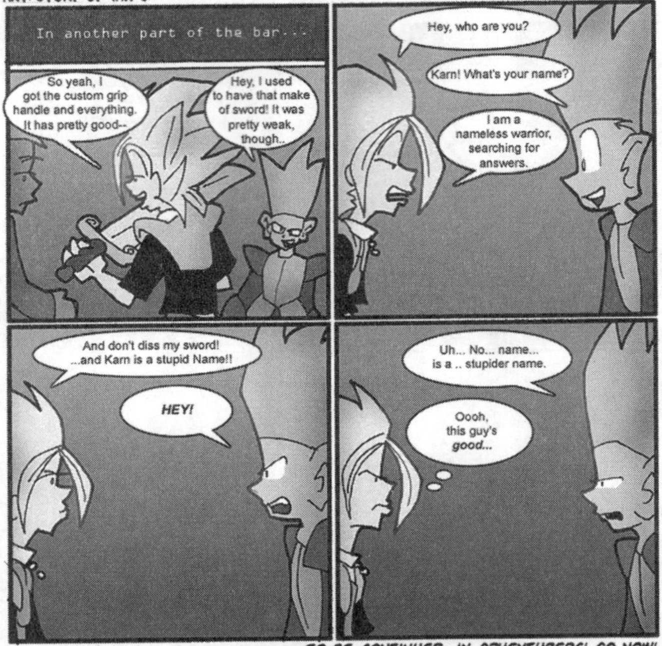

In another part of the bar...
So yeah, I got the custom grip handle and everything. It has pretty good--
Hey, I used to have that make of sword! It was pretty weak, though..
Hey, who are you?
Karn! What's your name?
I am a nameless warrior, searching for answers.
And don't diss my sword! ...and Karn is a stupid Name!!
HEY!
Uh... No... name... is a .. stupider name.
Oooh, this guy's good...

OOOOOH, THAT WAS COLD..!

TO BE CONTINUED- IN ADVENTURERS! GO NOW!

#321: Eh It Had to Happen: The ADV/RPG World Crossover part 4 — ADVENTURERS

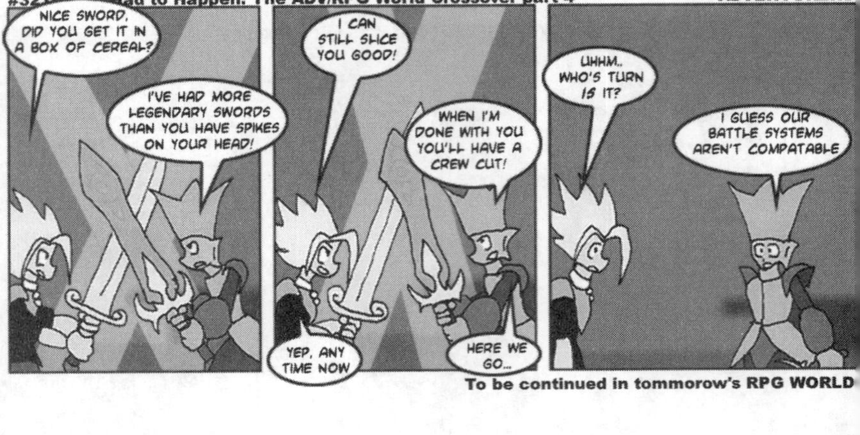

NICE SWORD, DID YOU GET IT IN A BOX OF CEREAL?
I'VE HAD MORE LEGENDARY SWORDS THAN YOU HAVE SPIKES ON YOUR HEAD!
I CAN STILL SLICE YOU GOOD!
WHEN I'M DONE WITH YOU YOU'LL HAVE A CREW CUT!
YEP, ANY TIME NOW
HERE WE GO...
UHHM.. WHO'S TURN IS IT?
I GUESS OUR BATTLE SYSTEMS AREN'T COMPATABLE

To be continued in tommorow's RPG WORLD

RPG WORLD

"EH, IT HAD TO HAPPEN"
THE ADVENTURERS / RPG WORLD CROSSOVER
PART FIVE

#106

ART/STORY BY IAN J.

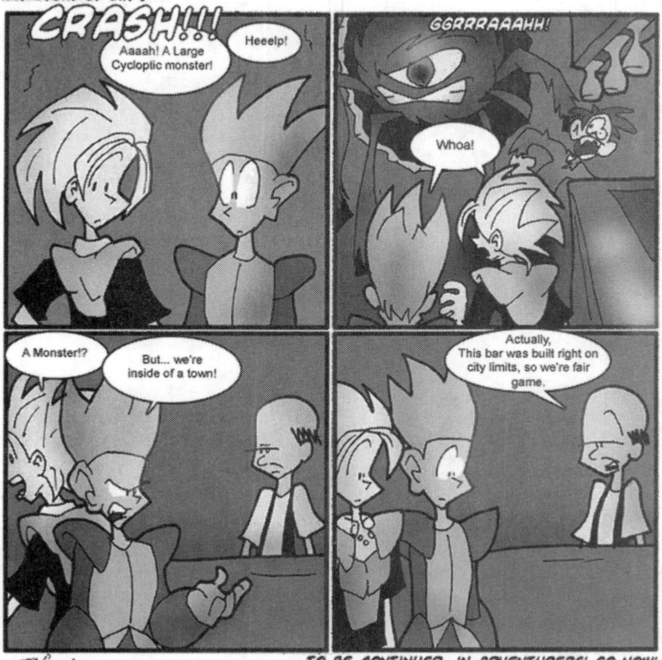
CRASH!!!
Aaaah! A Large Cycloptic monster!
Heeelp!
GGRRRAAAHH!
Whoa!
A Monster!?
But... we're inside of a town!
Actually, This bar was built right on city limits, so we're fair game.

TO BE CONTINUED- IN ADVENTURERS! GO NOW!

#322: Eh, It Had To Happen: The ADV/RPG World Crossover Part 6 **ADVENTURERS!**

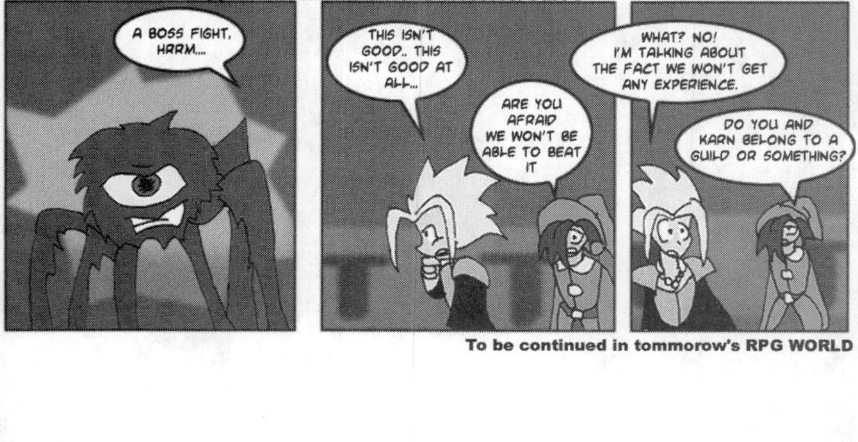
A BOSS FIGHT, HRRM...
THIS ISN'T GOOD.. THIS ISN'T GOOD AT ALL...
ARE YOU AFRAID WE WON'T BE ABLE TO BEAT IT
WHAT? NO! I'M TALKING ABOUT THE FACT WE WON'T GET ANY EXPERIENCE.
DO YOU AND KARN BELONG TO A GUILD OR SOMETHING?

To be continued in tommorow's RPG WORLD

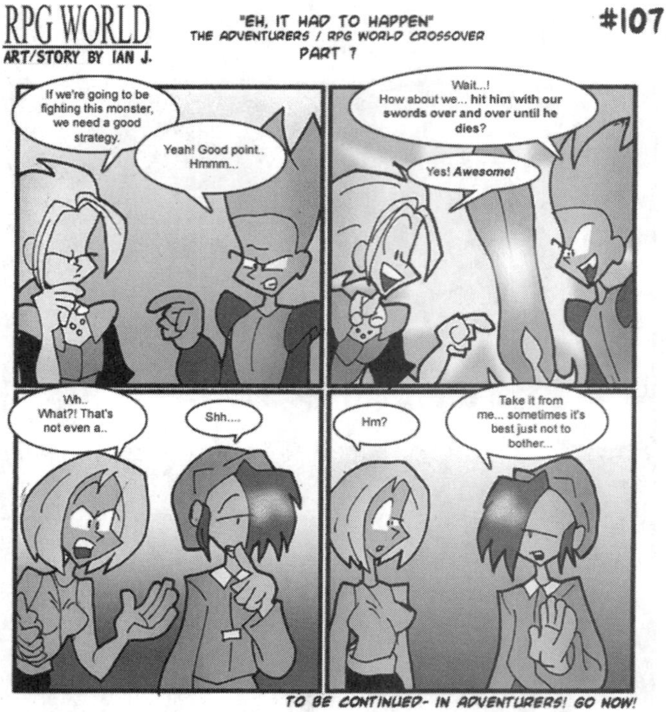
RPG WORLD
ART/STORY BY IAN J.
"EH, IT HAD TO HAPPEN"
THE ADVENTURERS / RPG WORLD CROSSOVER
PART 7
#107
If we're going to be fighting this monster, we need a good strategy.
Yeah! Good point.. Hmmm...
Wait...!
How about we... hit him with our swords over and over until he dies?
Yes! Awesome!
Wh..
What?! That's not even a..
Shh....
Hm?
Take it from me... sometimes it's best just not to bother...
TO BE CONTINUED- IN ADVENTURERS! GO NOW!

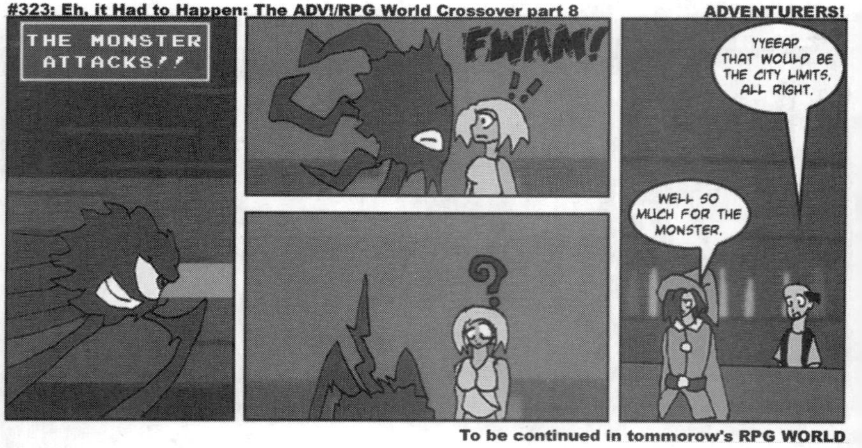
#323: Eh, it Had to Happen: The ADV!/RPG World Crossover part 8
ADVENTURERS!
THE MONSTER ATTACKS!!
FWAM!
!!
?
YYEEAP. THAT WOULD BE THE CITY LIMITS, ALL RIGHT.
WELL SO MUCH FOR THE MONSTER.
To be continued in tommorow's RPG WORLD

RPG WORLD
ART/STORY BY IAN J.

"EH, IT HAD TO HAPPEN"
THE ADVENTURERS / RPG WORLD CROSSOVER
PART 9

#108

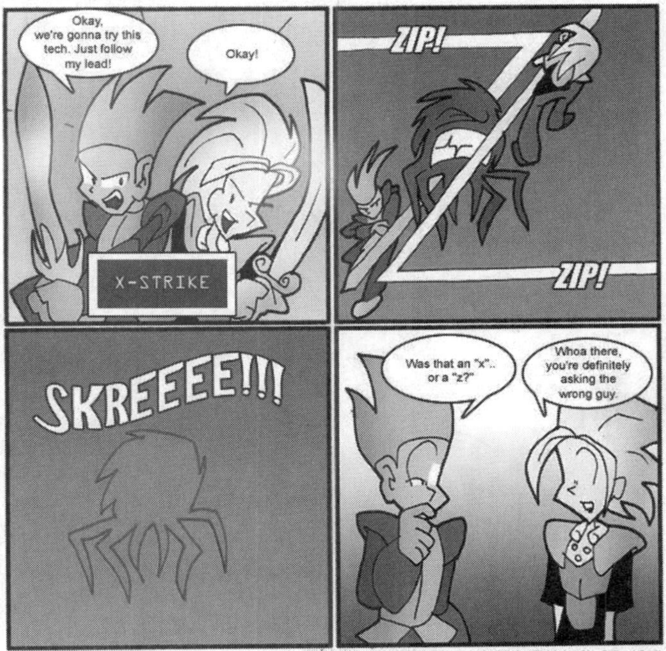

Okay, we're gonna try this tech. Just follow my lead!
Okay!
X-STRIKE
ZIP!
ZIP!
SKREEEEE!!!
Was that an "x".. or a "z?"
Whoa there, you're definitely asking the wrong guy.

TO BE CONTINUED- IN ADVENTURERS! GO NOW!

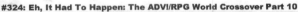

#324: Eh, It Had To Happen: The ADV!/RPG World Crossover Part 10 **ADVENTURERS!**

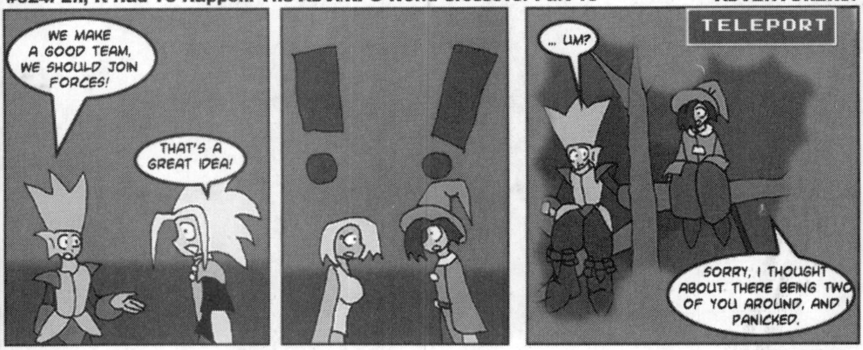

WE MAKE A GOOD TEAM, WE SHOULD JOIN FORCES!
THAT'S A GREAT IDEA!
!
!
TELEPORT
... UM?
SORRY, I THOUGHT ABOUT THERE BEING TWO OF YOU AROUND, AND I PANICKED.

~The End~

ASSORTED PINUPS AND OTHER PROMO GRAPHICS

RPG WORLD
ART/STORY BY IAN J.
#10.5

WE TAKE A TIMEOUT FROM OUR PLOTLINE TO SAY
HAPPY HALLOWEEN!

Featuring:
The Hero as Zidane Tribal (FF 9)
Cherry as Tifa Lockheart (FF7)
And The Dragobo as a Chocobo

(WITH MANY APOLOGIES TO SQUARESOFT.
NO, REALLY! I APOLOGIZE ABOUT THE ENTIRE
RPG WORLD COMIC, NOT JUST THE ONE ABOVE!)

HALLOWEEN 2000

RPG WORLD
ART/STORY BY IAN J.
"CHRISTMAS BONUS COMIC"
#32

RPG World wishes you a Merry Christmas and a Happy Holiday!

I WISH I SHOULD HAVE TRIED TO MAKE THIS COMIC FUNNY...

HAPPY HOLIDAYS!

CHRISTMAS 2000

SUMMER 2001

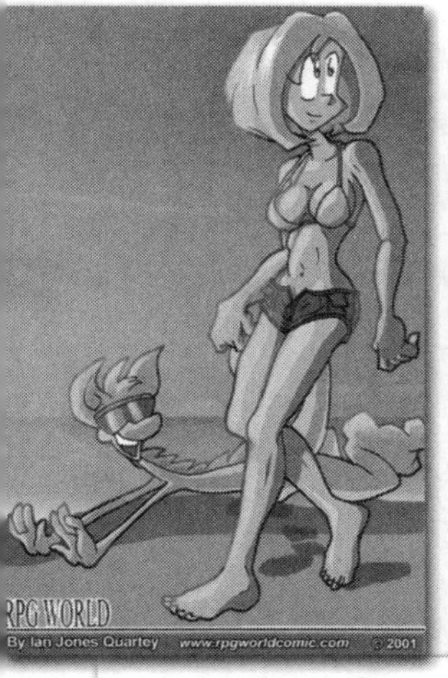
RPG WORLD
By Ian Jones Quartey
www.rpgworldcomic.com
© 2001

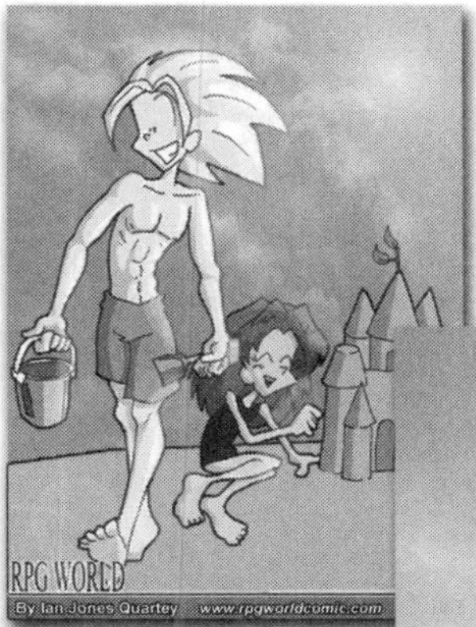
RPG WORLD
By Ian Jones Quartey
www.rpgworldcomic.com

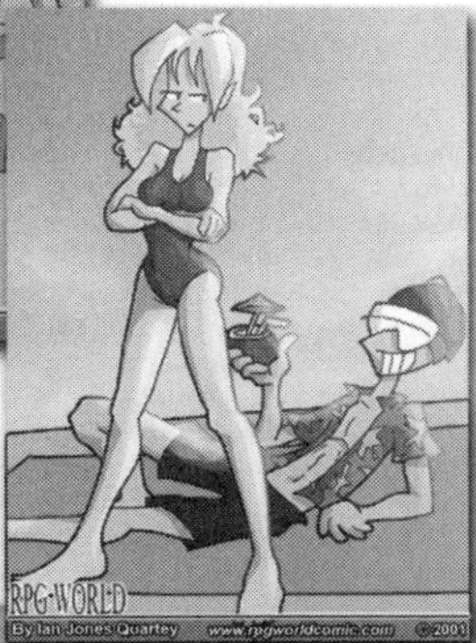
RPG WORLD
By Ian Jones Quartey
www.rpgworldcomic.com
© 2001

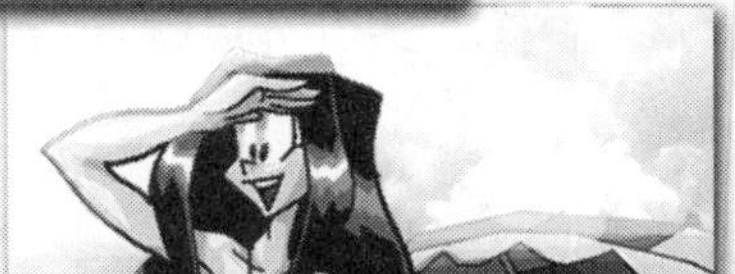
RPG WORLD
By Ian Jones Quartey

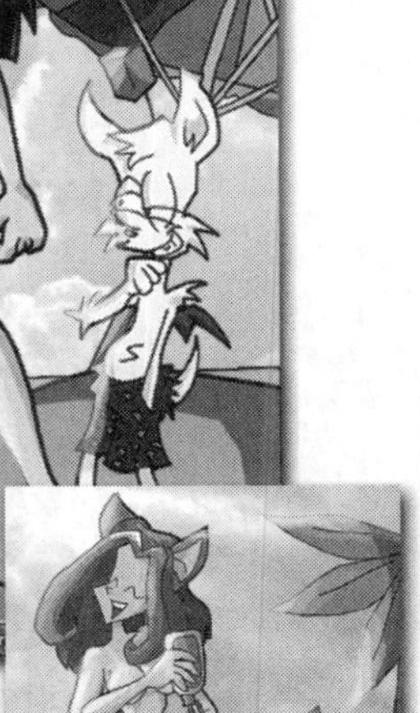
RPG WORLD
By Ian Jones Quartey
www.rpgworldcomic.com
© 2001

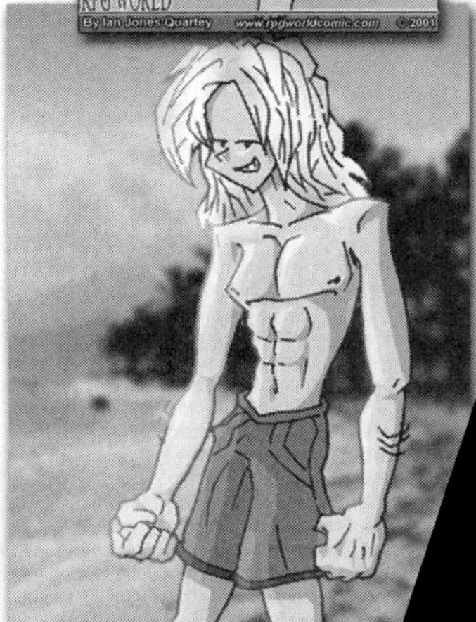
RPG WORLD
By Ian Jones Quartey

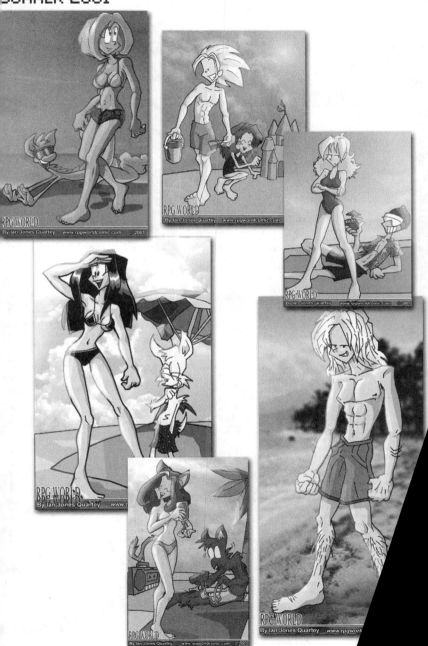

AFTERWORD

RPG World is a fictional Playstation game that was made sometime in the late 90's. This book collects the "First Disc". Were RPG World a real game, I'm pretty sure it wouldnt get that many good reviews. I mean, look at it. There's way too many cutscenes, and you know they make it so you can't skip them.

This comic is quite an experience to create. It forces me to try and create a coherent narrative and a consistent style. I don't know if I was very good at either of those things at the beginning, but drawing and writing RPG World has definitely made me practice.

To me the art in many of these comics looks extremely primitive and poorly rendered, but I hope that readers will be able to see how I grew and changed.

As I write this, RPG World has just started it's "third disc", and has recently passed four hundred comics. I've been at it a while and I'd like to think that these early comics are just as enjoyable as any of the others.

This book was a challenge to create because many of these early comics did not have high-quality copies. So there was a bit of touch-up here and there. If you're ever thinking of doing a print version of your webcomic, always remember to save high-quality versions of your art! It will save a lot of time in the long run.

The graphics are kinda iffy, there's no multiplayer support and the gameplay is annoying at times, but I hope that RPG World will have plenty of replay value for role playing game and comic fans all over the world.

~Ian J.

www.rpgworldcomic.com

IANCOMIX
"YOU READ IT. YOU CAN'T UN-READ IT."
THANKS SO MUCH FOR BUYING RPG WORLD VOLUME ONE!
WHEN PUTTING THIS BOOK TOGETHER, LOTS OF THOUGHTS WENT THROUGH MY HEAD.
THOUGHTS LIKE, "JEEZ, I CAN'T BELIEVE I USED TO DRAW LIKE THAT" AND "OH MAN, THAT JOKE WAS AWFUL!"
BUT YOU GUYS INSISTED THAT THIS STUFF WAS WORTH BUYING, SO WHO AM I TO ARGUE?
THANKS AGAIN!

THANKS

The list of people I want to thank is huge because it should logically include every single reader of RPG World from day one. My first ar was a bumpy ride but with your readership I kept on drawing grew a lot as an artist in a short time. I must have done some- ight because you guys continued coming to the site and support through fanart and emails. Thanks a lot. Thanks a k of a lot. And now some other shout-outs-

s for being a really cool big brother.

be no RPG World without you telling me that my nded like "some Playstation game". Thanks.

playing Jim and putting up with my constant

id Perducshins forever,

razy as hero but thankfully ten times as wise.

iration when the comic began.

est of the whole IanComix crew- you guys

ut we must represent.

#94

whole lot more.

allow, the artist of Adventurers!.

e I even took a crack at it, but

nt.

your character and use him

support.

lked with over the

y day(you know who

for letting me use

t to the publishers

ng my humble little strip

me in the face because

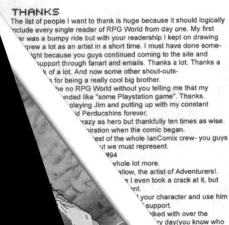

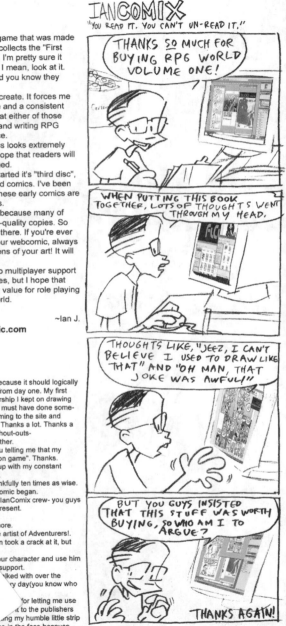

TO BE CONTINUED!

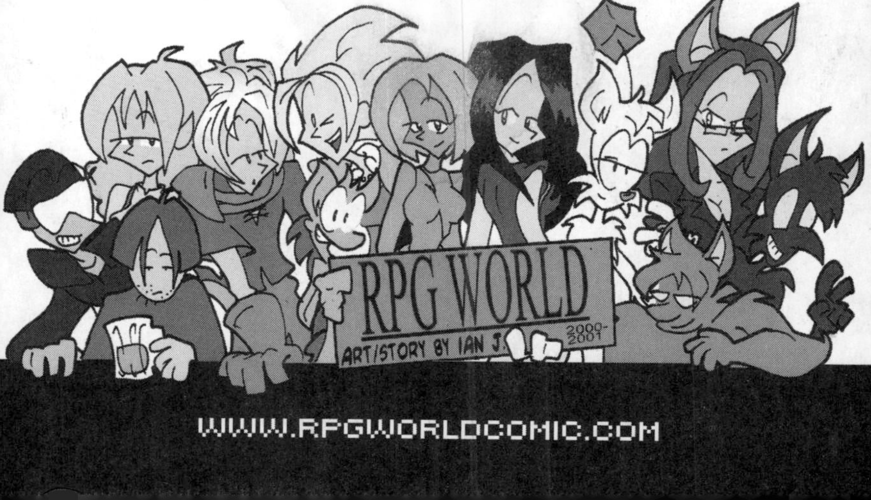
RPG WORLD
ART/STORY BY IAN J.
2000-2001
WWW.RPGWORLDCOMIC.COM